MW00340006

What's being said about MSP University?

"... (MSP University has) been on the cutting edge of the (MSP) movement and has helped many partners wade through the muddy waters. They continue to refine the process and share that information with their peers. We have gained much from our relationship with them and use their tools to continue growing our Managed Services practice."

- Arlin Sorensen, President/CEO, Heartland Technology Solutions, HTG Peer Groups, Iowa

"...I probably never would have been able to come up with a deal this creative if it wasn't for everything MSPU has taught me! You are totally changing the way I look at opportunities."

- Mark Sanders, President, AJMaddox Technologies, Texas

"...I am currently in the process of transitioning from a professional services model to a managed services provider here in south OC so that I can build up my company's client base and get more recurring revenue. These resources have proven to be very valuable in directing me towards my goals."

- Neil Richards, President, TotalTech Inc., California

"...MSPU has become the premier training house for managed services....."

- Karl Palachuk, Founder, KPEnterprises, Great Little Book, SMBBooks, California

What's being said about The Guide to a Successful Managed Services Practice?

"This book sits on my shelf and my service manager's shelf. You can't get $99 worth of consulting this valuable. It's a great reference, a great start, and worth looking at for everyone looking at managed services."

- Dave Sobel, President, Evolve Technologies, Virginia

"Every Small Business consultant needs to read this book. Yes, it's an awesome guide to managed services. But it's also a great guide to deciding which services to sell, how to price them, how to sell them, and how to "deliver" after you've inked the deal.

Did you need to know how to run a help desk? Or how to create an escalation procedure? It's all here.

You'll save literally hundreds -- maybe thousands of hours of work by reading this book. I run a very successful managed services business and I learned a great deal from this book. Simpson deserves a big hand for putting together such a valuable guide."

- Karl W. Palachuk, Founder, KP Enterprises, California

"...a "must-have" for any organization considering offering proactive, flat-rate I.T. Services"

"Packed with lots of valuable tools and other information that would have likely taken years to acquire on our own."

- Kurt Sippel, President, Applied Tech Solutions, Wisconsin

"This book was instrumental to getting our Managed Services practice to increase by about 2 1/2 times in less than 18 months. And I'm talking about a five figure number, too! The fundamental steps really work if you'll just stick to the plan outlined in the book. I recommend it to all my peers."

- Frances G. Miller, CEO, Dynamic Computer Solutions, Kansas

"What you don't know you don't know is in this book. Do yourself (and your clients) a favor, read this book and put to practice what you learn. I had to rethink the way I historically ran my business after reading (this) book and I am impressed with the results from the changes that I have made. My contracts, pricing structure, and how I handled different types of work were all reviewed and altered as a result of knowledge gained from this book.

You will be money and time ahead and proud that you invested such a small financial amount in your business and reaped so much in return."

- Travis B. Creighton, President, Computron, Florida

"This book provides the real world information and tools you need to understand and implement Managed Services in your company. The authors have obviously LIVED the transition from break fix to recurring revenue streams, and have provided a roadmap to success for others looking to make the same transition."

- Gavin Steiner, President, Interprom Inc., Canada

What's being said about The Best I.T. Sales & Marketing BOOK EVER!?

"The title to this book says it all. It really is the Best IT Sales and Marketing book ever. NUFF SAID!!!! YOU NEED TO BUY THIS BOOK if you want to turn your IT Business into a profitable one. I can't wait for (MSPU's) next book; hopefully (they) won't keep us waiting too long :-)"

- Chris Timm, Managing Director, TCG Computer Services, England, UK

"For those that have no formal marketing plan in place for their business this book is the how-to cookbook that will make it simple for you to be a great marketer. The tried and true approaches in this book are many of the tactics we use in our business. It is also laid out simply so that you don't need a marketing background to be able to understand and take action on the advice."

- Dan Hay, President/CEO, isoutsource.com, Washington

"This book is jam-packed with valuable insight to assist IT VAR's in selling and marketing to Small Business. It is required reading for my company's sales and marketing staff. I highly recommend it to anyone whether new to the business or an old veteran."

- Philip Kenealy, President, ACES, Iowa

If you want to grow a consistent services business, buy this book and start marketing now. You will recoup several times this book's cost with your first marketing campaign

- Mark Saum, President, Fidelis, TX

MSP University's

Managed Services Series

The Best I.T. Service Delivery BOOK EVER!

Hardware Warranty, Break-Fix, Professional and Managed Services

Erick Simpson
MCP, SBSC

MSP University
7077 Orangewood Avenue, Suite 104
Garden Grove, CA 92841
www.mspu.us

Voice: (714) 898-8195

Fax: (714) 898-8194

Printed in the United States of America

ISBN 978-0-9788943-2-0

Library of Congress Control Number: 2008937514

Library of Congress subject heading:

Computer Consulting
Information Technology Management
Information Technology Service

Contents

About the Author – Erick Simpson 17

Dedication 23

Acknowledgements 25

Foreword 29

Preface 31

Introduction 35

Build, Maintain, Maximize and Migrate 37

Identify or Determine Your I.T. Service Delivery Model 39

Section 1: The Hardware Warranty Services Delivery Model 43

   BUILD: THE HARDWARE WARRANTY SERVICES DELIVERY MODEL 45

      Characteristics 46

      Deliverables 46

      Warranty and SLA 46

      Tools and technology 48

      Pricing and positioning 48

      Staffing requirements 49

The Best I.T. Service Delivery BOOK EVER!

Table of Contents

Considerations 52

Target market 52

Customer satisfaction and loyalty 53

MAINTAIN: THE HARDWARE WARRANTY SERVICES DELIVERY MODEL 55

Focus 56

Technical implementation 56

Software and hardware tools 57

Effective processes and procedures 58

Parts and hardware inventory 59

Technical staff 59

Technical roles and responsibilities 60

Service delivery 64

Customer service 69

MAXIMIZE: THE HARDWARE WARRANTY SERVICES DELIVERY MODEL 71

Strategy 72

Tools and technology 72

Processes and procedures 73

The Best I.T. Service Delivery BOOK EVER!

Table of Contents

Scheduling 74

Service delivery 74

Inventory management 78

RMA processing 78

Staff utilization 79

Costs... 79

Vendors and distributors 80

Partnering.. 80

MIGRATE: THE HARDWARE WARRANTY SERVICES DELIVERY MODEL . 81

Migration choices 82

Strategies for migration to a break-fix services delivery
model.. 83

Strategies for migration to a managed services delivery
model.. 92

Strategies for migration to a professional services
delivery model 105

Section 2: The Break-Fix Services Delivery Model 117

BUILD: THE BREAK-FIX SERVICES DELIVERY MODEL 119

The Best I.T. Service Delivery BOOK EVER!

Table of Contents

Characteristics 120

Deliverables 121

Tools and technology 121

Pricing and positioning 122

Staffing requirements.. 123

Considerations... 126

Target market... 127

Customer satisfaction and loyalty 128

MAINTAIN: THE BREAK-FIX SERVICES DELIVERY MODEL 129

Focus... 130

Technical Implementation.. 130

Software and hardware tools.. 131

Effective processes and procedures 132

Parts and hardware inventory... 133

Technical staff 133

Technical roles and responsibilities................................... 133

Service delivery 138

The Best I.T. Service Delivery BOOK EVER!

Table of Contents

Customer service 143

MAXIMIZE: THE BREAK-FIX SERVICES DELIVERY MODEL 145

Strategy 146

Tools and technology 146

Processes and procedures 147

Scheduling 148

Service delivery 148

Equipment and parts ordering 152

RMA processing 153

Invoicing 153

Staff utilization 153

Costs... 154

Pricing... 154

Vendors and distributors 155

Partnering.. 155

Back office service desk support.............................. 155

Procurement services 156

The Best I.T. Service Delivery BOOK EVER!

Table of Contents

MIGRATE: THE BREAK-FIX SERVICES DELIVERY MODEL 157

Migration choices 158

Strategies for migration to a managed services delivery model 159

Strategies for migration to a professional services delivery model 172

Section 3: The Professional Services Delivery Model 183

BUILD: THE PROFESSIONAL SERVICES DELIVERY MODEL 185

Characteristics 186

Deliverables 187

Tools and technology 187

Pricing and positioning 188

Staffing requirements 189

Considerations 192

Target market 192

Customer satisfaction and loyalty 193

MAINTAIN: THE PROFESSIONAL SERVICES DELIVERY MODEL 195

The Best I.T. Service Delivery BOOK EVER!

Table of Contents

Focus.. 196

Technical implementation............................... 196

Software and hardware tools........................... 196

Effective processes and procedures 198

Parts and hardware inventory......................... 198

Technical staff 198

Technical roles and responsibilities................ 199

Sales engineers 199

Purchasing manager 200

Project managers 200

Inventory manager... 200

Service Delivery.. 203

Customer service 214

MAXIMIZE: THE PROFESSIONAL SERVICES DELIVERY MODEL 215

Strategy 216

Tools and technology 216

Processes and procedures 217

The Best I.T. Service Delivery BOOK EVER!

Table of Contents

Project scoping 218

Project quoting 218

Project planning 218

Equipment and parts ordering 219

Project management 220

Invoicing 220

Staff utilization 220

Costs 221

Pricing 221

Vendors and distributors 222

Partnering 222

MIGRATE: THE PROFESSIONAL SERVICES DELIVERY MODEL 223

Migration choices 224

Strategies for migration to a managed services delivery model 225

Section 4: The Managed Services Delivery Model 239

BUILD: THE MANAGED SERVICES DELIVERY MODEL 241

Characteristics 242

Deliverables 243

Agreement and SLA 244

Tools and technology 245

Pricing and positioning 247

Staffing requirements 250

Considerations 253

Target market 254

Customer satisfaction and loyalty 254

MAINTAIN: THE MANAGED SERVICES DELIVERY MODEL 257

Focus 258

Technical Implementation 259

Software and hardware tools 259

Effective processes and procedures 263

Parts and hardware inventory 263

Technical Staff 264

Technical roles and responsibilities 264

The Best I.T. Service Delivery BOOK EVER!

Table of Contents

Service Delivery 269

Customer Service 277

MAXIMIZE: THE MANAGED SERVICES DELIVERY MODEL 279

Strategy 280

Tools and technology 280

Processes and Procedures 281

Scheduling 282

Service Delivery 282

Equipment and parts ordering 286

RMA processing 287

Invoicing 287

Staff utilization 287

Costs 288

Pricing 289

Vendors and distributors 289

Partnering 289

Back office service desk support 290

The Best I.T. Service Delivery BOOK EVER!

Table of Contents

Hardware as a service (HaaS) *290*

Procurement services *291*

Section 5 – Hiring and Training Technical Staff **293**

WRITING EFFECTIVE EMPLOYMENT ADS FOR TECHNICAL STAFF 295

USING DISC BEHAVIORAL PROFILES BEFORE INTERVIEWING
CANDIDATES 303

THE INTERVIEW PROCESS FOR HIRING TECHNICAL STAFF 325

THE OFFER LETTER 339

THE EMPLOYMENT AGREEMENT 349

THE EQUIPMENT LOAN AGREEMENT 359

COMPENSATION PLANS 363

Help Desk Support Jr.-Sr. (Service Desk Staff) *364*

Service Dispatcher Jr.-Sr. *366*

Hardware Engineer I-V *367*

Field Service Engineer I-V *368*

Engineer I-V *369*

Purchasing Manager *370*

The Best I.T. Service Delivery BOOK EVER!

Table of Contents

Service Desk Manager..371

NOC Manager...372

Project Manager I-III 373

Sales Engineer I-V..374

Inventory Manager...375

TRAINING TECHNICAL STAFF...379

Role-Specific Training 383

Service desk staff...383

NOC staff 384

Field engineers/technicians...387

Bench engineers/technicians...389

Service dispatchers 390

Service managers 392

Sales engineers..393

Purchasing manager 394

Project managers 395

Inventory manager...396

The Best I.T. Service Delivery BOOK EVER!

Table of Contents

Section 6: Resources **399**

RMM SOLUTIONS 399

PSA SOLUTIONS 401

REMOTE DESKTOP CONTROL SOLUTIONS 402

I.T. AND MANAGED SERVICES TOOLS 402

BACK OFFICE SERVICE DESK PROVIDERS 403

TECHNICAL DRAWING SOLUTIONS 403

QUOTING SOLUTIONS 404

PROCUREMENT SERVICES 404

HAAS SOLUTIONS 404

DISC PROFILING SERVICES 404

BLOGS 405

PEER GROUPS 406

I.T. AND MANAGED SERVICES PUBLICATIONS 406

Section 7: Forms, Tools and Collateral **407**

HARDWARE WARRANTY SERVICES AGREEMENT EXAMPLE 413

MANAGED SERVICES AGREEMENT EXAMPLE 421

The Best I.T. Service Delivery BOOK EVER!

Table of Contents

I.T. SOLUTIONS AND MANAGED SERVICES PROPOSAL EXAMPLE 443

PROBLEM MANAGEMENT AND RESOLUTION PROCESS EXAMPLE 463

EMPLOYMENT AD FOR A SERVICE DESK ENGINEER 467

EMPLOYMENT AD FOR A NOC ENGINEER 471

EMPLOYMENT AD FOR A FIELD ENGINEER 475

EMPLOYMENT AD FOR A SERVICE DISPATCHER 479

EMPLOYMENT AD FOR A SERVICE MANAGER 483

EMPLOYMENT AD FOR A SALES ENGINEER 487

EMPLOYMENT AD FOR A PURCHASING MANAGER 491

EMPLOYMENT AD FOR AN INVENTORY MANAGER 495

EMPLOYMENT AD FOR A PROJECT MANAGER 499

HR HIRING CHECKLIST FOR A NEW TECHNICAL PERSON 503

HR INTERVIEW QUESTIONS FOR A NEW TECHNICAL PERSON 505

MANAGED SERVICES, YOUR BUSINESS PLAN AND YOU POWERPOINT PRESENTATION 511

MANAGED SERVICES BUSINESS PLAN TEMPLATE 533

MANAGED SERVICES BUSINESS PLAN WHITE PAPER 553

Table of Contents

MSP University 559

What's on the Download? 567

As always, every form, tool and piece of collateral discussed in this book is available as a download after registration at: **www.mspu.us/svcbookregistration**.

About the Author – Erick Simpson

As Co-founder, Vice President and CIO of Intelligent Enterprise and MSP University, Erick Simpson has experienced first-hand the challenges of growing an I.T. business. Intelligent Enterprise has been providing Information technology solutions to the Southern California SMB market since 1997. Their relationships with partners such as Microsoft, Cisco, Citrix and HP have allowed them the ability to design, scale and implement effective infrastructure solutions for their diverse client base.

Intelligent Enterprise, a Microsoft Gold Certified and Business Solutions partner and Small Business Specialist, and one of the first "pure-play" MSPs in the SMB space, successfully migrated to a managed services business model in January of 2005. Prior to this, they were operating as many other I.T. providers have – reacting to clients in "break-fix" mode, and dealing with the constant demand to recruit new clients and sell new solutions each and every month in order to meet their receivables goals.

The Best I.T. Service Delivery BOOK EVER!

About the Author – Erick Simpson

Intelligent Enterprise developed an "all you can eat" managed services approach focused on 3 core deliverables – remote help desk, proactive network monitoring, and they pioneered vendor management. Through the creation of a managed services sales and marketing approach unique to the industry, Intelligent Enterprise sold over $2MM worth of managed services agreements before being asked to share their managed services knowledge and expertise through their managed services university at www.mspu.us.

MSP University has helped numerous manufacturer, vendor, distributor and franchise membership organizations, their channels, and thousands of independent IT service organizations worldwide educate themselves in transitioning IT service businesses to successful, profitable managed services practices through its educational, training, fulfillment and consulting services.

A recognized author, speaker and trainer, and contributor to Microsoft's Small Business Channel Community Expert Column and presenter of a continuing series of Microsoft, Intel Cisco and Ingram Micro workshops, events and webcasts on managed services, Erick is the author of "The Guide to a Successful Managed Services Practice - *What Every SMB IT Service Provider Should Know...*", the definitive book on Managed Services, and the follow-up in MSP University's Managed Service Series; "The Best I.T. Sales & Marketing

BOOK EVER!", focused on helping I.T. and managed services providers grow their businesses through effective passive and direct marketing techniques proven to win business and increase revenues.

Erick's professional certifications include Microsoft MCP and SBSC, and affiliations include SMBTN and HTG1 Peer Group memberships. Erick has conducted nationwide managed services workshops, boot camps and presentations at industry events such as the Microsoft Worldwide Partner Conference, SMBNation, SMBSummit, ITPro Conference, ITAlliance, ICCA, MSPRevolution and others.

Erick also co-authored Arlin Sorensen's HTG Peer Group publication *"Peer Power – Powerful Ideas for Partners from Peers "*, available at www.htgmembers.com, and his recent articles on managed services are available at the following web urls:

Maximize Service Delivery Profits During Economic Downturns – Author, MSPMentor July 2008 - http://www.mspmentor.net/wp-content/uploads/2008/06/maximizing-service-delivery-profits-during-economic-downturnsdoc.pdf

---

We Can't Just Sell Managed Services – Author, MSPMentor June 2008 - http://www.mspmentor.net/wp-content/uploads/2008/06/we-can-t-just-sell-managed-servicesdoc.pdf

The Importance of Vertical-Specific Marketing for MSP's – Author, Focus On MSP May 2008 - http://www.focusonmsp.com/articles/20080415-3.aspx

Managed Services, your business plan and you – Author, SearchITChannel July 2007 - http://searchitchannel.techtarget.com/general/0,295582,sid96_gci1262243,00.html

Managed Services – What's All the Buzz About? Author, Microsoft Small Business Channel Community - https://partner.microsoft.com/us/40029753

Managed Services – It Makes Sense – Author, ChannelPro June 2007 – http://www.channelpro-digital.com/channelpro/200706/?folio=38

About the Author – Erick Simpson

An Introduction To Managed Services – Author, Infotech Update January 2007 – http://infotech.aicpa.org/NR/rdonlyres/AC23261D-D7F4-4459-A822-DFD4FDA8F999/0/it_jan_feb07.pdf

Erick lives in Orange County, California with his wife Susan and their two sons, Connor and Riley. His prior technical experience includes overseeing the design, development and implementation of Enterprise-level help desks and call centers for Fortune 1000 organizations.

Dedication

This book is dedicated first and foremost to my family – my wife Sue and our two boys, Connor and Riley. Without their love, tireless support and putting up with my long hours, hectic and sometimes extreme travel schedule, and general grumpiness when under a deadline (or when things just aren't going the way I wish they would)...I simply could not accomplish anything at all. I love you dearly.

Secondly, I'd like to dedicate this book to our MSPU partners, and all of the IT service providers who purchased our previous books, "The Guide to a Successful Managed Services Practice" and "The Best I.T. Service Delivery BOOK EVER!", and helped make them best-selling managed services publications. This follow-up to those books is in response to your positive reviews, encouragement and specific requests for the content contained herein. Thank you all.

Acknowledgements

There are so many people who have influenced, encouraged and continue to inspire us to succeed, and I'd like to personally thank them here.

First, I'd like to thank my business partner, Gary Beechum. It takes a special relationship to start a business with someone, and reflect back on all of the ups and downs, highs and lows 18 years later and know that you made the right decision. Gary and I haven't always been in the I.T. business, but in each successive entrepreneurial endeavor we've attempted over the years, our mutual respect, trust and friendship for each other continued to grow and become stronger and stronger. We're a good team – each of us balances the other's weaknesses and strengths to a point where we strike a natural balance, and are much more effective together than we would ever be apart. Thanks, Gary – it just keeps getting better and better.

I'd also like to thank Arlin Sorensen, and the incredible impact that being associated with him has had in our organization and for me personally; first as a member of his HTG1 Peer Group, then on a deeper, more personal level. Arlin is one of those rare individuals that lives his faith through every aspect

Acknowledgements

of his life, and uses it as his driving force in building relationships, utilizing the "servant-leader" philosophy to help those he touches realize the best in themselves and others. His dynamic HTG Peer Group concept has brought over 100 IT Organizations together in an open, sharing and mentoring relationship that is truly unique today. Check out www.htgmembers.com for more on Arlin's peer groups.

I'd also like to thank my peers in HTG1; Connie Arentson, Phil Kenealy, Mitch Miller, Kurt Sippel, Dave Cooksey, Don Miller, Dan Hay, Jim Strickland, John Pritchard, Don Miller, Dan Shundoff and Jack Safrit, as well as several members in succeeding groups; Dave Siebert, Erik Thorsell, Brad Schow, Aaron Booker, Stuart Crawford, Eric Adkins, Pat Dolan, Brad Kowerchuk, Robert Lindley, Brad Schow, Jane Cage, Michael Cocanower, Stuart Crawford, Larry Hedin, Wade Devore, John Endter, Richard Tubb, and Scott Scrogin, You've all been a great help and inspiration to me.

I've got a lot of folks at Microsoft to thank for their continuing support as well, including Chris Van Wesep, Ron Grattop, Tina Parkhouse, Fred Pullen, Stephen Deming, Mike Marshall, Mike Murphy, Paige Boesen, Suzanne Lavine, Tracye Foy, Glenn Osako, Eva Skidmore, Eric Ligman, Diane Golshan, Penelope Delgadillo, Arnie Mondloch, Charles Van Heusen, J.J. Antequino, Bernardo Alfredo Munoz, Aanal Bhatt, Paul Jensen, John Stroiney, Nicole Rau, Greg Randall, Allen

The Best I.T. Service Delivery BOOK EVER!

Acknowledgements

Goldberg, Peter Gallegher, Kevin Beares, Andrea Russell, Chris Almida, Marie Mcfadden and Steve VanRoekel, .

I owe a special thanks to Sameer Jayaker from Cisco, and John Hanna, Eric Townsend and Josh Hilliker from Intel – thanks so much for being our evangelists inside your respective organizations.

Thanks go out to Harry Brelsford, Beatrice Mulzer, Nancy Williams, Jeff Middleton, Susan Bradley, Jim Sterling, Amy and Steve Luby, Clinton Gatewood, Rajeev Laghate, Akash Saraf, Dan Shapero, Claudia Coleman, Justin Crotty, Ramsey Dellinger, Alex and Monique Rogers, Clark Crook, Matt Makowicz, Robin Robins, Chris Rue, Dana Epp, Jim Locke, Mike Iem, Joe Panettieri, Amy Katz, Paul Dippell and Ryan Morris for your continued support.

Special recognition goes out to Vlad "ABP" Mazek, Karl Palachuk, Dave Sobel, Mark Crall and Stuart Selbst, my ever-increasing conference posse and the kind of guys you can really feel comfortable "telling it like it is" to – and getting it right back. Also back in the posse category after a short hiatus is Anne Stanton – the universal connector – thank you all.

Extra special thanks go out to Mark Sanders – Mark, thanks for everything you've done to help us get to the next level.

The Best I.T. Service Delivery BOOK EVER!

Acknowledgements

Finally, I'd like to recognize our excellent staff for all the hard work they put in to keep our organizations moving forward; Flynn Bashford, Quyen Nguyen, Jessica Lopez, Nilo Nogueras, David Huynh, Roger Tang, Jerry Moran, Brandon Avillar, Cesar Ordaz, Dwight Blair, Danielle Fraley, Valerie Cano, James Wright, Rafael Sanguily, Jasmine Cano, Giovanni Sanguily and Dashmilia Guevara – we couldn't do it without you.

Foreword

Being the third book in our Managed Services Series, with the first (The Guide to a Successful Managed Services Practice) covering an overview of managed services, and the second (The Best I.T. Sales & Marketing BOOK EVER!) covering sales and marketing, this book covers the next logical area in an I.T. provider's business – service delivery.

As service providers, our ability to "slay dragons" in our client environments and come away with the spoils and accolades time and again sometimes overinflates our confidence to unrealistic levels. Can you remember the feeling of invincibility when attacking a new technical problem for the first time and the adrenaline rush once the issue was resolved? Those were good times, weren't they?

But all we needed to shake our newfound confidence was a situation that started off like all the others, but slowly and inexorably spiraled down an endless rabbit hole, with no light at the end of the tunnel...

So over time we learned to create and follow standardized processes in order to resolve issues – problem management and resolution strategies that we taught our technicians and engineers to follow as we grew our practices over time. These were duplicable steps that included problem identification, documentation, prioritization, escalation, remediation and communication, to name a few.

But the art of service delivery isn't just problem management and resolution, is it? Effective service delivery strategies must take into account factors such as our business model, our business mode of operation, our staff and their roles, our business goals, processes and procedures, the vertical markets we serve and the deliverables we offer, and numerous other considerations.

These and other topics will frame our discussion as we discover strategies to improve I.T. service delivery, and the results we should expect by doing so.

You will notice that throughout certain sections of this book, ideas and concepts are repeated, and may seem redundant.

This has been done intentionally, as there are those of you who may not read this book from start to finish, but instead jump directly to a specific section dealing with a particular service delivery model - each service delivery model's section has been written to stand independently of the others.

Preface

Here we are again, and I'm glad you could join us in our continuing exploration on how to improve our I.T. and managed services practices. It's hard to believe that another year has come and gone since we began this journey together, adding up to three so far; and for each, we've shared a new book and new discussion together.

This time around we're going to deep-dive into service delivery improvement, and we'll be exploring the characteristics, deliverables, pricing and positioning, staffing requirements, target markets, and maintenance, maximization and migration strategies for each of four different I.T. service delivery models, along with what it takes to hire, compensate, train and manage technical staff.

Our goal will be to provide a roadmap for successful service delivery in each of these models, and help you meet your goals and objectives in them.

So what are the secrets to service practice improvement? In our experience, there are several questions that need to be answered before we can develop a plan for improvement. The first question is: what service delivery **model** do we currently practice? In order to answer this question, we need to identify a core set of service delivery models to work from. For purposes of our discussion, let's establish these as:

1. Hardware warranty services providers
2. Break-fix services providers
3. Professional services providers
4. Managed services providers

Each of these service provider groups face their own unique challenges in terms of deliverables, staffing, marketing and sales and business operations. We will need to make decisions on internal and external business process modifications specific to our individual service delivery model in order to improve our practices. But prior to making these decisions; and in addition to identifying our service delivery model, we must also understand where we are in terms of our business **mode**, which will fall into one of the following categories:

- Build
- Maintain
- Maximize
- Migrate

If our business is in **Build** mode, we are currently working to start an I.T. services practice, or are in a very early stage of operation.

Preface

If our business is in **Maintain** mode, we are not currently seeking to actively grow the business, but instead simply to maintain the customers that we currently have, and not lose any. If we happen to pick up an occasional customer via referral, that's just icing on the cake. This might be characterized as a "lifestyle" business model by some.

If our business is in **Maximize** mode, we are actively seeking ways to improve our business processes, efficiencies and profitability, and are actively focused on investing in and growing our practice.

If our business is in **Migrate** mode, we are actively seeking to, or currently executing a migration strategy to adopt or move from one service delivery model to another.

A clear identification and understanding of all of these variables is required in order for us to develop our service improvement strategy; as a resultant combination of factors will dictate the specific modifications, timing and phasing of our service improvement plan. We will explore all of these considerations in this book

As always, every form, tool and piece of collateral discussed in this book is available as a download after registration at: www.mspu.us/svcbookregistration.

Introduction

If you've read any of the other books in this series you know the drill by now, right? Before we can bake our soufflé, we need to pick or create our recipe, identify and source all of our ingredients, then combine them in the right order (pinch of this, dash of that), modify to taste, and then maybe let the entire concoction set a while before popping it into the oven.

So we'll be baking some soufflé's before we're done with all of the discussions we'll be having in this book – and if we create and follow the right recipes, I'll bet they'll be mighty tasty ones, too...

As always, there is a recipe required for success and having a good time in all endeavors – even baking soufflé's...

So the chapters comprising the following sections will deal with building, maintaining, maximizing and migrating our service delivery models – everything that must be identified and understood before we can take the next steps in our service delivery practice. And finally, we'll explore what it takes to hire, train and manage technical staff, along with compensation considerations.

Ready? Let's get started...

Build, Maintain, Maximize and Migrate

Among the topics we will explore in this book are the concepts of building, maintaining and maximizing existing I.T. service delivery models, as well as migrating to different modes of service delivery. For our purposes, we will define these as:

Build Mode – the act of preparing to, or currently building a business concern by understanding the considerations necessary including its deliverables, tools and technology, pricing and positioning, staffing requirements, target markets and other key factors.

Maintain Mode – the act of operating a business concern without actively seeking to grow the business, but instead simply to maintain the current customer count without attrition. If the provider happens to pick up an occasional customer via referral, that's just icing on the cake. *This might be characterized as a "lifestyle" business model by some.*

Maximize Mode – the act of operating a business concern in growth mode, and actively seeking ways to improve business processes, efficiencies and profitability, while actively focusing on investing in and growing the practice.

Migrate Mode – the act of actively seeking to, or currently executing a migration strategy to transition from one service

---

---

delivery model to another, or adding components of an additional service delivery model to the current one (a hybrid strategy).

Identify or Determine Your I.T. Service Delivery Model

If you are a veteran service provider, you will have little trouble identifying your current I.T. service delivery model from the following:

1. Hardware warranty services provider
2. Break-fix services provider
3. Professional services provider
4. Managed services provider

In fact, you may operate a blended; or hybrid, model and deliver a combination of services, such as hardware warranty services and break-fix services, or break-fix and professional services, or all three – and if you're really a masochist, add managed services on top for good measure!

In our experience, the more models we juggled, the more difficult it became to focus and maximize profits in any individual one. It is for this reason we decided to focus primarily on delivering managed services, and partner with others to deliver professional services to our customers over time, as we evolved towards more of a "pure play" MSP model.

Identify Or Determine Your I.T. Service Delivery Model

For those of you that are thinking about starting, or have recently started an I.T. services practice, you may still need to determine which, or which combination of these service delivery models you will practice.

The reality is that each of these service delivery models has its own unique characteristics, deliverables, pricing models, target markets and marketing strategies, in addition to unique staffing and skill set requirements. For instance, operating a hardware warranty services practice is different in numerous ways from operating a managed services practice.

In fact, these differences may be so fundamental as to dictate disparate customer bases and value propositions, not to mention pricing and positioning considerations for these two very different service delivery models. If we take an objective view of these different service delivery models, we might surmise that the hardware warranty services delivery model and the break-fix services delivery model share more similarities to each other than to any of the other models.

Additionally, we might also surmise that the professional services and managed services delivery models share more similarities to each other than to the hardware warranty and break-fix models. Let's explore why we might think this way...

Both hardware warranty services and break-fix services delivery models share the following similarities:

Identify Or Determine Your I.T. Service Delivery Model

1. Operate a primarily reactive service delivery model
2. Sell a commodity
3. Profit margins are the lowest of the four service provider groups
4. Customer base is generally more focused on price than service or value
5. Experience minimal customer loyalty

In contrast, professional and managed services delivery models share these similarities:

1. Operate a proactive service delivery model
2. Services are less likely to be commoditized
3. Profit margins are the highest of the four service provider groups
4. Customer base is generally more focused on service and value than price
5. Experience greater customer loyalty than other service provider groups

Of course, each of these service delivery models have uniquely different characteristics as well, with the greatest distinction among them being the transaction-based nature of the hardware warranty, break-fix and professional services provider models as opposed to the annuity-based nature of the managed services delivery model, where each new customer added brings additional monthly revenues which compound over time, and add true value to the MSP's practice.

Section 1: The Hardware Warranty Services Delivery Model

For purposes of our discussion, the hardware warranty services delivery model is defined as being comprised of activities, processes and procedures that allow the service provider to deliver hardware troubleshooting and repair services for faulty equipment managed under a warranty services agreement. These services can be scheduled or reactive, unscheduled events.

Build: The Hardware Warranty Services Delivery Model

build [bild] – *to develop or give form to according to a plan or process; create*

In order to build a hardware warranty services delivery model, we must understand its characteristics – the nuts and bolts.

This section will explore the considerations necessary to build a hardware warranty services delivery model and discuss deliverables, tools and technology, pricing and positioning, staffing requirements, target markets and other concerns.

Build: The Hardware Warranty Services Delivery Model

Characteristics

Characteristics of a hardware warranty services delivery model include delivering a commodity service with the lowest profit margins of the four service delivery models in our discussion. This requires the "pure" hardware warranty services provider to make up for these low margins by selling warranty service agreements in high volume and keeping their overhead, parts and labor costs as low as possible, in addition to developing a standardized problem management and resolution process to deliver hardware warranty services in the most efficient manner.

Deliverables

The deliverables of a hardware warranty services provider may include providing remote, onsite and bench support to troubleshoot, remediate or replace faulty hardware components for warranted equipment.

The hardware warranty services provider's duties include conducting RMA activities and inventory management to insure appropriate levels of replacement parts and hardware components are maintained to service hardware failures for their customers.

Warranty and SLA

The hardware warranty services provider' service level agreement (SLA) is the contract that binds their level of

---

Build: The Hardware Warranty Services Delivery Model

---

warranty service between themselves and their customers, and records the common understanding regarding the following:

- Services
- Priorities
- Responsibilities
- Guarantees
- Availability
- Serviceability
- Performance
- Operation
- Response
- Resolution

Warranty SLA's commonly include the following:

- Definition of services
- Term of agreement
- Fees
- Taxes
- Coverage hours
- Exclusions
- Performance measurement
- Problem management, response and resolution times
- Limitation of liability
- Service requirements
- Covered equipment, components and/or services

Tools and technology

The hardware warranty services provider may invest in software tools to assist them in effective, efficient service delivery. A professional services automation (PSA) solution may provide them the following capabilities:

- Customer relationship management (CRM) capabilities
- Service request or trouble ticketing capabilities
- Scheduling & dispatching capabilities
- Time & expense tracking capabilities
- Inventory control capabilities
- Asset management capabilities
- Configuration & change management capabilities
- Knowledgebase capabilities
- Resource management capabilities
- Integration of quoting & invoicing with accounting systems capabilities
- Sales funnel capabilities
- Robust, customizable reporting capabilities

Pricing and positioning

Because of the competitive challenges faced by hardware warranty services providers, pricing for their services tends to be very aggressive, as it is difficult to build a unique value proposition for a commodity service which compels a prospect to choose one provider over another - hence the proclivity for many hardware warranty service providers to compete on price.

Positioning a hardware warranty services agreement as the answer to alleviating a prospect's pain points concerning hardware failure and its negative impact on efficiency, productivity and net profits may not be a persuasive enough message in the SMB space to secure enough business to meet the provider's revenue requirements. This is the reason that many service providers offer hardware warranty services in addition to break-fix, professional and managed services for equipment they have either installed or manage.

Staffing requirements
Depending upon the number of devices under warranty, and the size of the organization, the hardware warranty services provider will require a minimum number of staff that fulfill specific roles, and these may include:

- Owners
- Managers
- Administrative staff
- Technical staff
- Marketing/sales staff
- Other staff

Build: The Hardware Warranty Services Delivery Model

Owners

As in any organization; and based upon a number of factors, hardware warranty services provider owners may wear many hats, or merely a few. Their basic responsibility to the organization, its stakeholders, staff and customers is to manage and maintain a profitable business concern.

Managers

The size of the organization's management staff will be based upon the number of the organization's staff, among other factors, and may include:

- Operations management
- Office management
- HR management
- Marketing/sales management
- Service delivery management
- Vendor management
- Customer service management

Administration

Every organization, no matter how large or small requires some form of administrative support. These roles include:

- Front office staff
- HR staff
- Accounting staff

Build: The Hardware Warranty Services Delivery Model

- Customer service staff

Technical staff

We wouldn't have an I.T. organization without technical staff now, would we? For a hardware warranty services delivery practice these roles may include:

- Service desk staff
- Field engineers/technicians
- Bench engineers/technicians
- Service dispatchers

Marketing/sales staff

Although the marketing and sales roles are distinct, and in larger organizations segmented by business unit and resources, we'll group them together for purposes of our service delivery-focused discussion.

No matter what size the service provider's organization is, at one point or another, someone is going to have to market and sell the provider's services.

Other staff

Additional staff that may make up the hardware warranty service provider's organization may include:

- Purchasing manager
- Inventory manager

Considerations

The "pure" hardware warranty services delivery model requires a tremendous volume of warranty service business in order to operate due to low margins and high service delivery costs. These factors require providers serving the SMB market to expand their service offerings to augment their revenues and profits while meeting the hardware warranty services needs of their customers.

Target market

As mentioned, due to the volume required for profitability as a "pure" hardware warranty services provider, the provider's target market would tend to be the upper Mid to Enterprise customer with large enough equipment assets to make warranty services a requirement to maintain efficiencies and productivity, resulting in higher profitability.

For "hybrid" hardware warranty service providers, who deliver not only hardware warranty services, but perhaps break-fix, professional and managed services, or some combination thereof, the target market is much broader.

Typically, a more service-oriented delivery model (as opposed to a transaction-based model) will succeed in attracting more technology-strategic customers who view technology spending as strategic investments in their organizations and provide them a competitive advantage in their markets. To these customers, service and value rank higher than cost considerations.

On the other hand, a more transaction-based delivery model attracts less technology-strategic customers, and the more commoditized the products and services delivered, the more cost-conscious the customers become, reducing the ability for the provider to win business based on value and service.

Customer satisfaction and loyalty
As a result of the commodity nature of hardware warranty services, as long as the service provider is capable of meeting the customer's expectations in terms of service delivery, customer satisfaction should be easy to achieve and maintain.

Customer loyalty; however, may be another matter entirely, based yet again on the commodity nature of the deliverable, as well as the reactive, transaction-based nature of the relationship. How many times have you been able to win business away from a provider delivering hardware warranty services, or a hybrid deliverable including break-fix services? This proves the point that customers in a transaction-based relationship receiving a commoditized service have little loyalty to the existing provider, and reinforces the reality that we must modify our deliverables and relationships with customers to be perceived as indispensable trusted advisors.

Maintain: The Hardware Warranty Services Delivery Model

main · tain [meyn-**teyn**] – *to keep in an existing state; preserve or retain*

Now that we understand the nuts and bolts of the hardware warranty services delivery model and its characteristics and considerations, let's dive a bit deeper and explore what it takes to maintain it in terms of service delivery.

This section will cover implementing the hardware warranty services delivery model and discuss technical roles and responsibilities, as well as service delivery.

Maintain: The Hardware Warranty Services Delivery Model

Focus

The "pure" hardware warranty services delivery model focuses on allowing the provider the ability to effectively deliver scheduled and unscheduled hardware troubleshooting and repair services for equipment covered under warranty, respond to service requests dealing with hardware issues, deliver problem identification and remediation and meet established SLA's for service delivery.

Therefore, at a minimum, the provider and their staff must be able to document, inventory and manage assets for all warranted hardware in their customer locations, as well as provide problem management and resolution services for this equipment.

A hardware warranty services provider's services will generally have been paid for at the inception of the hardware warranty services agreement, potentially preventing the provider from billing their customers to meet their hardware warranty services SLA's, unless a provision excluding labor costs exists.

Technical implementation

In order to implement a hardware warranty services delivery model, the provider must possess:

- Software and hardware tools
- Effective processes and procedures
- Parts and hardware inventory

- Technical staff

Software and hardware tools

An effective hardware warranty services provider will be able to document, inventory and manage warranted assets in customer environments and execute a consistent problem management process, insuring service delivery remains within agreed-upon SLA's. Software tools utilized by the provider to accomplish these activities will include asset management, problem management and remote access/control and remediation solutions. Some remote monitoring and management (RMM) and professional service automation (PSA) solutions provide all of these capabilities.

The hardware warranty services provider's PSA solution may provide the following capabilities:

- Customer relationship management (CRM) capabilities
- Service request or trouble ticketing capabilities
- Scheduling & dispatching capabilities
- Time & expense tracking capabilities
- Inventory control capabilities
- Asset management capabilities
- Configuration & change management capabilities
- Knowledgebase capabilities
- Resource management capabilities

- Integration of quoting & invoicing with accounting systems capabilities
- Sales funnel capabilities
- Robust, customizable reporting capabilities

Dependent upon the specific hardware and associated components the provider warrants, there may be additional software test, update and remediation tools required or beneficial in order to provide diagnostic, troubleshooting and repair services for their customers. Leveraging these types of software tools help the hardware warranty services provider gain efficiency and speeds problem identification and resolution, increasing customer satisfaction.

In addition to software tools, the hardware warranty services provider will require both standard, as well as specialized hardware tools in order to service warranted equipment.

Effective processes and procedures
In order for the provider to cost-effectively deliver hardware warranty services to their customers, they must develop and implement consistent problem management and resolution processes and procedures.

By standardizing on their software and hardware tools, and fine-tuning their processes and procedures, the provider will

---

increase customer satisfaction as well as their own profitability.

Parts and hardware inventory
The hardware warranty service provider is required to maintain a sufficient quantity of replacement hardware and components to meet established customer SLA's for warranted equipment failure.

Accurate inventory management will be required in order to identify, determine and maintain minimum levels of spare replacement parts.

Technical staff
In order to meet customer expectations, SLA's and maximize profitability, the hardware warranty services provider will require a sufficient number of technical staff trained in effective hardware and software problem management and resolution processes. These processes should be tailored to support the provider's warranted hardware, and training specific to the provider's chosen software and hardware management and remediation tools, processes and procedures will be required for all technical staff.

Maintain: The Hardware Warranty Services Delivery Model

Technical roles and responsibilities

Depending upon the number of devices under warranty, and the size of the organization, the hardware warranty services provider's technical staff will fall into specific roles which may include:

- Purchasing managers
- Inventory managers
- Service dispatchers
- Service managers
- Service desk staff
- Bench engineers/technicians
- Field engineers/technicians

Purchasing manager

In this context, the purchasing manager participates in the provider's service delivery process by insuring pricing and availability of hardware, software licensing and services from vendors, distributors and fulfillment partners to meet the provider's service delivery requirements.

Inventory manager

In this context, the inventory manager participates in the provider's service delivery process by insuring adequate inventory availability of hardware, software licensing and services from vendors, distributors and fulfillment partners to

---

meet the provider's service delivery requirements, and handles all returns, RMAs and credits when necessary.

Service dispatchers
In this context, the service dispatcher participates in the provider's problem management and resolution process, and may assign resources to and schedule all remote, onsite or bench warranty services. The service dispatcher may also be included in the provider's escalation process and be alerted by their PSA solution should service requests become in danger of falling out of SLA.

Service dispatchers will utilize the provider's chosen software management tools, processes and procedures to manage dispatch functions during service delivery.

Service managers
In this context, the service manager is ultimately responsible for maintaining the provider's technical staffing levels, training and certification requirements, problem management and resolution processes and customer satisfaction by strict SLA management, among other responsibilities.

Service managers will utilize the provider's chosen software management tools, processes and procedures to manage service delivery.

Service desk staff

In this context, the service desk staff participates in the provider's problem management and resolution process, and can be assigned to deliver remote technical support services to end users. The service desk staff identifies, prioritizes and documents all service requests, and initiates problem management and resolution activity.

Service desk staff will execute the provider's problem management and resolution processes as well as utilize the provider's chosen software and hardware management and remediation tools, processes and procedures during remote service delivery.

Bench engineers/technicians

In this context, the bench engineer/technician participates in the provider's problem management and resolution process, and can be assigned to deliver technical support services for customer equipment brought into the provider's facilities when necessary.

Bench engineers/technicians will utilize the provider's hardware and software problem management and resolution processes as well as the provider's chosen software and hardware management and remediation tools, processes and procedures during service delivery.

Field engineers/technicians
In this context, the field engineer/technician participates in the provider's problem management and resolution process, and can be assigned to deliver technical support services at the customer's facilities when necessary.

Field engineers/technicians will utilize the provider's hardware and software problem management and resolution processes as well as the provider's chosen software and hardware management and remediation tools, processes and procedures during service delivery.

Maintain: The Hardware Warranty Services Delivery Model

Service delivery

Scheduled maintenance

The hardware warranty services provider may provide scheduled maintenance services if required by their hardware warranty services agreement and SLA.

Problem management and resolution

In order for the hardware warranty services provider to deliver effective hardware warranty services to customers, they must develop, implement and adhere to a consistent problem management and resolution process. This process can include the utilization of a service desk.

In this context, the service desk is defined as the central point of contact between the customer and the provider, and whose staff maintains and facilitates the restoration of normal service operation while minimizing impact to the customer within an agreed-upon SLA.

The hardware warranty services provider's service desk conducts hardware warranty services problem management and resolution, and service desk staff can be assigned to the following tiers for escalation:

- Tier 1
- Tier 2
- Tier 3

These tiers are utilized in the prioritization and escalation process per the provider's service desk escalation procedure. After an issue is identified and documented in the provider's PSA solution, non-critical support incidents are normally assigned to tier 1 for a technician to begin basic troubleshooting and problem resolution. Based upon priority and other factors, the issue will be escalated up through successive support tiers as necessary in order to adhere to applicable SLAs.

All support incidents that cannot be resolved within tier 1 are escalated to tier 2, where more complex support can be provided by more experienced staff.

Support incidents that cannot be resolved in tier 2 are escalated to tier 3, where support is provided by the most qualified and experienced staff that has the ability to collaborate with the provider's vendor support engineers to resolve the most complex issues.

In many cases, an onsite visit may be required to troubleshoot and remediate faulty hardware. In this scenario a field engineer /technician may be dispatched to continue the problem resolution process.

In other cases, the customer or a field engineer/technician may bring an affected piece of equipment in to the provider's offices for troubleshooting or remediation. In this scenario a

---

bench engineer/technician may be assigned to continue the problem resolution process.

The hardware warranty services provider's service desk's goals include:

- Providing a single point of contact for end-user issues
- Facilitating the restoration of normal service operation while minimizing impact to the end-user
- Delivering services within agreed-upon SLA's
- Receiving all incident notifications through the provider's preferred means - phone, fax, email, service desk portal, etc.
- Recording all incidents in the provider's PSA solution
- Classifying all incidents and correctly documenting the nature of the incident, including affected users, systems and hardware
- Prioritizing all incidents for effective escalation
- Troubleshooting all incidents according to best practices
- Escalating all incidents as necessary to maintain established SLA's
- Maintaining consistent communication with all parties including end-users, their managers and higher, as well as the provider's own internal management hierarchy

---

The hardware warranty services provider's service desk's staff's daily duties

The service desk staff's daily duties are determined by their service manager, whose responsibility includes the management of the hardware warranty services provider's service desk, and the proper prioritization and assignment of all service requests to the appropriate tier. The scheduling of all onsite and remote service work is ultimately the responsibility of the service manager, but this and other functions may be performed by a service dispatcher. It is the Service manager's ultimate responsibility to make certain the service desk is maintaining their SLA's.

In this context, a service desk staff's typical day may resemble the following:

- Log in to the hardware warranty services provider's PSA solution
- Review all newly-assigned service requests to him/her
- Review any service requests previously assigned and still open to insure they are not in danger of falling outside of SLA (service dispatcher and/or manager should be alerted to this status automatically by the PSA solution before it occurs)
- Work service requests in order of priority
  - Accept service request and time stamp
  - Review service request

- o Contact customer or end-user as needed to gather any necessary information in order to begin problem resolution
- o Consult information documented in PSA solution as needed in order to perform problem resolution
- o Qualify issue to determine if it can be resolved through tier 1 support within SLA
- o Work issue to successful resolution
- o Verify issue to be resolved to end-user's satisfaction
- o Document complete problem resolution details in PSA solution, mark status complete and time stamp
- o Service request is held in completed status for a minimum of 24 hours, after which the end-user is contacted to verify the issue has been resolved to their satisfaction and asked if the service request can be closed
- o Service request is closed
- If Service request cannot be resolved through tier 1 support, or is in danger of falling outside of SLA:
  - o Service request is escalated to Tier 2 and successive tiers of support, or an onsite visit is scheduled with a field engineer/technician as needed, and the problem resolution process continues

Maintain: The Hardware Warranty Services Delivery Model

Customer service

In order to establish, maintain and increase customer satisfaction, the hardware warranty services provider will need to educate their staff on delivering not only first-rate technical services, but excellent customer service as well. In fact, larger hardware warranty services providers may create and staff a customer service position to insure consistent customer service delivery.

Maximize: The Hardware Warranty Services Delivery Model

max · i · mize [**mak**-*suh*-mahyz] – *to increase to the greatest possible amount or degree*

Now that we understand the basics of what it takes to maintain the hardware warranty services delivery model in terms of service delivery, it's time to dive even deeper and identify how to maximize efficiencies, processes, procedures and profitability within this service delivery model.

Strategy

Although the "pure" hardware warranty services delivery model is challenged by factors such as low margins and the commodity-based nature its deliverables, areas where efficiencies, processes and procedures and profits can be maximized from a technical perspective include the following:

- Tools and technology
- Processes and procedures
- Scheduling
- Service delivery
- Inventory management
- RMA processing
- Staff utilization
- Costs
- Pricing
- Vendors
- Partners

Tools and technology

In order to provide the best services possible for customers, and continually improve their internal efficiencies and capabilities in order to scale, all service providers should consistently evaluate new tools and technologies and budget for investments in these yearly. These investments should be business decisions based upon a clear ROI or benefit to the provider and/or their customers.

Processes and procedures

No matter what service delivery model employed, there are always gains to be made by analyzing existing workflows to improve outcomes. Providers all too often neglect to turn the mirror upon themselves, or sample the Kool-Aid they are liberally drenching their customers with.

How often do providers practice what they preach to their customers and perform internal business needs analyses and technology assessments on themselves? *Not often enough.* In order to maximize their business models, they must understand that it is imperative to continue to invest in new tools and technology to offload labor-intensive processes from costly resources and continue to tweak and tune their processes and procedures to yield incremental gains in efficiency and productivity.

Service delivery maximization is not an event, but a continual process that never ends.

As intelligent business owners, providers need to grant their organizations the same type of consultative services as they do for customers. This will help insure that they can scale profitably to meet existing customers' needs and service new ones efficiently and gainfully.

Scheduling

Unfortunately, the reactive nature of the hardware warranty services delivery model challenges the service dispatcher in the scheduling department. Potential improvements in this area are relegated to forecasting realistic timelines for service delivery, especially when dispatching field engineers/technicians onsite to customer locations.

In these scenarios, it is incumbent for the service dispatcher to enforce a rigorous communication process between all field-dispatched resources and themselves. This can take the form of 30 minute check-in intervals where status is regularly communicated back to the service dispatcher during onsite problem remediation. This allows the service dispatcher to make informed decisions regarding the allocation of resources throughout the day.

Service delivery

Service delivery is an area where all service providers can always make improvements. The first step towards service delivery improvement is to map out the provider's existing service delivery process, beginning with the initial call or contact from the customer regarding a support issue, and following the problem management and resolution process all the way through to closure. An efficient problem management and resolution process will include escalation points to insure

---

---

that service requests don't end up in limbo for extended periods of time.

One thing to always keep in mind is the fact that the more services the provider can deliver remotely, the more profitable they will become.

It is a good idea for the provider to poll existing customers and get their candid feedback on their problem management and resolution process from start to finish. This will impress the customer's experience on the provider, and may help the provider identify ways to improve efficiency and customer satisfaction.

All technical support staff should always "start the clock", or timestamp a service request before they begin working on it, regularly documenting their activities and results in the provider's PSA solution. All too often technical resources forget to book their time during service delivery, and later have to "make up" their activities and timelines – *this is a major profitability killer.*

The following illustrates a basic problem management and resolution process:

1. Support request is received

2. Trouble ticket is created

---

3. Issue is identified and documented in PSA solution

4. Issue is qualified to determine if it can be resolved through tier 1 support

If issue can be resolved through tier 1 support:

5. Level 1 resolution - issue is worked to successful resolution

6. Quality control - Issue is verified to be resolved to customer's satisfaction

7. Trouble ticket is closed, after complete problem resolution details have been updated in PSA solution

If issue cannot be resolved through tier 1 support:

6. Issue is escalated to tier 2 support

7. Issue is qualified to determine if it can be resolved by tier 2 support

If issue can be resolved through tier 2 support:

8. Level 2 resolution - issue is worked to successful resolution

9. Quality control - issue is verified to be resolved to customer's satisfaction

10. Trouble ticket is closed, after complete problem resolution details have been updated in PSA solution

---

If issue cannot be resolved through tier 2 support:

9. Issue is escalated to tier 3 support

10. Issue is qualified to determine if it can be resolved through tier 3 support

If issue can be resolved through tier 3 support:

11. Level 3 resolution - issue is worked to successful resolution

12. Quality control - issue is verified to be resolved to customer's satisfaction

13. Trouble ticket is closed, after complete problem resolution details have been updated in PSA solution

If issue cannot be resolved through tier 3 support:

12. Issue is escalated to onsite support

13. Issue is qualified to determine if it can be resolved through onsite support

If issue can be resolved through onsite support:

14. Onsite resolution - issue is worked to successful resolution

15. Quality control - Issue is verified to be resolved to customer's satisfaction

---

16. Trouble ticket is closed, after complete problem resolution details have been updated in PSA solution

If issue cannot be resolved through onsite support:

17. Service manager decision point – request is updated in PSA solution with complete details of all activity performed

Inventory management

Improper inventory control and management can be a tremendous burden which ties up the hardware warranty services provider's cash flow and purchasing power, and may affect their ability to properly service their customers and meet SLA's.

The provider must be able to accurately forecast the equipment, parts and components needed on hand in order to support their customers, turn their inventory regularly and prevent out-of-stock situations.

RMA processing

It is incumbent upon the hardware warranty services provider to develop and implement an efficient procedure for dealing with RMA's so that they don't pile up in a back office or closet and miss their RMA replacement window. This is an area that can bleed profits for a provider over time, if not managed properly.

Staff utilization

The ability for the hardware warranty services provider to keep their technical staff fully utilized at better than 75% on a consistent basis is critical for profitability, and in most cases cannot be accomplished without a professional services automation (PSA) solution and the requirement for all staff to book each minute of their time in it. In fact, the proper implementation and use of a PSA solution has the potential of increasing staff utilization close to 100%, driving more revenue to the provider's bottom line.

The cost of low utilization is an extremely important concept to grasp, as 75% overall utilization means that the provider is paying their staff a full 3 months per year for non-billable time, and if this utilization number is lower, so are net profits.

Costs

As with any service delivery model, the ability to contain, control and reduce costs directly impacts the bottom line. The hardware services provider should review all of their overhead costs on a regular basis to make certain that they are getting the absolute best rates on services such as telco, broadband, cell service and HR costs as well as medical and other employee benefits.

Other ways to minimize costs are to find and utilize dependable contractors for periodic or temporary surges in business. This strategy may save on labor costs in the long run, and delay the necessity to hire additional full-time employees until absolutely necessary.

Vendors and distributors

Another area the hardware warranty services provider can explore is working with their vendors and distributors to obtain better pricing and discounts, or other benefits such as marketing development funds that can be used to market for new prospects and grow the provider's business.

Partnering

Another way to maximize and grow revenues for the hardware warranty services provider is to partner with other complementary services providers such as telco vendors, copier vendors and the like to trade warm leads. Similarly, the hardware warranty services provider can partner with other I.T. solution providers to deliver additional products and services to their customer base and earn added revenues as commissions, and reciprocally make available hardware warranty services to these providers if they do not offer these services to their own customers.

Migrate: The Hardware Warranty Services Delivery Model

mi · grate [mahy-greyt] – *to shift, as from one system, mode of operation, or enterprise to another*

No matter which service delivery model the provider practices, one way to increase revenues and opportunities is to adopt an additional service delivery model as a hybrid option, or completely migrate to it. In many situations, providers choose a hybrid model that allows them to provide a blend of hardware warranty, break-fix, professional and managed services all under one roof.

While the desire for the provider to have the capability to address all of their customers' needs in this fashion is strong, the most successful providers are those that focus on a smaller number of deliverables, allowing them to really fine-tune their processes and procedures to receive the greatest net profits. They may also specialize in vertical-specific markets in order to further increase their profits through service delivery familiarity and shorten their sales cycles.

The next section focuses on migration strategies for the hardware warranty services provider wishing to explore the grass on the other side of the fence.

Migrate: The Hardware Warranty Services Delivery Model

Migration choices

The hardware warranty services provider has their choice of three other service delivery models to migrate to or adopt into a new hybrid service delivery model:

1. The break-fix services delivery model
2. The managed services delivery model
3. The professional services delivery model

It will generally be easier for the "pure" hardware warranty services provider to adopt or migrate to the break-fix services delivery model first, rather than directly to the professional or managed services delivery models. This is due to the similarities shared between these models in terms of service delivery tools and processes and staffing and management roles and requirements. This strategy will allow the provider to obtain the experience and knowledge required to migrate to successive models in the least painful and challenging manner possible, if desired.

With this understanding, we will explore strategies for the hardware warranty services provider to migrate to all three models, with the break-fix services delivery model first, followed by the managed services and professional services delivery models.

Migrate: The Hardware Warranty Services Delivery Model

Strategies for migration to a break-fix services delivery model

Areas that the hardware warranty services provider will need to evaluate when migrating to the break-fix services delivery model may include:

- Tools and technology
- Processes and procedures
- Scheduling
- Service delivery
- Equipment and parts ordering
- RMA processing
- Invoicing
- Staffing
- Staff utilization
- Costs
- Pricing
- Vendors
- Partners

Tools and technology

The hardware warranty services provider should evaluate the suitability of their existing problem management and resolution, or PSA software solution for compatibility with the break-fix services delivery model. Key features to evaluate include:

- Customer relationship management (CRM) capabilities
- Service request or trouble ticketing capabilities
- Scheduling & dispatching capabilities
- Time & expense tracking capabilities
- Inventory control capabilities
- Asset management capabilities
- Configuration & change management capabilities
- Knowledge base capabilities
- Resource management capabilities
- Integration of quoting & invoicing with accounting systems capabilities
- Sales funnel capabilities
- Robust, customizable reporting capabilities

Processes and procedures

Similarities between the hardware warranty and break-fix services delivery models prove advantageous in this area, as the provider's problem management and resolution processes and procedures should transfer to the break-fix service delivery model without much modification, if they are based on best practices.

The primary difference here will be the support of a much wider variety of hardware and software applications, as well as networks and infrastructure, requiring the hardware

---

warranty services provider to add or create additional problem management procedures to handle the support and maintenance of these additional devices and services.

Scheduling

The process of scheduling resources for service delivery is similar and consistent across all service delivery models. The primary difference in this migration scenario is that the provider will be delivering a much broader set of maintenance and support services to their customers than they had previously, and so will need to carefully monitor and evaluate the time required to deliver these new services during and for some time after migration. This will provide them the information necessary to accurately forecast the time required to deliver these new services, and improve their scheduling effectiveness, resulting in increased efficiencies and profitability over time.

Service delivery

As mentioned, if the hardware warranty services provider's problem management and resolution process is based upon best practices, delivering support to a broader range of devices and services will only be challenged by the provider's service desk staff's problem-specific training and experience.

Migrate: The Hardware Warranty Services Delivery Model

Equipment and parts ordering

The provider's existing equipment and parts request and fulfillment process for ordering, tracking and paying for equipment and parts required for hardware warranty services delivery should be adequate for the break-fix services delivery model, with the requirement to add new vendors and distributors to support a wider variety of hardware and services a good possibility.

RMA processing

The hardware warranty services provider's existing RMA processing procedure should not require much modification, save for the likely need to identify the RMA procedures for additional vendors and/or distributors.

Invoicing

This is an area that might require some focused attention and modification for the "pure" hardware warranty services provider migrating to the break-fix services delivery model, as the provider may historically sell hardware warranties to customers in a single transaction, and not be accustomed to invoicing for additional services on a consistent basis afterwards.

The break-fix services delivery model; however, is much different in this respect, and requires the ability for the provider to bill daily for services rendered, if desired. With this reality comes the requirement for both the capability, as well as the process to manage this activity.

Staffing

Due to the similarities between the hardware warranty and break-fix services delivery models in terms of staff roles and responsibilities, existing roles should transfer to the new model with minimal modifications in this area.

Staff utilization

The same requirements for maintaining the highest possible utilization for billable resources exists in all service delivery models. As a result, the provider's need to extract every ounce of utilization from their staff does not change as a result of service delivery model migration.

Costs

The necessity for the provider to contain, reduce and control costs is not service delivery model-dependent. This migration scenario may require the provider to invest in training their existing staff to provide them the ability to support a wider range of solutions and environments, or to hire and train additional staff as needed to provide their customers break-fix services.

Pricing

The hardware warranty services provider will need to establish labor rates for break-fix services delivery.

The identification of the cost of service delivery is the first step in developing a labor rate pricing strategy. Factors to weigh when identifying the total cost of service delivery (TCSD) include the following:

- The provider's hourly cost of billable resources
- The provider's employer contributions
- The provider's overhead

Determining the hourly cost for 1 billable technician
In order to determine the provider's hourly cost for 1 billable technician, it is necessary to include the technician's hourly wages, the provider's employer contributions and overhead costs in a formula which yields an hourly value.

In the following table, the technician's hourly wage is added to the employer's payroll contributions. This value is then added to the provider's monthly overhead costs and divided by the monthly hours of service delivery, which is then divided by the number of billable technicians. The outcome is the provider's TCSD per hour.

Determining TCSD

Hourly cost for 1 billable technician		
Technician's hourly wage	$30.00	Hourly pay
+		
Employer payroll contributions	$10.00	Taxes, Insurance, etc.
+		
Total overhead cost	$18.75	$3k/mo ÷ 160hrs/mo ÷ 1
=		
TCSD per hour	$58.75	

Determining profit margins and labor rates

After the provider determines their TCSD per hour, it is now possible to determine a desired profit margin and final labor rate. In the previous example, the provider's TCSD per hour is $58.75, so it is now a simple matter to determine a desired profit margin in this example. If the provider wishes to

---

implement a 100% profit margin on their hourly TCSD, the result would be a billable labor rate of $117.50. Higher desired profit margins would yield higher billable labor rates.

Determining Labor Rates

100% Margin for 1 billable technician		
Cost per hour	$58.75	CPH
+		
Target margin	$58.75	100% of CPH
=		
Billable labor rate	$117.50	

Vendors and Distributors

The hardware warranty services provider will almost certainly need to build relationships with new vendors and distributors to support their customer environments with break-fix services.

Partnering

The hardware warranty services provider migrating to break-fix services delivery will benefit from partnering with other complementary services providers such as telco vendors, copier vendors and the like to trade warm leads with and grow their new business model.

Similarly, the provider should actively seek partnering opportunities with other I.T. solution providers to deliver additional products and services to their customer base and earn added revenues as commissions, increasing their value to their customers by marshalling the resources to meet their business needs.

Migrate: The Hardware Warranty Services Delivery Model

Strategies for migration to a managed services delivery model

Areas that the hardware warranty services provider will need to evaluate when migrating to the managed services delivery model may include:

- Agreement and SLA
- Tools and technology
- Processes and procedures
- Scheduling
- Service delivery
- Equipment and parts ordering
- RMA processing
- Invoicing
- Staffing
- Staff utilization
- Costs
- Pricing
- Vendors
- Partners

Agreement and SLA

The hardware warranty services provider will need to develop a managed services agreement and SLA in order to deliver proactive, flat fee managed I.T. services to their customers.

Migrate: The Hardware Warranty Services Delivery Model

Like hardware warranty services, managed I.T. services are delivered, measured and governed by strict SLAs.

Tools and technology

The hardware warranty services provider should evaluate the suitability of their existing problem management and resolution, or PSA software solution for compatibility with the managed services delivery model. Key features to evaluate include:

- Customer relationship management (CRM) capabilities
- Service request or trouble ticketing capabilities
- Scheduling & dispatching capabilities
- Time & expense tracking capabilities
- Inventory control capabilities
- Asset management capabilities
- Configuration & change management capabilities
- Knowledge base capabilities
- Resource management capabilities
- Integration of quoting & invoicing with accounting systems capabilities
- Sales funnel capabilities
- Robust, customizable reporting capabilities

In addition, the hardware warranty services provider will need to invest in a remote monitoring and management (RMM)

---

solution to allow them to proactively monitor critical devices, events and services within their customer environments and alert on operation outside of recommended parameters, allowing the provider to take action to maximize customer uptime and maintain SLA's.

The RMM solution will allow the provider to script, schedule and automatically execute otherwise costly, labor-intensive activities such as hardware and software patching and updating and system optimization. This solution may grant the provider the following capabilities:

- WMI/Syslog/SNMP monitoring capabilities
- Multiple alerting capabilities – email/text page/pager
- Configurable and customizable alerting capabilities
- Supports escalation
- Outputs detailed logging
- Supports multiple operating systems
- Supports critical server monitoring functions – Exchange, SQL, IIS, SharePoint, Linux, Novell
- Supports multiple types of hardware – PCs, Macs, servers, routers, switches, firewalls, Printers
- Supports Multiple 3rd-Party Software Monitoring
- Supports operating system and software patch management and updates
- Easily Integrates with PSA solutions
- Supports remote control of monitored devices

- Allows scripting, scheduling and automatic execution of otherwise costly, labor-intensive activities
- Robust, customizable reporting capabilities

Processes and procedures

Some similarities between the hardware warranty and managed services delivery models benefit the provider in this area, as their problem management and resolution processes and procedures are transferable to the managed services delivery model without much modification, if they are based on best practices.

The primary differences here will include the shift from a reactive to a proactive service delivery focus, as well as the development of NOC services to include a remote monitoring and management (RMM) solution's deployment, maintenance, response and remediation procedures.

Scheduling

The process of scheduling resources for service delivery is similar and consistent across all service delivery models. Modifications to the provider's scheduling process are negligible in this migration scenario due to the similarities between the service delivery models in this regard.

Migrate: The Hardware Warranty Services Delivery Model

Service delivery

As mentioned, if the hardware warranty services provider's problem management and resolution processes are based upon best practices, these are transferable to the managed services delivery model without extreme modification, with the exceptions being a mind-shift from delivering services reactively to a proactive service delivery focus, and the development of remote monitoring and management (RMM) processes and procedures.

Equipment and parts ordering

The hardware warranty provider's existing documented request and fulfillment process for ordering, tracking and paying for equipment, licensing and parts required for service delivery should suit their needs in delivering managed services.

Primary differences in this area may include expanding the number and types of manufacturers, vendors and distributors that customer equipment, licensing, services and solutions are sourced from as a managed services provider.

RMA processing

The hardware warranty services provider's existing RMA processing procedure should not require much modification when delivering managed services.

Migrate: The Hardware Warranty Services Delivery Model

Invoicing

The managed services delivery model requires the ability for the provider to invoice for services in advance of their delivery, and for a flat fee per month. This requires both the capability, as well as the process to manage invoicing in this manner.

Invoicing for additional services that fall outside of the provider's managed services agreement or SLA will occur as these services are delivered.

Staffing

Although similarities between the hardware warranty and managed services delivery models exist in terms of most existing staff roles and responsibilities, allowing them to transfer to the new model with minimal modifications, an additional NOC staff role will be required to support the proactive monitoring of critical devices and services in customer environments to maximize uptime and maintain SLA's.

NOC staff

In this context, the NOC (network operations center) staff participates in the provider's problem management and resolution process, and can be assigned to deliver proactive remote patching, updating and monitoring services for devices, software applications and operating systems and

---

---

services in customer environments. Whereas the provider's service desk staff works primarily with end-user issues, the NOC staff's main focus is on managing and delivering scheduled maintenance activities for critical devices and services and responding to alerts generated by the provider's remote monitoring and management (RMM) solution.

The NOC staff identifies, prioritizes and documents all service activity and will execute the provider's problem management and resolution processes as well as utilize the provider's chosen software and hardware management and remediation tools, processes and procedures during remote technical service delivery.

Staff utilization

The same requirements for maintaining the highest possible utilization for billable resources exists in all service delivery models. As a result, the provider's need to extract every ounce of utilization from their staff does not change due to service delivery model migration.

Costs

The necessity for the provider to contain, reduce and control costs is not service delivery model-dependent. This migration scenario may require the provider to invest in training their existing staff to provide them the ability to support a wider range of solutions and environments, or to hire and train

---

additional staff as needed to provide their customers managed services, as well as the costs to purchase, train on and maintain the provider's RMM solution.

Pricing

A consideration for the provider migrating to the managed services delivery model is the necessity to adopt a flat-fee pricing model for proactive service delivery. Whether the provider chooses a per-device, per user or tiered model, they must first understand what their total cost of service delivery is, in order to determine a desired profit margin and ultimate retail price for their services.

Factors to weigh when identifying the total cost of service delivery (TCSD) include the following:

- The provider's hourly cost of billable resources
- The provider's employer contributions
- The provider's overhead

Determining the hourly cost for 1 billable technician

In order to determine the provider's hourly cost for 1 billable technician, it is necessary to include the technician's hourly wages, the provider's employer contributions and overhead costs in a formula which yields an hourly value.

In the following table, the technician's hourly wage is added to the employer's payroll contributions. This value is then added to the provider's monthly overhead costs and divided by the monthly hours of service delivery, which is then divided by the number of billable technicians. The outcome is the provider's TCSD per hour.

Determining TCSD

Hourly cost for 1 billable technician		
Technician's hourly wage	$30.00	Hourly pay
+		
Employer payroll contributions	$10.00	Taxes, Insurance, etc.
+		
Total overhead cost	$18.75	$3k/mo ÷ 160hrs/mo ÷ 1
=		
TCSD per hour	$58.75	

Determining profit margins and labor rates

After the provider determines their TCSD per hour, it is now possible to determine a desired profit margin and final labor rate. In the previous example, the provider's TCSD per hour is $58.75, so it is now a simple matter to determine a desired profit margin in this example. If the provider wishes to implement a 100% profit margin on their hourly TCSD, the result would be a billable labor rate of $117.50 per hour. Higher desired profit margins would yield higher billable labor rates.

Determining Labor Rates

100% Margin for 1 billable technician		
Cost per hour	$58.75	CPH
+		
Target margin	$58.75	100% of CPH
=		
Billable labor rate	$117.50	

Quoting managed services per estimated monthly support hours

One method a provider may utilize in quoting a managed services maintenance plan to their customers would be to estimate the amount of hours required per month to perform the services agreed to in their SLA, then use their billable labor rate as the factor to yield the cost to deliver services.

The following example illustrates quoting a customer a flat fee for supporting a 30 pc and 2-server environment. The provider assumes a support requirement of a half hour per month per pc and two and a half hours per month per server, equaling a 20 hour per month service requirement.

Migrate: The Hardware Warranty Services Delivery Model

Quoting managed services by estimating support hours

Pricing for a 30 pc, 2 server environment at .5 hrs/mo support per pc and 2.5 hrs/mo support per server

Estimated support hours/mo	20
x	
Billable labor rate	$117.50/hr
=	_____
Flat monthly fee	$2,350.00/mo

Should the provider deliver a hybrid blend of services including break-fix services along with flat-fee managed services, these services would be invoiced separately to customers, along with any other services delivered that fall outside of the provider's flat-fee support and maintenance services.

Vendors and distributors
The hardware warranty services provider will almost certainly need to build relationships with new vendors and distributors

---

---

to support their customer environments with managed services.

Partnering

Other ways to maximize and grow revenues for the provider is to partner with other complementary services providers such as telco vendors, copier vendors and the like to trade warm leads. Similarly, the provider can partner with other I.T. solution providers to deliver additional products and services to their customer base and earn added revenues as commissions, increasing their value to their customers as a trusted advisor by marshalling the resources to meet their business needs.

Strategies for migration to a professional services delivery model

In order for the hardware warranty services provider to successfully migrate to the professional services delivery model, or add professional services to their existing deliverables, they will need to modify and/or add key tools and technologies, staff, and roles and responsibilities to their organization.

Areas that the hardware warranty services provider will need to evaluate when migrating to the professional services delivery model may include:

- Tools and technology
- Processes and procedures
- Project scoping
- Project quoting
- Project planning
- Equipment and parts ordering
- Project management
- Invoicing
- Staffing
- Staff utilization
- Costs
- Pricing
- Vendors and distributors

- Partners

Tools and technology

The provider may invest in software tools to assist them in effective, efficient professional services delivery. These software solutions may provide them the following capabilities:

- Customer relationship management (CRM) capabilities
- Project scoping capabilities
- Technical drawing capabilities
- Project quoting capabilities
- Project planning capabilities
- Equipment and parts ordering capabilities
- Project management capabilities
- Integration of quoting & invoicing with accounting systems capabilities
- Sales funnel capabilities
- Robust, customizable reporting capabilities

Processes and procedures

The provider migrating to the professional services delivery model will need to develop effective processes and procedures to:

- Conduct needs analyses and technology assessments

- Scope and quote projects and create proposals
- Create technical drawings
- Order equipment, software licensing and services
- Design project plans and timelines
- Manage project implementations
- Set and manage customer expectations

Project scoping
The provider must develop or hire resources with the capability to utilize the provider's preferred tools, technology and processes to conduct needs analyses and technology assessments, as well as resources to review the findings contained therein and work with manufacturers, vendors and distributors to design effective solutions to address customer needs.

Project quoting
The provider must develop or hire resources with the capability to utilize the provider's preferred tools, technology and processes to create accurate quotes and compelling proposals from project scopes and information and pricing received from manufacturers, vendors and distributors.

Project planning
The provider must develop or hire resources with the capability to utilize the provider's preferred tools, technology and processes to create effective project plans that identify

resources, tasks and timelines to insure a project's completion within its defined scope, schedule and budget.

Equipment and parts ordering

The provider should have a documented request and fulfillment process for ordering, tracking and paying for equipment, parts, licensing, services and solutions required for professional services delivery.

These processes may differ from their existing hardware warranty ordering procedures in areas such as number of sources and lead times and costs, requiring the provider to increase their flooring accounts, request credit from new sources or increase credit limits and modify payment terms with their existing vendors and distributors.

Project management

The provider must develop or hire resources with the capability to utilize the provider's preferred tools, technology and processes to manage projects, their resources and schedules to insure project completion within scope, timeline and budget.

Invoicing

The provider must determine how they will invoice for their professional services, and may choose to invoice the customer a portion of the project's overall value in advance to cover the costs of hardware, licensing and labor during the initial phases of project implementation, with the outstanding balance due upon completion, or accept progress payments for projects with extended timelines.

Staffing

Although similarities between the hardware warranty and professional services delivery models exist in terms of some existing staff roles and responsibilities, allowing them to transfer to the new model with minimal modifications, additional staff roles will be required to support the requirements of the professional services delivery model, and may include:

- Sales engineers
- Purchasing managers
- Project managers

Sales engineers

In this context, the sales engineer is perhaps the most versatile and important role in the professional services delivery model. The sales engineer participates in both the provider's pre- and post-sales and project planning processes, and can be assigned to assist in the business needs analysis, technology assessment and solution design and specification phases of professional services delivery. All of these functions are critical to insuring smooth project delivery.

Purchasing manager

In this context, the purchasing manager participates in the provider's project quoting and planning process by insuring pricing and availability of hardware, software licensing and services from vendors, distributors and fulfillment partners to meet the sales engineer's solution requirements, and handles all returns and credits when necessary.

Project managers

In this context, the project manager participates in the provider's project planning and management process by working with the sales engineer to develop a project scope, then specify methods to be utilized during project implementation, identify all tasks to be completed during project implementation, create a timeline and expected duration for each task's completion and estimate and allocate resources for each task's completion.

In addition, the project manager is normally responsible for creating the risk management plan, change control process and communication and status reporting process utilized during project implementation.

Staff utilization

The same requirements for maintaining the highest possible utilization for billable resources exists in all service delivery models. As a result, the provider's need to extract every ounce of utilization from their staff does not change due to service delivery model migration.

Costs

The necessity for the provider to contain, reduce and control costs is not service delivery model-dependent. This migration scenario may require the provider to invest in training their existing staff to provide them the ability to support a wider range of solutions and environments, or to hire and train additional staff as needed to provide their customers professional services, as well as the costs to purchase, train on and utilize the provider's professional services-specific tools and technology solutions.

Pricing

A consideration for the provider migrating to the professional services delivery model is the necessity to understand what their total cost of service delivery is, in order to determine a desired profit margin and ultimate retail price for their services.

Factors to weigh when identifying the total cost of service delivery (TCSD) include the following:

- The provider's hourly cost of billable resources
- The provider's employer contributions
- The provider's overhead

Determining the hourly cost for 5 billable resources

In order to determine the provider's hourly cost to deliver a project requiring 5 billable resources, it is necessary to include each resources' hourly wages, the provider's employer contributions and overhead costs in a formula which yields an hourly value.

In the following table, each of the resources' individual hourly wages are aggregated and added to the employer's payroll contributions. This value is then added to the provider's monthly overhead costs and divided by the monthly hours of service delivery, which is then divided by the number of billable resources. The outcome is the provider's TCSD per hour for this resource group.

Determining TCSD per Resource Group

Hourly cost for 5 billable resources		
Resources' aggregate hourly wages	$190.00	Hourly pay
+		
Employer payroll contributions	$57.00	Taxes, Insurance, etc.
+		
Total overhead cost	$3.75	$3k/mo ÷ 160hrs/mo ÷ 5
=		
TCSD per hour	$250.75	

Determining profit margins and labor rates

After the provider determines their TCSD per hour, it is now possible to determine a desired profit margin and final labor rate. In the previous example, the provider's TCSD per hour is $250.75, so it is now a simple matter to determine a desired

---

profit margin in this example. If the provider wishes to implement a 50% profit margin on their hourly TCSD, the result would be a billable labor rate of about $375.00 per hour. Higher desired profit margins would yield higher billable labor rates.

Determining Labor Rates

100% Margin for 5 billable resources		
Cost per hour	$250.75	CPH
+		
Target margin	$125.00	50% of CPH
=		
Billable labor rate	+/- $375.00	

Because each unique resource's contribution and cost per hour may differ from the others, for a professional services delivery quote, the provider would estimate how many hours each of their resources would contribute to the overall project, and may use their individual billable labor rates to come up with the final quote.

Vendors and distributors

The provider migrating to the professional services delivery model will almost certainly need to build relationships with new vendors and distributors in order to deliver professional services.

Partnering

Other ways to maximize and grow revenues for the provider migrating to a professional services delivery model is to partner with other I.T. solution providers to deliver additional products and services to their customer base to meet their customers' needs.

Section 2: The Break-Fix Services Delivery Model

For purposes of our discussion, the break-fix services delivery model is defined as being comprised of activities, processes and procedures that allow the service provider to deliver scheduled or unscheduled I.T. maintenance services to customers. These services are normally delivered on a time and materials basis, and some break-fix services providers sell these services in blocks of hours, which customers can pre-pay for in exchange for a discounted rate.

Build: The Break-Fix Services Delivery Model

build [bild] – *to develop or give form to according to a plan or process; create*

In order to build a break-fix services delivery model, we must understand its characteristics – the nuts and bolts.

This section will explore the considerations necessary to build a break-fix services delivery model and discuss deliverables, tools and technology, pricing and positioning, staffing requirements, target markets and other concerns.

Build: The Break-Fix Services Delivery Model

Characteristics

Although break-fix services providers experience higher profit margins than hardware warranty service providers, characteristics of a break-fix services delivery model include delivering a commodity service – and as such, it may be difficult to grow revenues during periods of economic uncertainty, when prospects and clients are trying to cut costs.

And since break-fix services are based on a time and materials billing model, there exists a finite amount of service that the provider's individual staff can deliver, making it difficult to scale without hiring, training and managing additional resources.

As break-fix services are generally reactive in nature (as the name denotes), the provider is challenged to break free from firefighter mode, and since reactive, emergency services are always the most costly for customers, the break-fix services provider may be perceived as enjoying increased profits when their customers are experiencing the most pain. Thus it is difficult for the provider in the break-fix services delivery model to demonstrate close alignment with their prospects' and customers' business goals and needs.

Deliverables

The deliverables of a break-fix services provider may include providing remote, onsite and bench support to troubleshoot and remediate hardware, software, service and user issues impacting their proper function and operations.

The break-fix services provider's duties may include quoting, ordering and implementing hardware and software solutions to meet their customers' needs, and they may blend professional services with their existing deliverables. The provider may also be prone to involvement with the customer's vendors from time to time. In this relationship, the customer generally manages their vendors, with the provider grouped into that category.

Tools and technology

The break-fix services provider may invest in software tools to assist them in effective, efficient service delivery. A professional services automation (PSA) solution may provide them the following capabilities:

- Customer relationship management (CRM) capabilities
- Service request or trouble ticketing capabilities
- Scheduling & dispatching capabilities
- Time & expense tracking capabilities
- Inventory control capabilities
- Asset management capabilities

- Configuration & change management capabilities
- Knowledge base capabilities
- Resource management capabilities
- Integration of quoting & invoicing with accounting systems capabilities
- Sales funnel capabilities
- Robust, customizable reporting capabilities

Pricing and positioning

Break-fix services providers share competitive challenges similar to those faced by hardware warranty services providers, and pricing for their time and materials-based services tends to be aggressive, as it is remains difficult to build a unique value proposition for a commodity service which can be sourced from a multitude of vendors. In this service delivery model, the provider may price their services in the following manner:

- Per hour
- Per hour based upon response time
- Per hour based upon service required
- Per hour based upon number of resources
- Per hour based upon skill set of resources
- Per hour based upon time of day
- Per hour based upon day of week or holiday

...or any combination thereof. In addition, the break-fix services provider may allow customers to receive reduced labor rates by offering the ability to purchase blocks of hours in advance. This is commonly referred to as "block time".

Positioning break-fix services as a necessity for prospects and customers whose businesses are reliant on technology is not a tremendously difficult task, and achieved more easily by a break-fix services provider than by a pure hardware warranty services provider – especially when targeting the SMB space. This being said, it is generally not difficult for the break-fix services provider to secure enough business to meet their revenue requirements.

Additional project revenue can be had by the provider that delivers professional services to their customers in addition to break-fix services, and these services are normally quoted on a per-project basis.

Staffing requirements
The break-fix services provider shares similar staffing requirements as the hardware warranty services provider (another similarity shared between these two models), and depending upon the vertical market, services offered, number of customers and the complexity of the environments serviced (among other factors), the break-fix services provider will

---

require a minimum number of staff who fall into specific roles, which may include:

- Owners
- Managers
- Administrative staff
- Technical staff
- Marketing/sales staff
- Other staff

Owners

As in any organization; and based upon a number of factors, break-fix services provider owners may wear many hats, or merely a few. Their basic responsibility to the organization, its stakeholders, staff and customers is to manage and maintain a profitable business concern.

Managers

The size of the organization's management staff will be based upon the number of the organization's staff, among other factors, and may include:

- Operations management
- Office management
- HR management
- Marketing/sales management
- Service delivery management

- Vendor management
- Customer service management

Administration

Every organization, no matter how large or small requires some form of administrative support. These roles include:

- Front office staff
- HR staff
- Accounting staff
- Customer service staff

Technical staff

Technical staff requirements for a break-fix services delivery practice may include:

- Service desk staff
- Field engineers/technicians
- Bench engineers/technicians
- Service dispatchers

Marketing/sales staff

Although the marketing and sales roles are distinct, and in larger organizations segmented by business unit and resources, we'll group them together for purposes of our service delivery-focused discussion.

No matter what size the service provider's organization is, at one point or another, someone is going to have to market and sell the provider's services.

Other staff

As in all service delivery models, other resources may be required and additional staff that may make up the break-fix services provider's organization may include:

- Purchasing manager
- Inventory manager

Considerations

The "pure" break-fix services delivery model can be very profitable, notwithstanding its placement in the pecking-order of service delivery profitability contained in this book. The challenge for the break-fix services provider quickly becomes the ability to scale their services profitably without going through the time and expense of interviewing, hiring, training and managing an ever-increasing amount of staff and dealing with the HR, customer service and quality control considerations this type of growth brings with it.

In addition, the break-fix services provider must continually find and demonstrate ways to prove their value to their customers in order to stave off competitors attempting to win their attention and business.

The Best I.T. Service Delivery BOOK EVER!

Build: The Break-Fix Services Delivery Model

Target market

Unlike the pure hardware warranty services provider, who must depend on high volume engagements which relegate them more towards Mid and Enterprise markets, the break-fix services provider's target market may be vertical or non-vertical specific, and can span the SMB and Mid markets. Enterprise customers are more than likely to have their own in-house staff to handle break-fix duties for their user environments, so the typical provider would probably not experience much traction there.

For "hybrid" break-fix services providers, who deliver not only break-fix services, but hardware warranty, professional and managed services, or some combination of these, their value to customers is greater, and therefore their target market is much broader.

Typically, a more service-oriented delivery model (as opposed to a transaction-based model) will succeed in attracting more technology-strategic customers who view technology spending as strategic investments in their organizations and provide them a competitive advantage in their markets. To these customers, service and value rank higher than cost considerations.

On the other hand, a more transaction-based delivery model attracts less technology-strategic customers, and the more

---

commoditized the products and services delivered, the more cost-conscious the customers become, reducing the ability for the provider to win business based on value and service.

Customer satisfaction and loyalty

As a result of the commodity nature of break-fix services, as long as the service provider is capable of meeting the customer's expectations in terms of service delivery, customer satisfaction should be easy to achieve and maintain.

Customer loyalty; however, may be another matter entirely, based yet again on the commodity nature of the deliverable, as well as the reactive, transaction-based nature of the relationship. How many times have you been able to win business away from a provider delivering break-fix services? This proves the point that customers in a transaction-based relationship receiving a commoditized service have little loyalty to the existing provider, and reinforces the reality that we must modify our deliverables and relationships with customers to be perceived as indispensable trusted advisors.

Maintain: The Break-Fix Services Delivery Model

main·tain [meyn-**teyn**] – *to keep in an existing state; preserve or retain*

Now that we understand the nuts and bolts of the break-fix services delivery model and its characteristics and considerations, let's dive a bit deeper and explore what it takes to maintain it in terms of service delivery.

This section will cover implementing the break-fix services delivery model and discuss technical roles and responsibilities, as well as service delivery.

Focus

The "pure" break-fix services delivery model focuses on allowing the provider the ability to effectively deliver scheduled and unscheduled break-fix maintenance services to their customers on a time and materials basis without establishing or adhering to an SLA.

The primary difference between the break-fix services provider's and the hardware warranty services provider's service delivery strategy is that the break-fix service provider will bill their customers on a time and materials basis for all problem management and remediation activity (remote, onsite or bench), whereas a hardware warranty services provider's services will generally have been paid for at the inception of the hardware warranty services agreement.

The break-fix services provider may also sell their customers a pre-paid block of hours at a reduced hourly labor rate, and bill service time against these hours until depleted, then sell their customers another pre-paid block of service hours.

Technical Implementation

In order to implement a break-fix services delivery model, the provider must possess:

- Software and hardware tools
- Effective processes and procedures
- Technical staff

Software and hardware tools
An effective break-fix services provider will be able to manage the I.T. infrastructure in their customer environments and execute a consistent problem management process.

Software tools utilized by the break-fix services provider to accomplish these activities may include asset management, problem management and remote access/control and remediation solutions. Some remote monitoring and management (RMM) and professional service automation (PSA) solutions provide all of these capabilities.

The break-fix services provider's PSA solution may provide them the following capabilities:

- Customer relationship management (CRM) capabilities
- Service request or trouble ticketing capabilities
- Scheduling & dispatching capabilities
- Time & expense tracking capabilities
- Inventory control capabilities
- Asset management capabilities
- Configuration & change management capabilities
- Knowledge base capabilities
- Resource management capabilities
- Integration of quoting & invoicing with accounting systems capabilities
- Sales funnel capabilities

- Robust, customizable reporting capabilities

The break-fix services provider may also utilize additional software test, update and remediation tools to provide diagnostic, troubleshooting and repair services for their customers. Leveraging these types of software tools help the break-fix services provider gain efficiency and speeds problem identification and resolution, increasing customer satisfaction, which is required in this commodity-based service delivery model.

In addition to software tools, the break-fix services provider will require both standard, as well as specialized hardware tools in order to service equipment in their customer environments.

Effective processes and procedures
In order for the provider to cost-effectively deliver break-fix services to their customers, they must develop and implement consistent problem management and resolution processes and procedures.

By standardizing on their software and hardware tools, and fine-tuning their processes and procedures, the provider will increase customer satisfaction as well as their own profitability.

Parts and hardware inventory

Unless the break-fix services provider is also building and supporting white box equipment for their customers, there really is no need to maintain the type of hardware inventory that a hardware warranty services provider would. Since the break-fix services provider does not sell or adhere to SLA's, their challenge is to readily source replacement hardware for their customers in a reasonable enough timeframe to maintain customer satisfaction.

Technical staff

In order to meet customer expectations and workload requirements, the break-fix services provider will require a sufficient number of technical staff trained in effective hardware and software problem management and resolution processes to support their customers' infrastructure and environments. The technical staff will also require training specific to the provider's chosen software and hardware management and remediation tools, processes and procedures.

Technical roles and responsibilities

Depending upon the number and size of customers served, and the size of the provider's organization, the break-fix services provider's technical staff will fall into specific roles which may include:

- Purchasing managers
- Inventory managers
- Service dispatchers
- Service managers
- Service desk staff
- Bench engineers/technicians
- Field engineers/technicians

Purchasing manager
In this context, the purchasing manager participates in the provider's service delivery process by insuring pricing and availability of hardware, software licensing and services from vendors, distributors and fulfillment partners to meet the provider's service delivery requirements.

Inventory manager
In this context, the inventory manager participates in the provider's service delivery process by insuring adequate inventory availability of hardware, software licensing and services from vendors, distributors and fulfillment partners to meet the provider's service delivery requirements, and handles all returns, RMAs and credits when necessary.

Service dispatchers
In this context, the service dispatcher participates in the provider's problem management and resolution process, and may assign resources to and schedule all remote, onsite or

---

bench warranty services. The service dispatcher may also be included in the provider's escalation process and be alerted by their PSA solution should service requests become in danger of falling out of SLA.

Service dispatchers will utilize the provider's chosen software management tools, processes and procedures to manage dispatch functions during service delivery.

Service managers
In this context, the service manager is ultimately responsible for maintaining the provider's technical staffing levels, training and certification requirements, problem management and resolution processes and customer satisfaction by strict SLA management, among other responsibilities.

Service managers will utilize the provider's chosen software management tools, processes and procedures to manage service delivery.

Service desk staff
In this context, the service desk staff participates in the provider's problem management and resolution process, and can be assigned to deliver remote technical support services to end users. The service desk staff identifies, prioritizes and documents all service requests, and initiates problem management and resolution activity.

Service desk staff will execute the provider's problem management and resolution processes as well as utilize the provider's chosen software and hardware management and remediation tools, processes and procedures during remote service delivery.

Bench engineers/technicians
In this context, the bench engineer/technician participates in the provider's problem management and resolution process, and can be assigned to deliver technical support services for customer equipment brought into the provider's facilities when necessary.

Bench engineers/technicians will utilize the provider's hardware and software problem management and resolution processes as well as the provider's chosen software and hardware management and remediation tools, processes and procedures during service delivery.

Field engineers/technicians
In this context, the field engineer/technician participates in the provider's problem management and resolution process, and can be assigned to deliver technical support services at the customer's facilities when necessary.

Field engineers/technicians will utilize the provider's hardware and software problem management and resolution processes as well as the provider's chosen software and hardware

---

management and remediation tools, processes and procedures during service delivery.

Service delivery

Scheduled maintenance
The break-fix services provider may provide scheduled maintenance services to their customers, and bill them on a time and materials basis, or deduct these hours from their pre-paid service block time.

Problem management and resolution
In order for the break-fix services provider to deliver effective break-fix services to customers, they must develop, implement and adhere to a consistent problem management and resolution process. This process can include the utilization of a service desk.

In this context, the service desk is defined as the central point of contact between the customer and the provider, and whose staff maintains and facilitates the restoration of normal service operation while minimizing impact to the customer.

The break-fix services provider's service desk conducts break-fix services problem management and resolution, and service desk staff can be assigned to the following tiers for escalation:

- Tier 1
- Tier 2
- Tier 3

These tiers are utilized in the prioritization and escalation process per the provider's service desk escalation procedure. After an issue is identified and documented in the provider's PSA solution, non-critical support incidents are normally assigned to tier 1 for service desk staff to begin basic troubleshooting and problem resolution. Based upon priority and other factors, the issue will be escalated up through successive support tiers as necessary in order to adhere to applicable SLAs.

All support incidents that cannot be resolved within tier 1 are escalated to tier 2, where more complex support can be provided by more experienced staff.

Support incidents that cannot be resolved in tier 2 are escalated to tier 3, where support is provided by the most qualified and experienced staff that has the ability to collaborate with the provider's vendor support engineers to resolve the most complex issues.

In some cases, an onsite visit may be required to troubleshoot and remediate issues. In this scenario a field engineer /technician may be dispatched to continue the problem resolution process.

In other cases, the customer or a field engineer/technician may bring an affected piece of equipment in to the provider's offices for troubleshooting or remediation. In this scenario a

---

bench engineer/technician may be assigned to continue the problem resolution process.

The break-fix services provider's service desk's goals include:

- Providing a single point of contact for end-user issues
- Facilitating the restoration of normal service operation while minimizing impact to the end-user
- Receiving all incident notifications through the provider's preferred means - phone, fax, email, service desk portal, etc.
- Recording all incidents in the provider's PSA solution
- Classifying all incidents and correctly documenting the nature of the incident, including affected users, systems, hardware and services
- Prioritizing all incidents for effective escalation
- Troubleshooting all incidents according to best practices
- Escalating all incidents as necessary for effective problem resolution
- Maintaining consistent communication with all parties including end-users, their managers and higher, as well as the provider's own internal management hierarchy
- Performing all scheduled activities such as moves/adds/changes, maintenance, patch management, documentation and reporting

The break-fix services provider's service desk's staff's daily duties

The service desk staff's daily duties are determined by their service manager, whose responsibility includes the management of the provider's service desk, and the proper prioritization and assignment of all service requests to the appropriate tier. The scheduling of all onsite and remote service work is ultimately the responsibility of the service manager, but this and other functions may be performed by a service dispatcher. It is the Service manager's ultimate responsibility to make certain the service desk is effective and efficient.

In this context, a service desk staff's typical day may resemble the following:

- Log in to the hardware warranty services provider's PSA solution
- Review all newly-assigned service requests to him/her
- Review any service requests previously assigned and still open to insure they are not in danger of falling outside of SLA (service dispatcher and/or manager should be alerted to this status automatically by the PSA solution before it occurs)
- Work service requests in order of priority
  - Accept service request and time stamp
  - Review service request

- o Contact customer or end-user as needed to gather any necessary information in order to begin problem resolution
- o Consult information documented in PSA solution as needed in order to perform problem resolution
- o Qualify issue to determine if it can be resolved through tier 1 support
- o Work issue to successful resolution
- o Verify issue to be resolved to end-user's satisfaction
- o Document complete problem resolution details in PSA solution, mark status complete and time stamp
- o Service request is held in completed status for a minimum of 24 hours, after which the end-user is contacted to verify the issue has been resolved to their satisfaction and asked if the service request can be closed
- o Service request is closed
- If Service request cannot be resolved through tier 1 support:
  - o Service request is escalated to Tier 2 and successive tiers of support, or an onsite visit is scheduled with a field engineer/technician as needed, and the problem resolution process continues

---

Customer service

In order to establish, maintain and increase customer satisfaction within this highly competitive service delivery model, the break-fix services provider will need to educate their staff on delivering not only first-rate technical services, but excellent customer service as well. This is so important that larger break-fix services providers may create and staff a customer service position to insure consistent customer service delivery.

Maximize: The Break-Fix Services Delivery Model

max · i · mize [mak-s*uh*-mahyz] – *to increase to the greatest possible amount or degree*

Now that we understand the basics of what it takes to maintain the break-fix services delivery model in terms of service delivery, it's time to dive even deeper and identify how to maximize efficiencies, processes, procedures and profitability within this service delivery model.

Maximize: The Break-Fix Services Delivery Model

Strategy

Although the break-fix services delivery model is challenged by factors such the commodity-based nature its deliverables, areas where efficiencies, processes and procedures and profits can be maximized from a technical perspective include the following:

- Tools and technology
- Processes and procedures
- Scheduling
- Service delivery
- Equipment and parts ordering
- RMA processing
- Invoicing
- Staff utilization
- Costs
- Pricing
- Vendors
- Partners
- Back office service desk support
- Procurement services

Tools and technology

In order to provide the best services possible for customers, and continually improve their internal efficiencies and capabilities in order to scale, all service providers should

---

---

consistently evaluate new tools and technologies and budget for investments in these yearly. These investments should be business decisions based upon a clear ROI or benefit to the provider and/or their customers.

Processes and procedures
No matter what service delivery model employed, there are always gains to be made by analyzing existing workflows to improve outcomes. Providers all too often neglect to turn the mirror upon themselves, or sample the Kool-Aid they are liberally drenching their customers with.

How often do providers practice what they preach to their customers and perform internal business needs analyses and technology assessments on themselves? *Not often enough.* In order to maximize their business models, they must understand that it is imperative to continue to invest in new tools and technology to offload labor-intensive processes from costly resources and continue to tweak and tune their processes and procedures to yield incremental gains in efficiency and productivity.

Service delivery maximization is not an event, but a continual process that never ends.

As intelligent business owners, providers need to grant their organizations the same type of consultative services as they do for customers. This will help insure that they can scale

---

profitably to meet existing customers' needs and service new ones efficiently and gainfully.

Scheduling

Unfortunately, the reactive nature of the break-fix services delivery model challenges the service dispatcher in the scheduling department. Potential improvements in this area are relegated to forecasting realistic timelines for service delivery, especially when dispatching field engineers/technicians onsite to customer locations.

In these scenarios, it is incumbent for the service dispatcher to enforce a rigorous communication process between all field-dispatched resources and themselves. This can take the form of 30 minute check-in intervals where status is regularly communicated back to the service dispatcher during onsite problem remediation. This allows the service dispatcher to make informed decisions regarding the allocation of resources throughout the day.

Service delivery

Service delivery is an area where all service providers can always make improvements. The first step towards service delivery improvement is to map out the provider's existing service delivery process, beginning with the initial call or contact from the customer regarding a support issue, and following the problem management and resolution process all

---

the way through to closure. An efficient problem management and resolution process will include escalation points to insure that service requests don't end up in limbo for extended periods of time.

One thing to always keep in mind is the fact that the more services the provider can deliver remotely, the more profitable they will become.

It is a good idea for the provider to poll existing customers and get their candid feedback on their problem management and resolution process from start to finish. This will impress the customer's experience on the provider and may help the provider identify ways to improve efficiency and customer satisfaction.

All technical support staff should always "start the clock", or timestamp a service request before they begin working on it, consistently documenting their activities and results in the provider's PSA solution. All too often technical resources forget to book their time during service delivery, and later have to "make up" their activities and timelines – this is a major profitability killer.

The following illustrates a basic problem management and resolution process:

1. Support request is received

2. Trouble ticket is created

3. Issue is identified and documented in PSA solution

4. Issue is qualified to determine if it can be resolved through tier 1 support

If issue can be resolved through tier 1 support:

5. Level 1 resolution - issue is worked to successful resolution

6. Quality control - Issue is verified to be resolved to customer's satisfaction

7. Trouble ticket is closed, after complete problem resolution details have been updated in PSA solution

If issue cannot be resolved through tier 1 support:

6. Issue is escalated to tier 2 support

7. Issue is qualified to determine if it can be resolved by tier 2 support

If issue can be resolved through tier 2 support:

8. Level 2 resolution - issue is worked to successful resolution

---

9. Quality control - issue is verified to be resolved to customer's satisfaction

10. Trouble ticket is closed, after complete problem resolution details have been updated in PSA soluton

If issue cannot be resolved through tier 2 support:

9. Issue is escalated to tier 3 support

10. Issue is qualified to determine if it can be resolved through tier 3 support

If issue can be resolved through tier 3 support:

11. Level 3 resolution - issue is worked to successful resolution

12. Quality control - issue is verified to be resolved to customer's satisfaction

13. Trouble ticket is closed, after complete problem resolution details have been updated in PSA solution

If issue cannot be resolved through tier 3 support:

12. Issue is escalated to onsite support

13. Issue is qualified to determine if it can be resolved through onsite support

---

If issue can be resolved through onsite support:

14. Onsite resolution - issue is worked to successful resolution

15. Quality control - Issue is verified to be resolved to customer's satisfaction

16. Trouble ticket is closed, after complete problem resolution details have been updated in PSA solution

If issue cannot be resolved through onsite support:

17. Service manager decision point – request is updated in PSA solution with complete details of all activity performed

Equipment and parts ordering

The provider should have a documented request and fulfillment process for ordering, tracking and paying for equipment and parts required for service delivery. Providers can lose valuable scheduling opportunities if this process is not adhered to, not to mention the negative impact to customer satisfaction. It is also vitally important to have a consistent customer billing process for all new hardware installed – the faster the invoice goes out, the faster it will be paid.

RMA processing

As with all service delivery models, it is incumbent upon the break-fix services provider to develop and implement an efficient procedure for dealing with RMA's so that they don't pile up in a back office or closet and miss their RMA replacement window. This is an area that can bleed profits for a provider over time, if not managed properly.

Invoicing

One area that should never impact the provider's cash flow is invoicing. The provider should maintain a scheduled, consistent invoicing and accounts receivable collections process. Some break-fix providers are so proficient at this that invoicing occurs daily for all services delivered. Customers won't pay without an invoice, and the faster the invoice gets to them, the faster they can process it.

Staff utilization

The ability for the break-fix services provider to keep their technical staff fully utilized at better than 75% on a consistent basis is critical for profitability, and in most cases cannot be accomplished without a professional services automation (PSA) solution and the requirement for all staff to book each minute of their time in it. In fact, the proper implementation and use of a PSA solution has the potential of increasing staff utilization close to 100%, driving more revenue to the provider's bottom line.

The cost of low utilization is an extremely important concept to grasp, as 75% overall utilization means that the provider is paying their staff a full 3 months per year for non-billable time, and if this utilization number is lower, so are net profits.

Costs

As with any service delivery model, the ability to contain, control and reduce costs directly impacts the bottom line. The break-fix services provider should review all of their overhead costs on a regular basis to make certain that they are getting the absolute best rates on services such as telco, broadband, cell service and HR costs as well, including medical and other employee benefits.

Other ways to minimize costs are to find and utilize dependable contractors for periodic or temporary surges in business. This strategy may save on labor costs in the long run, and delay the necessity to hire additional full-time employees until absolutely necessary.

Pricing

An area that is often overlooked by break-fix services providers and the fastest way to increase revenues across the board in a single day is the practice of raising their rates and other pricing on a yearly basis. Customers will not balk at a 5% to 8% yearly labor rate increase, but they will if the provider

---

---

tries to raise rates 25% to make up for several years without a rate increase.

Vendors and distributors

Another area the break-fix services provider can explore is working with their vendors and distributors to obtain better pricing and discounts, or other benefits such as marketing development funds that can be used to market for new prospects and grow the provider's business.

Partnering

Other ways to maximize and grow revenues for the break-fix services provider is to partner with other complementary services providers such as telco vendors, copier vendors and the like to trade warm leads. Similarly, the break-fix services provider can partner with other I.T. solution providers to deliver additional products and services to their customer base and earn added revenues as commissions, increasing their value to their customers by marshalling the resources to meet their business needs.

Back office service desk support

With the advent of affordable, 3rd-party back office service desk organizations, the provider has the opportunity to scale their services to a much broader range of customers, and prolong the necessity to hire, train and manage internal full-time staff. This allows a consistent support experience for

---

customers and in many cases increases the provider's profitability due to the low cost of these services. In addition, these organizations are private-labeled services, and represent the provider's organization throughout all communications and problem management and resolution activities with their customers.

Procurement services
A new service for providers gaining momentum is that of procurement services, where a provider partners with an organization to handle the research, pricing, quoting, order fulfillment, invoicing and accounts receivable activities for any and all infrastructure purchases required by the provider for their customers. The management of complex licensing programs, authorizations and support renewals for the provider's customers is also handled by these organizations.

These services streamline the buying and fulfillment process for providers and increase profitability by lowering the expense of procurement by significantly reducing the labor hours currently expended by the provider, as well as leveraging the buying power of the procurement service vendor to reduce costs.

Migrate: The Break-Fix Services Delivery Model

mi · grate [mahy-greyt] – *to shift, as from one system, mode of operation, or enterprise to another*

No matter which service delivery model the provider practices, one way to increase revenues and opportunities is to adopt an additional service delivery model as a hybrid option, or completely migrate to it. In many situations, providers choose a hybrid model that allows them to provide a blend of hardware warranty, break-fix, professional and managed services all under one roof.

While the desire for the provider to have the capability to address all of their customers' needs in this fashion is strong, the most successful providers are those that focus on a smaller number of deliverables, allowing them to really fine-tune their processes and procedures to receive the greatest net profits. They may also specialize in vertical-specific markets in order to further increase their profits through service delivery familiarity and shorten their sales cycles.

The next section focuses on migration strategies for the break-fix services provider wishing to explore the grass on the other side of the fence.

Migration choices
The break-fix services provider has their choice of two service delivery models to migrate to or adopt into a new hybrid service delivery model:

1. The professional services delivery model
2. The managed services delivery model

It may be easier for the "pure" break-fix services provider to adopt or migrate to the managed services delivery model than the professional services delivery model. This is due to greater similarities shared between these models in terms of service delivery tools and processes and staffing and management roles and requirements, than between the break-fix and professional services delivery models.

With this understanding, we will explore strategies for the break-fix services provider to migrate to both models, with the managed services delivery model first.

Strategies for migration to a managed services delivery model

Areas that the break-fix services provider will need to evaluate when migrating to the managed services delivery model may include:

- Agreement and SLA
- Tools and technology
- Processes and procedures
- Scheduling
- Service delivery
- Equipment and parts ordering
- RMA processing
- Invoicing
- Staffing
- Staff utilization
- Costs
- Pricing
- Vendors
- Partners

Agreement and SLA

The break-fix services provider will need to develop a managed services agreement and SLA in order to deliver proactive, flat fee managed I.T. services to their customers, as

---

unlike break-fix services, managed I.T. services are delivered, measured and governed by strict SLAs.

Tools and technology

The break-fix services provider should evaluate the suitability of their existing problem management and resolution, or PSA software solution for compatibility with the managed services delivery model. Key features to evaluate include:

- Customer relationship management (CRM) capabilities
- Service request or trouble ticketing capabilities
- Scheduling & dispatching capabilities
- Time & expense tracking capabilities
- Inventory control capabilities
- Asset management capabilities
- Configuration & change management capabilities
- Knowledge base capabilities
- Resource management capabilities
- Integration of quoting & invoicing with accounting systems capabilities
- Sales funnel capabilities
- Robust, customizable reporting capabilities

In addition, the break-fix services provider will need to invest in a remote monitoring and management (RMM) solution to allow them to proactively monitor critical devices, events and

---

---

services within their customer environments and alert on operation outside of recommended parameters, allowing the provider to take action to maximize customer uptime and maintain SLA's.

The RMM solution will allow the provider to script, schedule and automatically execute otherwise costly, labor-intensive activities such as hardware and software patching and updating and system optimization. This solution may grant the managed services provider the following capabilities:

- WMI/Syslog/SNMP monitoring capabilities
- Multiple alerting capabilities – email/text page/pager
- Configurable and customizable alerting capabilities
- Supports escalation
- Outputs detailed logging
- Supports multiple operating systems
- Supports critical server monitoring functions – Exchange, SQL, IIS, SharePoint, Linux, Novell
- Supports multiple types of hardware – PCs, Macs, servers, routers, switches, firewalls, Printers
- Supports Multiple 3rd-Party Software Monitoring
- Supports operating system and software patch management and updates
- Easily Integrates with PSA solutions
- Supports remote control of monitored devices
- Allows scripting, scheduling and automatic execution of otherwise costly, labor-intensive activities

---

- Robust, customizable reporting capabilities

Processes and procedures

Similarities between the break-fix and managed services delivery models benefit the provider in this area, as their problem management and resolution processes and procedures are transferable to the managed services delivery model without much modification, if they are based on best practices.

The primary differences here will include the shift from a reactive to a proactive service delivery focus, as well as the development of NOC services to include a remote monitoring and management (RMM) solution's deployment, maintenance, response and remediation procedures.

Scheduling

The process of scheduling resources for service delivery is similar and consistent across all service delivery models. Modifications to the provider's scheduling process are negligible in this migration scenario due to the similarities between the service delivery models in this regard.

Service delivery

As mentioned, if the break-fix services provider's problem management and resolution processes are based upon best practices, these are transferable to the managed services

---

delivery model without drastic modification, with the exceptions being a mind-shift from delivering services reactively to a proactive service delivery focus, and the development of remote monitoring and management (RMM) processes and procedures.

Equipment and parts ordering

The break-fix provider's existing documented request and fulfillment process for ordering, tracking and paying for equipment, licensing and parts required for service delivery should suit their needs in delivering managed services.

The primary differences here may include expanding the number and types of manufacturers, vendors and distributors that customer equipment, licensing, services and solutions are sourced from.

RMA processing

The break-fix services provider's existing RMA processing procedure should not require much modification when delivering managed services.

Invoicing

This is an area that will require some focused attention and modification for the break-fix services provider migrating to the managed services delivery model, as the provider may be accustomed to invoicing for services after they have been

---

delivered, or possibly selling blocks of service hours at a reduced rate to their customers.

The managed services delivery model; however, is much different in this respect, and requires the ability for the provider to invoice for services in advance of their delivery, and for a flat fee per month. This requires both the capability, as well as the process to manage invoicing in this manner.

Invoicing for additional services that fall outside of the provider's managed services agreement or SLA will occur as these services are delivered.

Staffing
Although similarities between the break-fix and managed services delivery models exist in terms of most existing staff roles and responsibilities, allowing them to transfer to the new model with minimal modifications, an additional NOC staff role will be required to support the proactive monitoring of critical devices and services in customer environments to maximize uptime and maintain SLA's.

NOC staff
In this context, the NOC (network operations center) staff participates in the provider's problem management and resolution process, and can be assigned to deliver proactive remote patching, updating and monitoring services for devices, software applications and operating systems and

---

services in customer environments. Whereas the provider's service desk staff works primarily with end-user issues, the NOC staff's main focus is on managing and delivering scheduled maintenance activities for critical devices and services and responding to alerts generated by the provider's remote monitoring and management (RMM) solution.

The NOC staff identifies, prioritizes and documents all service activity and will execute the provider's problem management and resolution processes as well as utilize the provider's chosen software and hardware management and remediation tools, processes and procedures during remote technical service delivery.

Staff utilization
The same requirements for maintaining the highest possible utilization for billable resources exists in all service delivery models. As a result, the provider's need to extract every ounce of utilization from their staff does not change due to service delivery model migration.

Costs
The necessity for the provider to contain, reduce and control costs is not service delivery model-dependent. This migration scenario may require the provider to invest in training their existing staff to provide them the ability to support a wider range of solutions and environments, or to hire and train

---

additional staff as needed to provide their customers managed services, as well as the costs to purchase, train on and maintain the provider's RMM solution.

Pricing

A consideration for the provider migrating to the managed services delivery model is the necessity to adopt a flat-fee pricing model for proactive service delivery. Whether the provider chooses a per-device, per user or tiered model, they must first understand what their total cost of service delivery is, in order to determine a desired profit margin and ultimate retail price for their services.

Factors to weigh when identifying the total cost of service delivery (TCSD) include the following:

- The provider's hourly cost of billable resources
- The provider's employer contributions
- The provider's overhead

Determining the hourly cost for 1 billable technician

In order to determine the provider's hourly cost for 1 billable technician, it is necessary to include the technician's hourly wages, the provider's employer contributions and overhead costs in a formula which yields an hourly value.

In the following table, the technician's hourly wage is added to the employer's payroll contributions. This value is then added

---

to the provider's monthly overhead costs and divided by the monthly hours of service delivery, which is then divided by the number of billable technicians. The outcome is the provider's TCSD per hour.

Determining TCSD

Hourly cost for 1 billable technician		
Technician's hourly wage	$30.00	Hourly pay
+		
Employer payroll contributions	$10.00	Taxes, Insurance, etc.
+		
Total overhead cost	$18.75	$3k/mo ÷ 160hrs/mo ÷ 1
=		
TCSD per hour	$58.75	

Determining profit margins and labor rates

After the provider determines their TCSD per hour, it is now possible to determine a desired profit margin and final labor rate. In the previous example, the provider's TCSD per hour is $58.75, so it is now a simple matter to determine a desired profit margin in this example. If the provider wishes to implement a 100% profit margin on their hourly TCSD, the result would be a billable labor rate of $117.50. Higher desired profit margins would yield higher billable labor rates.

Determining Labor Rates

100% Margin for 1 billable technician		
Cost per hour	$58.75	CPH
+		
Target margin	$58.75	100% of CPH
=		
Billable labor rate	$117.50	

Quoting Managed Services per estimated monthly support hours

One method a provider may utilize in quoting a managed services maintenance plan to their customers would be to estimate the amount of hours required per month to perform the services agreed to in their SLA, then use their billable labor rate as the factor to yield the cost to deliver services.

The following example illustrates quoting a customer a flat fee for supporting a 30 pc and 2-server environment. The provider assumes a support requirement of a half hour per month per pc and two and a half hours per month per server, equaling a 20 hour per month service requirement.

Migrate: The Break-Fix Services Delivery Model

Quoting managed services by estimating support hours

Pricing for a 30 pc, 2 server environment at .5 hrs/mo support per pc and 2.5 hrs/mo support per server	
Estimated support hours/mo	**20**
x	
Billable labor rate	**$117.50/hr**
=	_____
Flat monthly fee	**$2,350.00/mo**

Should the provider continue to deliver break-fix services along with flat-fee managed services, these services would be invoiced separately to customers, along with any other services delivered that fall outside of the provider's flat-fee support and maintenance services.

Vendors and distributors
The break-fix services provider will almost certainly need to build relationships with new vendors and distributors to support their customer environments with managed services.

Partnering
Other ways to maximize and grow revenues for the provider is to partner with other complementary services providers such as telco vendors, copier vendors and the like to trade warm leads. Similarly, the provider can partner with other I.T. solution providers to deliver additional products and services to their customer base and earn added revenues as commissions, increasing their value to their customers as a trusted advisor by marshalling the resources to meet their business needs.

Strategies for migration to a professional services delivery model

In order for the break-fix services provider to successfully migrate to the professional services delivery model, or add professional services to their existing deliverables, they will need to modify and/or add key tools and technologies, staff, and roles and responsibilities to their organization.

Areas that the break-fix services provider will need to evaluate when migrating to the professional services delivery model may include:

- Tools and technology
- Processes and procedures
- Project scoping
- Project quoting
- Project planning
- Equipment and parts ordering
- Project management
- Invoicing
- Staffing
- Staff utilization
- Costs
- Pricing
- Vendors and distributors
- Partners

Tools and technology

The provider may invest in software tools to assist them in effective, efficient professional services delivery. These software solutions may provide them the following capabilities:

- Customer relationship management (CRM) capabilities
- Project scoping capabilities
- Technical drawing capabilities
- Project quoting capabilities
- Project planning capabilities
- Equipment and parts ordering capabilities
- Project management capabilities
- Integration of quoting & invoicing with accounting systems capabilities
- Sales funnel capabilities
- Robust, customizable reporting capabilities

Processes and procedures

The provider migrating to the professional services delivery model will need to develop effective processes and procedures to:

- Conduct needs analyses and technology assessments
- Scope and quote projects and create proposals
- Create technical drawings

- Order equipment, software licensing and services
- Design project plans and timelines
- Manage project implementations
- Set and manage customer expectations

Project scoping
The provider must develop or hire resources with the capability to utilize the provider's preferred tools, technology and processes to conduct needs analyses and technology assessments, as well as resources to review the findings contained therein and work with manufacturers, vendors and distributors to design effective solutions to address customer needs.

Project quoting
The provider must develop or hire resources with the capability to utilize the provider's preferred tools, technology and processes to create accurate quotes and compelling proposals from project scopes and information and pricing received from manufacturers, vendors and distributors.

Project planning
The provider must develop or hire resources with the capability to utilize the provider's preferred tools, technology and processes to create effective project plans that identify resources, tasks and timelines to insure a project's completion within its defined scope, schedule and budget.

Equipment and parts ordering
The provider should have a documented request and fulfillment process for ordering, tracking and paying for equipment, parts, licensing, services and solutions required for professional services delivery.

These processes may differ from their existing break-fix ordering procedures in areas such as number of sources and lead times and costs, requiring the provider to increase their flooring accounts, request credit from new sources or increase credit limits and modify payment terms with their existing vendors and distributors.

Project management
The provider must develop or hire resources with the capability to utilize the provider's preferred tools, technology and processes to manage projects, their resources and schedules to insure completion within scope, timeline and budget.

Invoicing
The provider must determine how they will invoice for their professional services, and may choose to invoice the customer a portion of the project's overall value in advance to cover the costs of hardware, licensing and labor during the initial phases of project implementation, with the outstanding balance due

---

---

upon completion, or accept progress payments for projects with extended timelines.

Staffing

Although similarities between the break-fix and professional services delivery models exist in terms of some existing staff roles and responsibilities, allowing them to transfer to the new model with minimal modifications, additional staff roles will be required to support the requirements of the professional services delivery model, and may include:

- Sales engineers
- Purchasing managers
- Project managers

Sales engineers

In this context, the sales engineer is perhaps the most versatile and important role in the professional services delivery model. The sales engineer participates in both the provider's pre- and post-sales and project planning processes, and can be assigned to assist in the business needs analysis, technology assessment and solution design and specification phases of professional services delivery. All of these functions are critical to insuring smooth project delivery.

Purchasing manager

In this context, the purchasing manager participates in the provider's project quoting and planning process by insuring pricing and availability of hardware, software licensing and services from vendors, distributors and fulfillment partners to meet the sales engineer's solution requirements, and handles all returns and credits when necessary.

Project managers

In this context, the project manager participates in the provider's project planning and management process by working with the sales engineer to develop a project scope, then specify methods to be utilized during project implementation, identify all tasks to be completed during project implementation, create a timeline and expected duration for each task's completion and estimate and allocate resources for each task's completion.

In addition, the project manager is normally responsible for creating the risk management plan, change control process and communication and status reporting process utilized during project implementation.

Staff utilization

The same requirements for maintaining the highest possible utilization for billable resources exists in all service delivery models. As a result, the provider's need to extract every ounce

---

---

of utilization from their staff does not change due to service delivery model migration.

Costs

The necessity for the provider to contain, reduce and control costs is not service delivery model-dependent. This migration scenario may require the provider to invest in training their existing staff to provide them the ability to support a wider range of solutions and environments, or to hire and train additional staff as needed to provide their customers professional services, as well as the costs to purchase, train on and utilize the provider's professional services-specific tools and technology solutions.

Pricing

A consideration for the provider migrating to the professional services delivery model is the necessity to understand what their total cost of service delivery is, in order to determine a desired profit margin and ultimate retail price for their services.

Factors to weigh when identifying the total cost of service delivery (TCSD) include the following:

- The provider's hourly cost of billable resources
- The provider's employer contributions
- The provider's overhead

Determining the hourly cost for 5 billable resources

In order to determine the provider's hourly cost to deliver a project requiring 5 billable resources, it is necessary to include each resources' hourly wages, the provider's employer contributions and overhead costs in a formula which yields an hourly value.

In the following table, each of the resources' individual hourly wages are aggregated and added to the employer's payroll contributions. This value is then added to the provider's monthly overhead costs and divided by the monthly hours of service delivery, which is then divided by the number of billable resources. The outcome is the provider's TCSD per hour for this resource group.

Determining TCSD per Resource Group

Hourly cost for 5 billable resources		
Resources' aggregate hourly wages	$190.00	Hourly pay
+		
Employer payroll contributions	$57.00	Taxes, Insurance, etc.
+		
Total overhead cost	$3.75	$3k/mo ÷ 160hrs/mo ÷ 5
=		
TCSD per hour	$250.75	

Determining profit margins and labor rates

After the provider determines their TCSD per hour, it is now possible to determine a desired profit margin and final labor rate. In the previous example, the provider's TCSD per hour is $250.75, so it is now a simple matter to determine a desired

---

profit margin in this example. If the provider wishes to implement a 50% profit margin on their hourly TCSD, the result would be a billable labor rate of about $375.00. Higher desired profit margins would yield higher billable labor rates.

Determining Labor Rates

100% Margin for 5 billable resources		
Cost per hour	$250.75	CPH
+		
Target margin	$125.00	50% of CPH
=		
Billable labor rate	$375.00	

Because each unique resource's contribution and cost per hour may differ from the others, for a professional services delivery quote, the provider would estimate how many hours each of their resources would contribute to the overall project, and may use their individual billable labor rates to come up with the final quote.

Vendors and distributors

The provider migrating to the professional services delivery model will almost certainly need to build relationships with new vendors and distributors in order to deliver professional services.

Partnering

Another way to maximize and grow revenues for the provider migrating to a professional services delivery model is to partner with other I.T. solution providers to deliver additional products and services to their customer base to meet their customers' needs.

Section 3: The Professional Services Delivery Model

For purposes of our discussion, the professional services delivery model is defined as being comprised of activities, processes and procedures that allow the service provider to deliver scheduled project-based services and outcomes to customers. These services are normally delivered through a consistent, managed process which involves careful project planning, scheduling, resource allocation and assignment of roles and responsibilities, risk management and change control, and a clear communication and status reporting process.

Build: The Professional Services Delivery Model

build [bild] – *to develop or give form to according to a plan or process; create*

In order to build a professional services delivery model, we must understand its characteristics – the nuts and bolts.

This section will explore the considerations necessary to build a professional services delivery model and discuss deliverables, tools and technology, pricing and positioning, staffing requirements, target markets and other concerns.

Characteristics

Professional services providers are among the most profitable of the four service provider categories in our discussion, and this level of profitability can be directly attributed to the provider's strict, process-oriented approach to conducting the preparatory work required in the business needs analysis and technology assessment phases of projects, as well as through the precise scoping, planning, delivery and assessment phases of their services to insure the customer's expected outcomes are achieved.

As a result of their experience and service planning and delivery process, the professional services provider is able to quote services to successfully come in on time and budget while meeting their profitability goals.

Since professional services are really based on a time and materials quoting model, akin to the break-fix services delivery model, there exists a finite amount of service that the provider's individual staff can deliver, making it difficult to scale without hiring, training and managing additional resources.

As professional services are generally competitive in nature, the provider faces challenges such as having their proposals "shopped", and since these services are transaction-based deliverables, the provider must continually market for and win

---

new business each month in order to meet their revenue goals.

To make things more challenging for the provider, professional services I.T. projects are among the first to be put on hold during times of economic uncertainty.

Deliverables

The deliverables of a professional services provider really know no bounds, as they can specialize in so many different technologies and solutions, be they vertical-specific or otherwise. Because of the fact that the provider is solution-oriented and strives to improve I.T. processes and services to their customers while measuring project and program outcomes, their deliverables are sought after by both technology-strategic customers, as well as technology-dependent verticals and customers.

The professional services provider's duties include handling the complete lifecycle of a project; from initial assessment to final acceptance, including ordering, managing, implementing, assessing and reporting on each aspect of service and project delivery.

Tools and technology

The professional services provider may invest in software tools to assist them in effective, efficient service delivery.

These software solutions may provide them the following capabilities:

- Customer relationship management (CRM) capabilities
- Project scoping capabilities
- Technical drawing capabilities
- Project quoting capabilities
- Project planning capabilities
- Equipment and parts ordering capabilities
- Project management capabilities
- Integration of quoting & invoicing with accounting systems capabilities
- Sales funnel capabilities
- Robust, customizable reporting capabilities

Pricing and positioning

Unless the professional services provider delivers highly specialized services, their service delivery model is not immune to competitive challenges. Depending upon their ability to demonstrate to their customers a unique value proposition which differentiates them in their market, their pricing can range from very reasonable to very expensive, based on this uniqueness and what their markets will bear.

Experienced professional services providers with a solid change management process will normally price their deliverables as a firm quote containing very specific detail regarding the work scope to be delivered, and will do an excellent job of setting and re-setting customer expectations throughout the project lifecycle. This not only guarantees profitability, but increases customer satisfaction as well.

Positioning professional services solutions as the answers to meeting prospects' and customers' needs in areas such as increasing efficiency, productivity, alleviating business pain and mitigating risk is not normally a difficult goal to achieve, and becomes easier the more vertical-specific or specialized these solutions are.

Staffing requirements
The professional services provider shares some of the staffing requirements as the break-fix services provider; however, certain roles will differ, and the professional services provider will add additional roles. As with any service model, dependent upon factors such as the vertical or target market, solutions offered, number of concurrent and scheduled projects and the complexity of same, the professional services provider will require a minimum number of staff that fall into specific roles, which may include:

- Owners
- Managers
- Administrative staff
- Technical staff

- Marketing/sales staff
- Other staff

Owners

As in any organization; and based upon a number of factors, professional services provider owners may wear many hats, or merely a few. Their basic responsibility to the organization, its stakeholders, staff and customers is to manage and maintain a profitable business concern.

Managers

The size of the organization's management staff will be based upon the number of the organization's staff and concurrent and scheduled projects, among other factors, and may include:

- Operations management
- Office management
- HR management
- Marketing/sales management
- Service delivery management
- Project management
- Vendor management
- Customer service management

Administration

Every organization, no matter how large or small requires some form of administrative support. These roles include:

- Front office staff
- HR staff
- Accounting staff
- Customer service staff

Technical staff

Technical staff requirements for a professional services delivery practice may include:

- Sales engineers
- Bench engineers/technicians
- Field engineers/technicians

Marketing/sales staff

Although the marketing and sales roles are distinct, and in larger organizations segmented by business unit and resources, we'll group them together for purposes of our service delivery-focused discussion.

No matter what size the service provider's organization is, at one point or another, someone is going to have to market and sell the provider's services.

Other staff

As in all service delivery models, other resources may be required, and additional staff that may make up the professional services provider's organization may include:

- Purchasing manager
- Inventory manager

Considerations

As mentioned, the "pure" professional services delivery model can be very profitable. The challenge for the professional services provider is similar to that experienced by the break-fix services provider, in that they are constrained in their ability to scale their services profitably without going through the time and expense of interviewing, hiring, training and managing an ever-increasing number of staff and dealing with the HR, customer service and quality control considerations this type of growth brings with it.

And true to the nature of the transaction-based model that it is, the professional services delivery model requires the provider to continually market for and close new opportunities in order to meet their revenue goals.

Target market

The professional services provider's target market may be vertical or non-vertical specific, and can span not only the SMB and Mid markets, but the Enterprise markets as well, as

---

professional services providers can bring much greater specialization, experience and skill sets to bear to scope and implement solutions in situations where the prospect and customer do not have these capabilities in-house.

As a result, professional services providers are more apt to attract technology-strategic customers who view technology spending as strategic investments in their organizations and provide them a competitive advantage in their markets. To these customers, service and value rank higher than cost considerations. As a result, the professional services provider aligns closely with their prospects' and customers' I.T. goals.

Customer satisfaction and loyalty
As a result of the professional services provider's effective and efficient service management and delivery process, customer satisfaction and loyalty rank higher than in the hardware warranty and break-fix services delivery models, leading to additional opportunities between the provider and their customers in the future.

These factors lead customers to perceive the professional services provider more as a trusted advisor than just another I.T. vendor or resource.

Maintain: The Professional Services Delivery Model

main · tain [meyn-**teyn**] – *to keep in an existing state; preserve or retain*

Now that we understand the nuts and bolts of the professional services delivery model and its characteristics and considerations, let's dive a bit deeper and explore what it takes to maintain it in terms of service delivery.

This section will cover implementing the professional services delivery model and discuss technical roles and responsibilities, as well as service delivery.

Focus

The "pure" professional services delivery model focuses on allowing the provider the ability to effectively deliver scheduled project-based services/solutions and outcomes to their customers on a quote and proposal basis.

The professional services provider will normally conduct a comprehensive business needs analysis and technology assessment in order to completely understand their customer's needs and current state of technology in order to develop a recommended solution and implementation strategy.

Technical implementation

In order to implement a professional services delivery model, the provider must possess:

- Software and hardware tools
- Effective processes and procedures
- Technical staff

Software and hardware tools

An effective professional services provider will be able to implement solutions in their customer environments and execute a consistent project planning and management process.

Software tools utilized by the professional services provider to accomplish these activities may include project planning, project management, technical drawing, quoting and pricing tools. Some professional service automation (PSA) solutions provide many of these capabilities.

These software tools may grant the professional services provider the following capabilities:

- Customer relationship management (CRM) capabilities
- Project scoping capabilities
- Technical drawing capabilities
- Project quoting capabilities
- Project planning capabilities
- Equipment and parts ordering capabilities
- Project management capabilities
- Integration of quoting & invoicing with accounting systems capabilities
- Sales funnel capabilities
- Robust, customizable reporting capabilities

The professional services provider may also utilize additional software imaging, updating and data and account migration tools during service delivery. Leveraging these types of software tools help the professional services provider gain

---

efficiency and speed implementation to bring solutions in on time and within budget, increasing customer satisfaction.

In addition to software tools, the professional services provider will require both standard, as well as specialized hardware tools in order to implement solutions in their customer environments.

Effective processes and procedures

In order for the provider to cost-effectively deliver services to their customers, they must develop and implement consistent project planning and management processes and procedures.

By standardizing and fine-tuning their processes and procedures, the professional services provider will increase customer satisfaction as well as their own profitability.

Parts and hardware inventory

There is normally no need for the professional services provider to stock replacement hardware for solutions they deliver to their customers, unless they build and include white box pc's and servers in their solutions and provide warranty services for same.

Technical staff

In order to meet customer expectations and workload requirements, the professional services provider will require a sufficient number of technical staff trained in effective project

---

planning, management and implementation processes to support their customers' solution delivery. The technical staff will also require training specific to the provider's chosen software and hardware management and delivery tools, processes and procedures.

Technical roles and responsibilities

Depending upon the number and size of the professional services provider's concurrent projects, and the size of the provider's organization, their technical staff will fall into specific roles which may include:

- Sales engineers
- Purchasing managers
- Project managers
- Inventory managers
- Bench engineers/technicians
- Field engineers/technicians

Sales engineers

In this context, the sales engineer is perhaps the most versatile and important role in the provider's practice. The sales engineer participates in both the provider's pre- and post-sales and project planning processes, and can be assigned to assist in the business needs analysis, technology assessment and solution design and specification phases of

---

professional services delivery. All of these functions are critical to insuring smooth project delivery.

Purchasing manager

In this context, the purchasing manager participates in the provider's project quoting and planning process by insuring pricing and availability of hardware, software licensing and services from vendors, distributors and fulfillment partners to meet the provider's requirements.

Project managers

In this context, the project manager participates in the provider's project planning and management process by working with the sales engineer to develop a project scope, then specify methods to be utilized during project implementation, identify all tasks to be completed during project implementation, create a timeline and expected duration for each task's completion and estimate and allocate resources for each task's completion.

In addition, the project manager is normally responsible for creating the risk management plan, change control process and communication and status reporting process utilized during project implementation.

Inventory manager

In this context, the inventory manager participates in the provider's service delivery process by insuring adequate inventory availability of hardware, software licensing and services from vendors, distributors and fulfillment partners to meet the provider's service delivery requirements, and handles all returns, RMAs and credits when necessary.

Field engineers/technicians
In this context, the field engineer/technician participates in the provider's problem management and resolution process, and can be assigned to deliver services at the customer's facilities when necessary.

Field engineers/technicians will utilize the provider's hardware and software problem management and resolution processes as well as the provider's chosen software and hardware management and remediation tools, processes and procedures during service delivery.

Bench engineers/technicians
In this context, the bench engineer/technician participates in the provider's problem management and resolution process, and can be assigned to deliver services for customer equipment brought in to the provider's facilities when necessary.

Bench engineers/technicians will utilize the provider's hardware and software problem management and resolution processes as well as the provider's chosen software and hardware management and remediation tools, processes and procedures during service delivery.

Service Delivery

Project scoping

In order to properly scope a project, the professional services provider must first perform a business needs analysis and technology assessment in order to completely understand their customer's needs and their current state of technology in order to develop a recommended solution and implementation strategy.

Normally conducted by the provider's account manager or salesperson, the goals of business needs analysis phase of the project include building an understanding of the customer's short, medium and long-term business goals, their current business processes and workflows, and their existing business risk and pain points.

The goals of the technology assessment phase of the project are understand the state of physical health and readiness of the customer's infrastructure. Normally conducted by a field engineer/technician, activities normally performed during a technology assessment include:

- Identifying and documenting the topology and interconnectivity of all devices in the customer's environment

---

- Identifying and documenting all hardware and its role and configuration in the customer's environment
- Identifying and documenting all software, its role and service pack and patch level in the customer's environment
- Identifying and documenting all processes and services and their roles in the customer's environment
- Identifying risks, vulnerabilities and bottlenecks which may impact service availability and end-user productivity in the customer's environment

The results of the business needs analysis and technology assessment are used by the sales engineer to prepare a project scope to meet the customer's business needs.

Project quoting

Once the project has been scoped, the sales engineer may work with the purchasing manager to begin the quoting process for the solution. This is first accomplished by working with vendors and fulfillment partners to establish the best solution(s) that align(s) with the project scope requirements, then determining pricing and availability of all required hardware, software licensing and external services.

Once this has been accomplished, the sales engineer may work with the project manager to break the solution into

---

---

phases and create a high-level project plan to determine with a high degree of certainty based upon experience the number of resources and amount of labor hours required to deliver the solution.

After this is achieved and based upon the professional services provider's desired profit margin on hardware, licensing, external services, and internal labor, the quote can be finalized with a standard 20% cushion to account for the unforeseen.

Let's take a look at a typical scenario where an account manager has made the initial contact with a new prospect for an infrastructure upgrade. The account manager has performed a business needs analysis, and a field engineer/technician has completed a technology assessment. The result is that the prospect will need to migrate from Microsoft Windows Server 2003 to a Microsoft Essential Business Server 2008 solution, and replace all 20 of the users' desktops with new ones running Microsoft Windows Vista Business. Because the prospect has an aging analog phone system, the account manager would like to quote a VoIP solution as well. The account manager and field engineer/technician have done a good job at gathering all of the necessary information the sales engineer will need to review to scope the project and propose a solution, including

---

---

network documentation and asset and software licensing information.

The sales engineer will discuss the project scope with the account manager and technician in order to get a clear understanding of the "lay of the land" at the prospect's location, and ask specific clarifying questions in order to shape the final solution and proposal. In many cases, sales staff will put together standard proposals for say, managed services agreements or simple services and solutions, but the sales engineer may review any and all quotes and proposals for approval before they are presented to a prospect or client. This process can save countless tens of thousands of dollars over the years, as it reduces the chance of quoting the wrong service, solution, equipment and/or price, which always affects client satisfaction. In addition, it sets appropriate prospect and customer expectations in terms of provisioning, implementation and turn-up schedules.

Based upon the complexity of the proposed solution or other factors, the sales engineer may meet with the prospect or client themselves, and always with the account manager, whose job it is to build and maintain the client relationship. It is the account manager's responsibility to marshal the support necessary to meet the prospect's or client's needs, and they must constantly be operating in this fashion – we always want the account manager to be the client contact in the

---

relationship, deepening their bond in order to build the trust necessary to continue to sell solutions deep into their environment as the trusted advisor.

Once the sales engineer understands the prospect's or client's needs completely, and has all of the information required in order to scope the solution, they can move from the discovery to the design phase of the project.

The sales engineer will work with the purchasing manager to leverage the relationships they've built with their distributors, vendors and fulfillment partners in order to price, quote and deliver this infrastructure upgrade. Their distributors will provide the best quotes they can on server and desktop hardware, as well as licensing. Since the solution requires a VoIP quote, the sales engineer and purchasing manager will engage their VoIP vendor, as well as their T-1 vendor, who will be upgrading the bandwidth at the location in order to support the prospect's new voice and data requirements.

Once the purchasing manager has received several different quotes from the distributor, VoIP and broadband vendor, the sales engineer will determine whether or not to present the prospect with different options, or present a single quote in their proposal reflecting their preferred solution. This decision will be based upon the professional services provider's current

---

company policy, as well as the overall profit goal for the solution.

We've found that the closing percentage for solutions is closely related to the quality of the proposal. This is why it is always a good idea to include a technical drawing of the proposed solution from a "before" and "after" perspective, as well as a breakdown of the phases of the project, along with an estimated timeline of the proposed work scope in professional services quotes and proposals.

The sales engineer next works with the project manager to break the solutions into phases, identify resources and task timelines to estimate total labor hours. The sales engineer then creates the quote with desired margins and writes the proposal.

Once the quote and proposal have been created, the sales engineer briefs the account manager on the solution and goes over the proposal with them in detail.

Once the account manager has been briefed on and agrees with the proposal; and based upon the complexity of the solution, the sales engineer may become involved in the final presentation of the proposed solution to the prospect. Their intimate understanding of all facets of any solution they've designed makes them an invaluable asset in many client presentations.

Let's take a look at the process the sales engineer will go through in this scenario:

- Receives business needs analysis and technology assessment information/documentation from the account manager and field engineer/technician
- Meets with the account manager and field engineer/technician in order to understand the basic needs and spell out the preliminary scope of the proposed solution
- May meet with the prospect along with the account manager in order to clarify specifics of the prospect's needs
- Meets with the account manager to finalize the work scope before beginning the design phase of the project
- Works with the purchasing manager to contact distributors, vendors and fulfillment partners for price quotes
- Receives distributor, vendor and fulfillment partner quotes back from purchasing manager and determines the best method of creating the proposal with input from the account manager
- Works with the project manager to determine phases, resources and total labor hours to complete project delivery

- Creates the proposal with technical drawings, phases of the project and an estimated timeline
- Briefs the account manager on the completed solution and proposal
- Becomes a resource to be called upon during future client presentations

Project planning

Once the customer has agreed to the proposal and its terms, the project manager can begin the process of planning for project implementation. Project planning is the first component of project management – the effective organization and management of resources to insure a project is completed within scope, timeline and budget. Effective project planning includes developing a project scope, specifying methods to be utilized during project implementation, identifying all tasks to be completed during project implementation, creating a timeline and expected duration for each task's completion and estimating and allocating resources for each task's completion.

The overall objectives that the project plan must insure are:

- Specific
- Measurable
- Achievable
- Realistic

- Time-bound

Determination of the project's success at meeting these objectives occurs at project closure; however, effective project management increases the potential for their achievement.

Once the project plan has been created, it is presented to the customer for:

- Approval of the overall project plan
- Reconciling scheduling against the customer's calendar
- Customer resource identification and allocation required for successful project implementation
- Agreement as to roles, responsibilities and task assignments between all parties
- Agreement upon the provider's risk management plan
- Agreement upon the provider's change control process
- Agreement upon the provider's communication and status reporting process

Prior to project implementation, it is required that the customer approve the overall project plan, which includes the project scope, implementation methods, timeline and schedule, as well as the involvement of any customer staff or

---

vendors that may be required as assets during project implementation.

The provider's risk management plan is used as a contingency strategy should the need to roll back during any phase of the project becomes necessary. The provider's change control process is a requirement, and utilized when additional tasks or services outside of the agreed-upon project plan and proposal require authorization by the customer to assure project completion.

A solid communication and status reporting process must be agreed to by all parties in order to keep all affected resources continually apprised of project status and facilitate effective decision-making throughout the project lifecycle.

Only after all resources have agreed to their roles and responsibilities and project milestones and timelines can accountability to tasks and their timely completion be enforced.

Project implementation and management
After the customer has agreed to the project, and the purchasing manager has ordered and received the necessary hardware, software and services, the project manager can begin project implementation. This will include managing their

---

own internal as well as external customer resources, and vendors and fulfillment partners allocated to the project.

To manage resources, tasks and timelines, the project manager will rely on the professional services provider's project management solution and processes to allow them and their resources to track and report on each task and its status throughout the project's lifecycle.

Dependent upon the project plan, tasks may be conducted at the provider's, customer's, vendors' or fulfillment partners' location(s).

In many cases, it is more efficient for bench engineers/technicians to prepare and build out as much of a project as possible at the provider's location to minimize service interruption for the customer, and then have field engineers/technicians deliver that phase of the solution to the customer's location during a cutover.

In other scenarios, a portion of the project plan may call for a Datacenter migration, in which case that phase of the project would be implemented at the vendor's location.

The project manager must monitor each phase of project implementation carefully and insure their risk management plan is in place at each step of the way, should the outcome of a particular project phase not match its objective.

The project manager should also be keen to document each and every deviation from the project plan, and strictly adhere to the provider's change control process, requiring the customer to approve all change orders before modification of the project and implementation plan is allowed to occur.

Customer service

As with all service delivery models in our discussion, in order to establish, maintain and increase customer satisfaction within this service delivery model, the professional services provider will need to educate their staff on delivering not only first-rate technical implementation services, but excellent customer service as well.

Maximize: The Professional Services Delivery Model

max · i · mize [**mak**-s*uh*-mahyz] – *to increase to the greatest possible amount or degree*

Now that we understand the basics of what it takes to maintain the professional services delivery model in terms of service delivery, it's time to dive even deeper and identify how to maximize efficiencies, processes, procedures and profitability with this service delivery model.

Strategy

Although the professional services delivery model is less challenged in terms of profitability than the hardware warranty and break-fix services delivery models, areas where efficiencies, processes and procedures and profits can be maximized from a technical perspective include the following:

- Tools and technology
- Processes and procedures
- Project scoping
- Project quoting
- Project planning
- Equipment and parts ordering
- Project management
- Invoicing
- Staff utilization
- Costs
- Pricing
- Vendors
- Partners

Tools and technology

In order to provide the best services possible for customers, and continually improve their internal efficiencies and capabilities in order to scale, all service providers should consistently evaluate new tools and technologies and budget

---

for investments in these yearly. These investments should be business decisions based upon a clear ROI or benefit to the provider and/or their customers.

Processes and procedures

No matter what service delivery model employed, there are always gains to be made by analyzing existing workflows to improve outcomes. Providers all too often neglect to turn the mirror upon themselves, or sample the Kool-Aid they are liberally drenching their customers with.

How often do providers practice what they preach to their customers and perform internal business needs analyses and technology assessments on themselves? *Not often enough.* In order to maximize their business models, they must understand that it is imperative to continue to invest in new tools and technology to offload labor-intensive processes from costly resources and continue to tweak and tune their processes and procedures to yield incremental gains in efficiency and productivity.

Service delivery maximization is not an event, but a continual process that never ends.

As intelligent business owners, providers need to grant their organizations the same type of consultative services as they do for customers. This will help insure that they can scale

---

profitably to meet existing customers' needs and service new ones efficiently and profitably.

Project scoping

For the professional services provider, the degree of project profitability begins in the scoping process and continues through successive phases. If the project is not scoped correctly to deliver a solution that aligns with the customer's business needs and expectations, not only is profitability jeopardized, but the customer relationship as well.

Project quoting

Equally, if not more important than proper project scoping is accurate quoting. Customers rely on the professional services provider to deliver their solutions on time and within the quoted cost. The professional services provider should spend the required time necessary to verify and insure not only their cost for equipment, software licensing and services, but also the availability of same, and include a "quoted price good until" clause in their quotes and proposals. This will help protect them in situations of vendor and distributor pricing increases and availability challenges.

Project planning

Successful project implementation and customer satisfaction and sign-off can only be achieved through the development of and adherence to a solid project plan. To insure the customer's satisfaction of the outcome and maintain maximum profitability, no project, no matter how small, should be delivered without a project plan that incorporates the following:

- A project scope
- A project implementation method
- The identification of all project tasks
- The creation of a timeline and expected duration for each task's completion
- The estimation and allocation of resources for each task's completion
- The identification of roles, responsibilities and task assignments between all resources
- A risk management plan
- A change control process
- A communication and status reporting process

Equipment and parts ordering

The provider should have a documented process for ordering, tracking and paying for equipment and parts required for project implementation. Professional services providers can ill afford to miss scheduling windows due to poor adherence to this established process, not to mention the negative impact to customer satisfaction.

Project management

An effective project management process provides management of resources to insure a project's completion within its defined scope, timeline and budget.

To manage resources, tasks and timelines, the project manager will rely on the professional services provider's project management solution to manage the successful completion of specific project goals and objectives.

Invoicing

One area that should never impact the professional services provider's cash flow is invoicing. The provider may choose to invoice the customer a portion of the project's overall value in advance to cover the costs of hardware and labor during the initial phases of project implementation, with the outstanding balance due upon completion, or accept progress payments for projects with extended timelines.

Staff utilization

The ability for the professional services provider to maintain enough new project work to keep their technical staff fully utilized at better than 75% on a consistent basis is critical for profitability, and in most cases cannot be accomplished without a professional services automation (PSA) solution and the requirement for all staff to book each minute of their time in it. In fact, the proper implementation and use of a PSA

---

solution has the potential of increasing staff utilization close to 100%, driving more revenue to the provider's bottom line.

The cost of low utilization is an extremely important concept to grasp, as 75% overall utilization means that the provider is paying their staff a full 3 months per year for non-billable time, and if this utilization number is lower, so are net profits.

Costs

As with any service delivery model, the ability to contain, control and reduce costs directly impacts the bottom line. The professional services provider is no exception, and should review all of their overhead costs on a regular basis to make certain that they are getting the absolute best rates on services such as telco, broadband, cell service and HR costs as well, including medical and other employee benefits.

Other ways to minimize costs are to find and utilize dependable contractors for periodic or temporary surges in business. This strategy may save on labor costs in the long run, and delay the necessity to hire additional full-time employees until absolutely necessary.

Pricing

An area that is often overlooked by professional services providers and the fastest way to increase revenues across the board in a single day is the practice of raising their rates and other pricing on a yearly basis. Customers will not balk at a 5%

---

to 8% yearly labor rate increase, but they will if the provider tries to raise rates 25% to make up for several years without a rate increase.

Vendors and distributors

Another area the professional services provider can explore is working with their vendors and distributors to obtain better pricing and discounts, or other benefits such as marketing development funds that can be used to market for new prospects and grow the provider's business.

Partnering

Another way to maximize and grow revenues for the professional services provider is to partner with other complementary services providers such as telco vendors, copier vendors and the like to trade warm leads. Similarly, the professional services provider can partner with other I.T. solution providers to deliver additional solutions to their customer base and earn added revenues as commissions, increasing their value to their customers by marshalling the resources to meet their business needs.

Migrate: The Professional Services Delivery Model

mi · grate [mahy-greyt] – *to shift, as from one system, mode of operation, or enterprise to another*

No matter which service delivery model the provider practices, one way to increase revenues and opportunities is to adopt an additional service delivery model as a hybrid option, or completely migrate to it. In many situations, providers choose a hybrid model that allows them to provide a blend of hardware warranty, break-fix, professional and managed services all under one roof.

While the desire for the provider to have the capability to address all of their customers' needs in this fashion is strong, the most successful providers are those that focus on a smaller number of deliverables, allowing them to really fine-tune their processes and procedures to receive the greatest net profits. They may also specialize in vertical-specific markets in order to further increase their profits through service delivery familiarity and shorten their sales cycles.

The next section focuses on migration strategies for the professional services provider wishing to explore the grass on the other side of the fence.

Migration choices

The professional services provider has their choice of three other service delivery models to migrate to or adopt into a new hybrid service delivery model:

1. The hardware warranty services delivery model
2. The break-fix services delivery model
3. The managed services delivery model

For purposes of our discussion; however, we will focus on migration strategies to the managed services model only. Should the professional services provider wish to provide reactive, break-fix or hardware warranty services as well, they can easily adopt the build, manage and maintain strategies of those service delivery models found in the appropriate sections of this book.

It will generally be easier for the "pure" professional services provider to adopt or migrate to the managed services delivery model. This is due to the provider's existing process-based focus for delivering professional services. In many cases, the creation or adoption of and adherence to process and procedure is the most difficult challenge faced by providers in general.

Strategies for migration to a managed services delivery model

Areas that the professional services provider will need to evaluate when migrating to the managed services delivery model may include:

- Agreement and SLA
- Tools and technology
- Processes and procedures
- Scheduling
- Service delivery
- Equipment and parts ordering
- RMA processing
- Invoicing
- Staffing
- Staff utilization
- Costs
- Pricing
- Vendors
- Partners

Agreement and SLA

The professional services provider will need to develop a managed services agreement and SLA in order to deliver proactive, flat fee managed I.T. services to their customers, as

---

managed I.T. services are delivered, measured and governed by strict SLAs.

Tools and technology

The professional services provider will need to evaluate the suitability of their existing problem management and resolution, or PSA software solution for suitability with the managed services delivery model. If they do not currently own or utilize a solution for problem management and resolution, they will need to invest in one.

Key features for a problem management and resolution or PSA solution to evaluate include:

- Customer relationship management (CRM) capabilities
- Service request or trouble ticketing capabilities
- Scheduling & dispatching capabilities
- Time & expense tracking capabilities
- Inventory control capabilities
- Asset management capabilities
- Configuration & change management capabilities
- Knowledge base capabilities
- Resource management capabilities
- Integration of quoting & invoicing with accounting systems capabilities
- Sales funnel capabilities
- Robust, customizable reporting capabilities

In addition, the professional services provider will need to invest in a remote monitoring and management (RMM) solution to allow them to proactively monitor critical devices, events and services within their customer environments and alert on operation outside of recommended parameters, allowing the provider to take action to maximize customer uptime and maintain SLA's.

The RMM solution will allow the provider to script, schedule and automatically execute otherwise costly, labor-intensive activities such as hardware and software patching and updating and system optimization. This solution may grant the provider the following capabilities:

- WMI/Syslog/SNMP monitoring capabilities
- Multiple alerting capabilities – email/text page/pager
- Configurable and customizable alerting capabilities
- Supports escalation
- Outputs detailed logging
- Supports multiple operating systems
- Supports critical server monitoring functions – Exchange, SQL, IIS, SharePoint, Linux, Novell
- Supports multiple types of hardware – PCs, Macs, servers, routers, switches, firewalls, Printers
- Supports Multiple 3rd-Party Software Monitoring
- Supports operating system and software patch management and updates

---

- Easily Integrates with PSA solutions
- Supports remote control of monitored devices
- Allows scripting, scheduling and automatic execution of otherwise costly, labor-intensive activities
- Robust, customizable reporting capabilities

Processes and procedures

The professional services provider will need to develop and implement effective best practices-based problem management and resolution processes and procedures for delivery of managed services to their customers.

The provider's service delivery development process should focus on proactive services delivered by a well-trained service desk and NOC staff to deliver services powered by a remote monitoring and management (RMM) solution, including maintenance and response and remediation procedures which are managed and documented in the provider's PSA solution.

Scheduling

The process of scheduling resources for service delivery is similar and consistent across all service delivery models. Modifications to the provider's scheduling process are negligible in this migration scenario due to the similarities between the service delivery models in this regard.

Service delivery

The professional services provider's problem management and resolution processes should be based upon best practices, and support a proactive service delivery focus, supported by the development and execution of remote monitoring and management (RMM) processes and procedures.

Equipment and parts ordering

The professional provider's existing documented request and fulfillment process for ordering, tracking and paying for equipment, licensing and parts required for professional service delivery should suit their needs in delivering managed services.

Primary differences in this area may include expanding the number and types of manufacturers, vendors and distributors that customer equipment, licensing, services and solutions are sourced from as a managed services provider.

RMA Processing

The professional services provider may need to develop or modify existing RMA processing procedures when delivering managed services.

Primary differences in this area may include expanding the number and types of manufacturers, vendors and distributors for whom RMA processes and procedures need to be

---

developed for in order to support a wider variety of solutions as a managed services provider.

Invoicing
The managed services delivery model requires the ability for the provider to invoice for services in advance of their delivery, and for a flat fee per month. This requires both the capability, as well as the process to manage invoicing in this manner.

Invoicing for additional services that fall outside of the provider's managed services agreement or SLA will occur as these services are delivered.

Staffing
Although similarities between the professional and managed services delivery models exist in terms of most existing staff roles and responsibilities, allowing them to transfer to the new model with minimal modifications, additional service roles will be required to support the ongoing service request and proactive monitoring and maintenance functions of a managed services provider to maximize customer uptime and maintain SLA's.

Service desk staff
In this context, the service desk staff participates in the managed services provider's problem management and resolution process, and can be assigned to deliver remote

---

technical support services to end users. The service desk staff identifies, prioritizes and documents all service requests, and initiates problem management and resolution activity.

Service desk staff will execute the provider's problem management and resolution processes as well as utilize the provider's chosen software and hardware management and remediation tools, processes and procedures during remote service delivery.

NOC Staff
In this context, the NOC (network operations center) staff participates in the provider's problem management and resolution process, and can be assigned to deliver proactive remote patching, updating and monitoring services for devices, software applications and operating systems and services in customer environments. Whereas the provider's service desk staff works primarily with end-user issues, the NOC staff's main focus is on managing and delivering scheduled maintenance activities and responding to alerts generated by the provider's remote monitoring and management (RMM) solution.

The NOC staff identifies, prioritizes and documents all service activity and will execute the provider's problem management and resolution processes as well as utilize the provider's chosen software and hardware management and remediation

---

tools, processes and procedures during remote service delivery.

Service dispatchers

In this context, the service dispatcher participates in the provider's problem management and resolution process, and assigns resources to and schedules all onsite or bench warranty services. The service dispatcher may also be included in the provider's escalation process and be alerted by their PSA solution should service requests become in danger of falling out of SLA.

As with all service staff, service dispatchers will utilize the provider's chosen software management tools, processes and procedures to manage dispatch functions during service delivery.

Service managers

In this context, the service manager is ultimately responsible for maintaining the provider's technical staffing levels, training and certification requirements, problem management and resolution processes and customer satisfaction by strict SLA management, among other responsibilities.

As with all service staff, service managers will utilize the provider's chosen software management tools, processes and procedures to manage service delivery.

Staff utilization

The same requirements for maintaining the highest possible utilization for billable resources exists in all service delivery models. As a result, the provider's need to extract every ounce of utilization from their staff does not change due to service delivery model migration.

Costs

The necessity for the provider to contain, reduce and control costs is not service delivery model-dependent. This migration scenario may require the provider to invest in training their existing staff to provide them the ability to support a wider range of solutions and environments, or to hire and train additional staff as needed to provide their customers managed services, as well as the costs to purchase, train on and maintain the provider's PSA and RMM solutions.

Pricing

A consideration for the provider migrating to the managed services delivery model is the necessity to adopt a flat-fee pricing model for proactive service delivery. Whether the provider chooses a per-device, per user or tiered model, they must first understand what their total cost of service delivery is, in order to determine a desired profit margin and ultimate retail price for their services.

Factors to weigh when identifying the total cost of service delivery (TCSD) include the following:

- The provider's hourly cost of billable resources
- The provider's employer contributions
- The provider's overhead

Determining the hourly cost for 1 billable technician

In order to determine the provider's hourly cost for 1 billable technician, it is necessary to include the technician's hourly wages, the provider's employer contributions and overhead costs in a formula which yields an hourly value.

In the following table, the technician's hourly wage is added to the employer's payroll contributions. This value is then added to the provider's monthly overhead costs and divided by the monthly hours of service delivery, which is then divided by the number of billable technicians. The outcome is the provider's TCSD per hour.

Determining TCSD

Hourly cost for 1 billable technician		
Technician's hourly wage	$30.00	Hourly pay
+		
Employer payroll contributions	$10.00	Taxes, Insurance, etc.
+		
Total overhead cost	$18.75	$3k/mo ÷ 160hrs/mo ÷ 1
=		
TCSD per hour	$58.75	

Determining profit margins and labor rates

After the provider determines their TCSD per hour, it is now possible to determine a desired profit margin and final labor rate. In the previous example, the provider's TCSD per hour is $58.75, so it is now a simple matter to determine a desired profit margin in this example. If the provider wishes to

---

implement a 100% profit margin on their hourly TCSD, the result would be a billable labor rate of $117.50 per hour. Higher desired profit margins would yield higher billable labor rates.

Determining Labor Rates

100% Margin for 1 billable technician		
Cost per hour	$58.75	CPH
+		
Target margin	$58.75	100% of CPH
=		
Billable labor rate	$117.50	

Quoting Managed Services per estimated monthly support hours

One method a provider may utilize in quoting a managed services maintenance plan to their customers would be to estimate the amount of hours required per month to perform the services agreed to in their SLA, then use their billable labor rate as the factor to yield the cost to deliver services.

The following example illustrates quoting a customer a flat fee for supporting a 30 pc and 2-server environment. The provider assumes a support requirement of a half hour per month per pc and two and a half hours per month per server, equaling a 20 hour per month service requirement.

Quoting managed services by estimating support hours

Pricing for a 30 pc, 2 server environment at .5 hrs/mo support per pc and 2.5 hrs/mo support per server	
Estimated support hours/mo	20
x	
Billable labor rate	$117.50/hr
=	_____
Flat monthly fee	$2,350.00/mo

Should the provider deliver a hybrid blend of services including break-fix services along with flat-fee managed services, these services would be invoiced separately to customers, along with any other services delivered that fall outside of the provider's flat-fee support and maintenance services.

Vendors and distributors
The professional services provider will almost certainly need to build relationships with new vendors and distributors to support their customer environments with managed services.

Partnering
Another way to maximize and grow revenues for the provider is to partner with other complementary services providers such as telco vendors, copier vendors and the like to trade warm leads. Similarly, the provider can partner with other I.T. solution providers to deliver additional products and services to their customer base and earn added revenues as commissions, increasing their value to their customers as a trusted advisor by marshalling the resources to meet their business needs.

Section 4: The Managed Services Delivery Model

For purposes of our discussion, the managed services delivery model is defined as being comprised of activities, processes and procedures that allow the service provider to deliver a defined set of proactive network, device, component, service and application monitoring and I.T. maintenance services governed by Service Level Agreement (SLA) to customers for a flat monthly fee. These services can be delivered remotely or onsite at the customer's location, and are scheduled, preventative and proactive. Furthermore, managed services are not measured by time invested, nor are they reactive, break-fix services that are billed on a time and materials basis. The managed services provider invests in tools and technology to extend the capabilities of their staff and develops consistent processes and procedures to improve service delivery efficiency and profitability.

In addition, the managed services provider utilizes their service desk and remote monitoring solutions' reporting capabilities to both identify and address issues in customer networks before they become work-stopping outages, and to demonstrate the value of their services to their customers.

Build: The Managed Services Delivery Model

build [bild] – *to develop or give form to according to a plan or process; create*

In order to build a managed services delivery model, we must understand its characteristics – the nuts and bolts.

This section will explore the considerations necessary to build a managed services delivery model and discuss deliverables, tools and technology, pricing and positioning, staffing requirements, target markets and other concerns.

Characteristics

Managed services providers are the most profitable of the four service provider categories in our discussion, and this level of profitability can be attributed to many factors, including the provider's strict, process-oriented approach to conducting the preparatory work required in the business needs analysis and technology assessment phases of the discovery process prior to on-boarding new customers, as well as their requirement for minimum baseline environmental standards for service delivery (the customer is billed to bring their environment up to these minimum standards for service). This eliminates the "gotcha" factor, and allows the provider to price and deliver their services for maximum profitability. In addition, managed services providers receive annuity-based revenues that compound month after month as new customers are acquired, eliminating the peaks and valleys of reactive break-fix or transaction-based professional services revenue over time. Furthermore, invoicing for managed services occurs in advance of service delivery, positively impacting cash flow for the provider.

Over time, the managed services provider's evolution to the role of trusted advisor allows them to increase the trust and loyalty of their customers and sell additional services and solutions to them more easily, further increasing their revenues.

Build: The Managed Services Delivery Model

The managed services delivery model is extremely attractive to prospects and customers due to the fact that the customer's and provider's business goals are in perfect alignment, unlike the break-fix services delivery model, where the provider may be perceived to profit from the customer's pain – *the more pain, the more profit.*

With the managed services delivery model, the provider is *most profitable when their customers experience the least pain*, and are productive and efficient, experiencing maximum uptime; for if their customer is down, the provider must become reactive, and since their services are billed as a flat fee, the longer the downtime, the more it hurts the customer *as well as the provider.* Thus, the managed services provider is most profitable when their customers are most profitable, meaning that they are both working towards the same goal – *a true business partnership* instead of a vendor relationship.

These are just a few reasons that the managed services delivery model is the most profitable of those in our discussion, and whose services are the most attractive to customers due to their flat-fee pricing model – especially during times of economic uncertainty.

Deliverables

Much like the professional services delivery model, the deliverables of a managed services provider can include

---

supporting just about any technology, be it vertical-specific or otherwise. Because of the fact that the managed services provider as the trusted advisor is focused on not only service but business outcomes, and strives to improve business processes and services to their customers by creating and managing synergies across business units, and bringing to bear not only technical, but also business acumen to achieve these goals, their deliverables are in high demand by both technology-strategic customers, as well as technology-dependent verticals and customers.

The managed services provider's duties include assuming responsibility for and managing their customers' I.T. infrastructure environments as documented in their managed services agreements.

Agreement and SLA

The managed services provider' service level agreement (SLA) is the contract that binds their level of service between themselves and their customers, and records the common understanding regarding the following:

- Services
- Priorities
- Responsibilities
- Guarantees
- Availability
- Serviceability

- Performance
- Operation
- Response
- Resolution

SLAs commonly include the following:

- Definition of services
- Term of agreement
- Fees and payment schedule
- Taxes
- Coverage hours
- Exclusions
- Performance measurement
- Problem management, response and resolution times
- Limitation of liability
- Service requirements
- Covered equipment and/or services

Tools and technology
The managed services provider may invest in software tools to assist them in effective, efficient service delivery. A professional services automation (PSA) solution may provide them the following capabilities:

- Customer relationship management (CRM) capabilities
- Service request or trouble ticketing capabilities
- Scheduling & dispatching capabilities

- Time & expense tracking capabilities
- Inventory control capabilities
- Asset management capabilities
- Configuration & change management capabilities
- Knowledge base capabilities
- Resource management capabilities
- Integration of quoting & invoicing with accounting systems capabilities
- Sales funnel capabilities
- Robust, customizable reporting capabilities

A remote monitoring and management (RMM) solution may grant the managed services provider the following capabilities:

- WMI/Syslog/SNMP monitoring capabilities
- Multiple alerting capabilities – email/text page/pager
- Configurable and customizable alerting capabilities
- Supports escalation
- Outputs detailed logging
- Supports multiple operating systems
- Supports critical server monitoring functions – Exchange, SQL, IIS, SharePoint, Linux, Novell
- Supports multiple types of hardware – PCs, Macs, servers, routers, switches, firewalls, Printers
- Supports Multiple 3rd-Party Software Monitoring

- Supports operating system and software patch management and updates
- Easily Integrates with PSA solutions
- Supports remote control of monitored devices
- Allows the ability to script, schedule and automatically execute otherwise costly, labor-intensive activities
- Robust, customizable reporting capabilities

Pricing and positioning

Sold in SMB, as well as Mid and Enterprise environments, flat-fee managed services may be priced in any number of ways, including but not limited to:

1. Monitoring Only
2. Per DEVICE
3. Per USER
4. Tiered
5. All You Can EAT

In the *Monitoring Only* scenario, several different service levels can be employed; from an SMB-focused offering which provides operating system and software application patch management, antivirus and anti-spam updates, disk optimization and backup monitoring for a flat fee per month, allowing the managed services provider to bill for additional remediation activities identified through monitoring, to a Mid/Enterprise offering which forwards all alerts to the customer's in-house IT staff only, allowing them to address

---

---

and perform all incident resolution, to a scenario where the provider participates in basic incident resolution or even more advanced support.

The *Per Device* pricing model is fairly simple, and many managed services providers utilize it primarily for its simplicity. The premise is to develop a flat fee for each type of device that is supported in a customer environment. For instance, a basic per device pricing model might designate a flat fee of $79 per desktop, $399 per server, $39 per network printer and $99 per network managed.

The benefits of this pricing model include the fact that it is very easy to quote and illustrate costs for prospects, as well as the facility it affords the provider to modify the monthly service fee as the customer adds additional devices in the future.

The *Per User* pricing model is similar to the *Per Device* pricing model, with the difference being that the flat fee is billed per end-user per month, and covers support for all devices used by each end-user. This may entail supporting an office pc, laptop, PDA or Smartphone, home pc and connectivity and communication from hotels and kiosks for the user while they are traveling or away from the office.

The *Tiered* pricing model may be the most popular among managed services providers. The premise for this pricing model is to create several bundled packages of services, with each increasingly more expensive package providing more services to the customer.

For instance, a "Bronze" desktop managed services package may include basic phone and remote support, patch management and virus and adware removal for an entry-level price. Bumping up to the higher-priced "Silver" desktop managed services package may include onsite visits, and the "Gold" package may include emergency after-hours support, being the highest-priced package.

The *All You Can Eat* pricing model is extremely flexible, and includes all remote support, onsite support and lab or bench time for an entire organization for a flat fee per month, and may provide 24x7x365 support, or services during specific hours and/or days of the month only, with additional charges billed for services rendered outside of those times. The primary goal is to provide the customer the ability to realistically budget their IT support costs over a year's time, and experience no extraordinary billing fluctuations.

For technology-strategic and -dependent prospects and customers, positioning flat-fee managed services as the answer to increasing efficiency, productivity and mitigating business pain and risk while reducing overall I.T. costs is not a difficult task to accomplish.

Staffing requirements

If delivering maintenance services as well as professional services, the managed services provider will share some of the staffing requirements as the hardware warranty, break-fix and professional services providers; however, certain roles will differ, and the managed services provider will add additional roles. As with any service model, dependent upon factors such as the vertical or target market, solutions and services offered, number of concurrent and scheduled projects and the complexity of same, and size of their customer base, the managed services provider will require a minimum number of staff that fall into specific roles, and may include:

- Owners
- Managers
- Administrative staff
- Technical staff
- Marketing/sales staff
- Other staff

Owners

As in any organization; and based upon a number of factors, managed services provider owners may wear many hats, or merely a few. Their basic responsibility to the organization, its stakeholders, staff and customers is to manage and maintain a profitable business concern.

Managers
The size of the organization's management staff will be based upon the number of the organization's staff and concurrent and scheduled projects, among other factors, and may include:

- Operations management
- Office management
- HR management
- Marketing/sales management
- Service delivery management
- Project management
- Vendor management
- Customer service management

Administration
Every organization, no matter how large or small requires some form of administrative support. These roles include:

- Front office staff
- HR staff
- Accounting staff
- Customer service staff

Technical staff

Technical staff requirements for a professional services delivery practice may include:

- Service desk staff
- NOC staff
- Field engineers/technicians
- Bench engineers/technicians
- Service dispatchers

Marketing/sales staff

Although the marketing and sales roles are distinct, and in larger organizations segmented by business unit and resources, we'll group them together for purposes of our service delivery-focused discussion.

No matter what size the service provider's organization is, at one point or another, someone is going to have to market and sell the provider's services.

Other staff

As in all service delivery models, other resources may be required, and additional staff that may make up the managed services provider's organization may include:

- Purchasing manager
- Inventory manager

Considerations

The managed services delivery model is in its infancy, and being the least challenged of all models in our discussion, enjoys the highest profit potential. It is not difficult for the managed services provider to illustrate real cost savings to their prospects and clients, convincing them to outsource responsibility for managing their I.T. infrastructure and environments for quantifiable benefit.

The managed services provider invests in and relies on their tools and technology to monitor for and alert on potential problems within their customer environments before they can affect user productivity, and to automatically deliver patch management, software update, disk optimization and other historically labor-intensive maintenance services to devices under management.

In addition, the provider develops and implements effective processes and procedures to deliver I.T. maintenance and problem management and remediation services to their customers' environments and users. These factors allow the managed services provider to scale their services much more broadly and profitably than other service delivery models, as their services are not delivered on a time and materials basis. As a result of being able to do much more with less, the managed services provider can delay interviewing, hiring,

---

training and managing additional staff beyond the capability of other service delivery models.

Target market

Akin to the professional service provider, the managed services provider's target market may be vertical or non-vertical specific, and span not only the SMB and Mid markets, but the Enterprise markets as well, as like professional services providers, managed services providers can bring specialization, experience and skill sets to bear to support very simple to very complex infrastructures.

As a result of these capabilities and the flat-fee nature of the managed services pricing model, providers are more apt to attract technology-strategic customers who view technology spending as strategic investments in their organizations and provide them a competitive advantage in their markets, as well as technology-dependent customers looking to reduce their I.T. support costs. To these customers, the opportunity to receive service and value along with cost savings through a provider that aligns directly with their I.T. and business goals becomes an extremely attractive consideration.

Customer satisfaction and loyalty

As a result of the managed services provider's effective, efficient and proactive service management and delivery process, and the investment made in understanding their

---

customer's business, goals and pain points, customer satisfaction and loyalty rank highest among all other service delivery models in our discussion. This leads to a trusted advisor relationship between the customer and provider, resulting in consistent opportunities for additional service and solution delivery.

These factors lead customers to perceive the managed services provider as a trusted advisor and business partner, rather than just another I.T. vendor or resource.

Maintain: The Managed Services Delivery Model

main · tain [meyn-**teyn**] – *to keep in an existing state; preserve or retain*

Now that we understand the nuts and bolts of the managed services delivery model and its characteristics and considerations, let's dive a bit deeper and explore what it takes to maintain it in terms of service delivery.

This section will cover implementing the managed services delivery model and discuss technical roles and responsibilities, as well as service delivery.

Focus

The managed services delivery model allows the provider the ability to effectively deliver a defined set of proactive network, device, component, service and application monitoring and I.T. maintenance services governed by Service Level Agreement (SLA), which are prepaid for by customers and delivered on a recurring basis. These services can be delivered remotely, at the provider's offices or onsite at the customer's location, and are scheduled, preventative and proactive.

Managed services are not measured by time invested, nor are they reactive, break-fix services that are billed on a time and materials basis. The managed services provider invests in tools and technology to extend the capabilities of their staff and provide comprehensive real-time monitoring and management of data and voice devices and services in customer environments, and develops consistent processes and procedures to improve service delivery responsiveness, efficiency and profitability.

In addition, the managed services provider utilizes their service desk and remote monitoring solutions' reporting capabilities to both identify and address issues in customer networks before they become work-stopping outages, and to demonstrate the value of their services to their customers.

In order to provide these value-added services, the managed services provider and their staff rely on their professional services automation (PSA) and remote monitoring and management (RMM) solutions to help document, inventory, manage, maintain and update hardware, software and services in their customer environments per their SLA's, in addition to providing problem management and resolution services for end-users.

The managed services provider's services will generally be paid for in advance of service delivery, and these payments may be collected on a monthly, quarterly or yearly basis.

Technical Implementation

In order to implement a managed services delivery model, a "pure-play" managed services provider must possess:

- Software and hardware tools
- Effective processes and procedures
- Technical staff

Software and hardware tools

In order to provide a well-rounded approach to proactive service delivery, the managed services provider must be equipped to monitor and service customer equipment, services and networks, and document the results of their actions. In addition, their profitability increases the more they are able to provide these services remotely.

An effective managed services provider will be able to manage, update and maintain hardware, software and services in customer environments and execute a consistent problem management process, insuring service delivery remains within agreed-upon SLA's. Software tools utilized by the provider to accomplish these activities will include asset management, problem management and remote access/control and remediation solutions.

A professional services automation (PSA) solution may provide them the following capabilities:

- Customer relationship management (CRM) capabilities
- Service request or trouble ticketing capabilities
- Scheduling & dispatching capabilities
- Time & expense tracking capabilities
- Inventory control capabilities
- Asset management capabilities
- Configuration & change management capabilities
- Knowledge base capabilities
- Resource management capabilities
- Integration of quoting & invoicing with accounting systems capabilities
- Sales funnel capabilities
- Robust, customizable reporting capabilities

Maintain: The Managed Services Delivery Model

The ability for the managed services provider to proactively monitor critical devices and services is a fundamental necessity to maintain and increase customer uptime. Many remote monitoring and management (RMM) solutions allow the capability to receive information from customer environments such as:

- Hardware asset, role and inventory information
- Operating system, application software and licensing and patch level information
- Device IP address information
- Physical system information (memory, disk, NIC, etc.)
- Running processes
- Up/down device status

These RMM solutions allow the configuration of pre-set thresholds for critical devices and services to alert on operation outside of recommended parameters, allowing the provider to take action to maximize customer uptime and maintain SLA's.

A remote monitoring and management (RMM) solution may grant the managed services provider the following capabilities:

- WMI/Syslog/SNMP monitoring capabilities

- Multiple alerting capabilities – email/text page/pager
- Configurable and customizable alerting capabilities
- Supports escalation
- Outputs detailed logging
- Supports multiple operating systems
- Supports critical server monitoring functions – Exchange, SQL, IIS, SharePoint, Linux, Novell
- Supports multiple types of hardware – PCs, Macs, servers, routers, switches, firewalls, Printers
- Supports Multiple 3rd-Party Software Monitoring
- Supports operating system and software patch management and updates
- Easily Integrates with PSA solutions
- Supports remote control of monitored devices
- script, schedule and automatically execute otherwise costly, labor-intensive activities
- Robust, customizable reporting capabilities

In addition to these tools, the managed services provider may invest in and utilize additional software test, update and remediation tools in order to provide diagnostic, troubleshooting and repair services for their customers. Leveraging these types of tools helps the managed services provider gain efficiency and speeds problem identification and resolution, increasing customer satisfaction. In addition to software tools, the professional services provider will require

---

both standard, as well as specialized hardware tools in order to deliver maintenance services to their customers.

Effective processes and procedures
In order for the provider to cost-effectively deliver managed services to their customers, they must develop and implement consistent problem management and resolution processes and procedures.

By standardizing on their software and hardware tools, and fine-tuning their processes and procedures, the provider will increase customer satisfaction as well as their own profitability.

Parts and hardware inventory
There is normally no need for the managed services provider to stock replacement hardware for equipment in their customer locations. In fact, experienced providers require vendor hardware warranties to be in place for all critical devices in their customer environments such as servers, routers, switches, firewalls, backup solutions and laptops as a prerequisite to managed services delivery.

In most cases, this guarantees the fastest parts replacement and remediation time for hardware and service failure and allows the provider to work with the vendor's support staff directly to identify and troubleshoot issues as needed.

Technical Staff

In order to meet customer expectations, SLA's and maximize profitability, the managed services provider will require a sufficient number of technical staff trained in effective hardware and software problem management and resolution processes tailored to support the provider's customer base, as well as training specific to the provider's chosen software and hardware management and remediation tools, processes and procedures.

Technical roles and responsibilities

Depending upon the number of devices, users and networks under management, and the size of the organization, the managed services provider's technical staff will fall into specific roles which may include:

- Purchasing managers
- Inventory managers
- Service dispatchers
- Service managers
- Service desk staff
- NOC staff
- Bench engineers/technicians
- Field engineers/technicians

Purchasing manager

In this context, the purchasing manager participates in the provider's service delivery process by insuring pricing and availability of hardware, software licensing and services from vendors, distributors and fulfillment partners to meet the provider's service delivery requirements.

Inventory manager

In this context, the inventory manager participates in the provider's service delivery process by insuring adequate inventory availability of hardware, software licensing and services from vendors, distributors and fulfillment partners to meet the provider's service delivery requirements, and handles all returns, RMAs and credits when necessary.

Service dispatchers

In this context, the service dispatcher participates in the provider's problem management and resolution process, and will assign resources to and schedule all onsite or bench warranty services. The service dispatcher may also be included in the provider's escalation process and be alerted by their PSA solution should service requests become in danger of falling out of SLA.

Service dispatchers will utilize the provider's chosen software management tools, processes and procedures to manage dispatch functions during service delivery.

Service managers

In this context, the service manager is ultimately responsible for maintaining the provider's technical staffing levels, training and certification requirements, problem management and resolution processes and customer satisfaction by strict SLA management, among other responsibilities.

Service managers will utilize the provider's chosen software management tools, processes and procedures to manage service delivery.

Service desk staff

In this context, the service desk staff participates in the provider's problem management and resolution process, and can be assigned to deliver remote technical support services to end users. The service desk staff identifies, prioritizes and documents all service requests, and initiates problem management and resolution activity.

Service desk staff will execute the provider's problem management and resolution processes as well as utilize the provider's chosen software and hardware management and remediation tools, processes and procedures during remote service delivery.

NOC staff

In this context, the NOC (network operations center) staff participates in the provider's problem management and resolution process, and can be assigned to deliver proactive remote patching, updating and monitoring services for devices, software applications and operating systems and services in customer environments. Whereas the provider's service desk staff works primarily with end-user issues, the NOC staff's main focus is on managing and delivering scheduled maintenance activities to critical devices and services and responding to alerts generated by the provider's remote monitoring and management (RMM) solution.

The NOC staff identifies, prioritizes and documents all service activity and will execute the provider's problem management and resolution processes as well as utilize the provider's chosen software and hardware management and remediation tools, processes and procedures during remote service delivery.

Bench engineers/technicians

In this context, the bench engineer/technician participates in the provider's problem management and resolution process, and can be assigned to deliver technical support services for customer equipment brought into the provider's facilities when necessary.

Bench engineers/technicians will utilize the provider's hardware and software problem management and resolution processes as well as the provider's chosen software and hardware management and remediation tools, processes and procedures during service delivery.

Field engineers/technicians

In this context, the field engineer/technician participates in the provider's problem management and resolution process, and can be assigned to deliver services at the customer's facilities when necessary.

Field engineers/technicians will utilize the provider's hardware and software problem management and resolution processes as well as the provider's chosen software and hardware management and remediation tools, processes and procedures during service delivery.

Service Delivery

Scheduled maintenance

The managed services provider will provide scheduled, preventative maintenance services for all devices, software and services under management according to vendor, manufacturer and provider best practices per the provider's SLA.

Remote monitoring and maintenance

The managed services provider will monitor critical devices and services within their customers' environments in order to maintain and increase customer uptime. Utilizing the provider's RMM solution, the NOC staff may install software agents within customer networks to gather and report information such as:

- Hardware asset, role and inventory information
- Operating system, application software and licensing and patch level information
- Device IP address information
- Physical system information (memory, disk, NIC, etc.)
- Running processes
- Up/down device status

The NOC staff will utilize the provider's RMM solution to configure alert thresholds for critical devices, processes and services in order to respond to operation outside of the norm before it can affect customer or user productivity.

The provider's RMM tool can also be utilized to script and automatically conduct common, labor intensive maintenance tasks such as patch management and updating and disk optimization. The automatic restart of failed services can also be scripted to occur through the RMM solution. These capabilities allow the provider to maximize customer uptime and staff utilization while increasing internal efficiency and profitability. All RMM activity, whether delivered automatically or physically by the NOC staff, is documented in the provider's PSA solution.

Problem management and resolution

In order for the managed services provider to deliver effective technical support and maintenance services to customers, they must develop, implement and adhere to a consistent problem management and resolution process. This process can include the utilization of a service desk.

In this context, the service desk is defined as the central point of contact between the customer and the managed services provider, and whose staff maintains and facilitates the restoration of normal service operation while minimizing impact to the customer within agreed-upon SLA's. The service

---

desk may provide the following services to the customer according to their SLA:

- Incident Management
- Problem Management
- Configuration Management
- Change Management
- Release Management
- Service Level Management
- Availability Management
- Capacity Management
- IT Service Continuity Management
- Security Management

The service desk's responsibilities include:

- Responding to service requests
- Following best practices for problem management and resolution
- Delivering services within established SLA's

The managed services provider's service desk conducts problem management and resolution, and all technical and engineering staff can be assigned to the following tiers for escalation:

- Tier 1
- Tier 2
- Tier 3

These tiers are utilized in the prioritization and escalation process per the provider's service desk escalation procedure. After an issue is identified and documented in the provider's PSA solution, non-critical hardware support incidents are normally assigned to tier 1 for service desk staff to begin basic troubleshooting and problem resolution. Based upon priority and other factors, the issue will be escalated up through successive support tiers as necessary in order to adhere to applicable SLAs.

All support incidents that cannot be resolved within tier 1 are escalated to tier 2, where more complex support can be provided by more experienced staff.

Support incidents that cannot be resolved in tier 2 are escalated to tier 3, where support is provided by the most qualified and experienced staff that has the ability to collaborate with the provider's vendor support engineers to resolve the most complex issues.

In many cases, an onsite visit may be required to troubleshoot and remediate issues. In this scenario a field engineer /technician may be dispatched to continue the problem resolution process.

In other cases, the customer or a field engineer/technician may bring an affected piece of equipment in to the provider's offices for troubleshooting or remediation. In this scenario a

---

bench engineer/technician may be assigned to continue the problem resolution process.

The managed services provider's service desk's goals include:

- Providing a single point of contact for end-user issues
- Facilitating the restoration of normal service operation while minimizing impact to the end-user
- Delivering services within agreed-upon SLA's
- Receiving all incident notifications through the provider's preferred means - phone, fax, email, service desk portal, etc.
- Recording all incidents in the provider's PSA solution
- Classifying all incidents and correctly documenting the nature of the incident, including affected users, systems and hardware
- Prioritizing all incidents for effective escalation
- Troubleshooting all incidents according to best practices
- Escalating all incidents as necessary to maintain established SLA's
- Maintaining consistent communication with all parties including end-users, their managers and higher, as well as the provider's own internal management hierarchy
- Perform all scheduled activities such as moves/adds/changes, maintenance, patch management, documentation and reporting

---

The managed services provider's NOC staff's daily duties

The NOC staff's daily duties are determined by their service manager, whose responsibility includes the management of the managed services provider's NOC and service desk, and the proper prioritization and assignment of all service requests to the appropriate tier.

In this context, and since all of the provider's RMM solutions alerts generate service requests in the provider's PSA solution, the NOC staff's typical day may resemble the following:

- Log in to the managed services provider's PSA solution
- Review all newly-assigned service requests to him/her
- Review any service requests previously assigned and still open to insure they are not in danger of falling outside of SLA (service dispatcher and/or manager should be alerted to this status automatically by the PSA solution before it occurs)
- Work service requests in order of priority
  - o Accept service request and time stamp
  - o Review service request
  - o Consult information documented in PSA solution as needed in order to perform problem resolution
  - o Qualify issue to determine if it can be resolved through tier 1 support within SLA
  - o Work issue to successful resolution
  - o Verify issue to be resolved

- - Document complete problem resolution details in PSA solution, mark status complete and time stamp
  - Service request is closed
- If service request cannot be resolved through tier 1 support, or is in danger of falling outside of SLA:
  - Service Request is escalated to Tier 2 and successive tiers of support, or an onsite visit is scheduled with a field engineer/technician as needed, and the problem resolution process continues

The managed services provider's service desk's staff's daily duties

The service desk staff's daily duties are determined by their service manager, whose responsibility includes the management of the managed services provider's NOC and service desk, and the proper prioritization and assignment of all service requests to the appropriate tier. The scheduling of all onsite and remote service work is ultimately the responsibility of the service manager, but this and other functions may be performed by a service dispatcher. It is the Service manager's ultimate responsibility to make certain the service desk is maintaining their SLA's.

In this context, a service desk staff's typical day may resemble the following:

Maintain: The Managed Services Delivery Model

- Log in to the managed services provider's PSA solution
- Review all newly-assigned service requests to him/her
- Review any service requests previously assigned and still open to insure they are not in danger of falling outside of SLA (service dispatcher and/or manager should be alerted to this status automatically by the PSA solution before it occurs)
- Work service requests in order of priority
  - Accept service request and time stamp
  - Review service request
  - Contact customer or end-user as needed to gather any necessary information in order to begin problem resolution
  - Consult information documented in PSA solution as needed in order to perform problem resolution
  - Qualify issue to determine if it can be resolved through tier 1 support within SLA
  - Work issue to successful resolution
  - Verify issue to be resolved to end-user's satisfaction
  - Document complete problem resolution details in PSA solution, mark status complete and time stamp
  - Service request is held in completed status for a minimum of 24 hours, after which the end-user is contacted to verify the issue has been resolved to their satisfaction and asked if the service request can be closed
  - Service request is closed

- If service request cannot be resolved through tier 1 support, or is in danger of falling outside of SLA:
  - Service Request is escalated to Tier 2 and successive tiers of support, or an onsite visit is scheduled with a field engineer/technician as needed, and the problem resolution process continues

Customer Service

In order to establish, maintain and increase customer satisfaction, the managed services provider will need to educate their staff on delivering not only first-rate technical services, but excellent customer service as well. In fact, larger managed services providers may create and staff a customer service position to insure consistent customer service delivery.

Maximize: The Managed Services Delivery Model

max · i · mize [mak-s*uh*-mahyz] – *to increase to the greatest possible amount or degree*

Now that we understand the basics of what it takes to maintain the managed services delivery model in terms of service delivery, it's time to dive even deeper and identify how to maximize efficiencies, processes, procedures and profitability within this service delivery model.

Strategy

Although the managed services delivery model is the least challenged in terms of profitability than the other service delivery models in our discussion, areas where efficiencies, processes and procedures and profits can be maximized from a technical perspective include the following:

- Tools and technology
- Processes and procedures
- Scheduling
- Service delivery
- Equipment and parts ordering
- RMA processing
- Invoicing
- Staff utilization
- Costs
- Pricing
- Vendors
- Partners
- Back office service desk support
- Hardware as a service
- Procurement services

Tools and technology

In order to provide the best services possible for customers, and continually improve their internal efficiencies and capabilities in order to scale, all service providers should consistently evaluate new tools and technologies and budget for investments in these yearly. These investments should be business decisions based upon a clear ROI or benefit to the provider and/or their customers.

Processes and Procedures

No matter what service delivery model employed, there are always gains to be made by analyzing existing workflows to improve outcomes. Providers all too often neglect to turn the mirror upon themselves, or sample the Kool-Aid they are liberally drenching their customers with.

How often do providers practice what they preach to their customers and perform internal business needs analyses and technology assessments on themselves? *Not often enough.* In order to maximize their business models, they must understand that it is imperative to continue to invest in new tools and technology to offload labor-intensive processes from costly resources and continue to tweak and tune their processes and procedures to yield incremental gains in efficiency and productivity.

Service delivery maximization is not an event, but a continual process that never ends.

As intelligent business owners, providers need to grant their organizations the same type of consultative services as they do for customers. This will help insure that they can scale profitably to meet existing customers' needs and service new ones efficiently and profitably.

Scheduling

Fortunately, the proactive nature of the managed services delivery model allows the service dispatcher the ability to schedule remote, bench and onsite support activity in ways that maximize utilization and profitability. Suggestions for potential improvements in this area are to schedule onsite service delivery as far out as possible in order to be in a position to take advantage of opportunities to group onsite service calls for customers in close proximity to each other when they occur.

In these scenarios, it is incumbent for the service dispatcher to enforce a rigorous communication process between all field-dispatched resources and themselves. This can take the form of 30 minute check-in intervals where status is regularly communicated back to the service dispatcher during onsite problem remediation. This allows the service dispatcher to make informed decisions regarding the allocation of resources throughout the day.

Service Delivery

Service delivery is an area where all service providers can always make improvements. The first step towards service

---

delivery improvement is to map out the provider's existing service delivery process, beginning with the initial call or contact from the customer regarding a support issue, and following the problem management and resolution process all the way through to closure. An efficient problem management and resolution process will include escalation points to insure that service requests don't end up in limbo for extended periods of time.

One thing to always keep in mind is the fact that the more services the provider can deliver remotely, the more profitable they will become.

It is a good idea for the provider to poll existing customers and get their candid feedback on their problem management and resolution process from start to finish. This will impress the customer's experience upon the provider and may help them identify ways to improve efficiency and customer satisfaction.

All technical support staff should always "start the clock", or timestamp a service request before they begin working on it, continually documenting their activities and results in the provider's PSA solution. All too often technical resources forget to book their time during service delivery, and later have to "make up" their activities and timelines – *this is a major profitability killer.*

The following illustrates a basic problem management and resolution process:

1. Support request is received

2. Trouble ticket is created

3. Issue is identified and documented in PSA solution

4. Issue is qualified to determine if it can be resolved through tier 1 support

If issue can be resolved through tier 1 support:

5. Level 1 resolution - issue is worked to successful resolution

6. Quality control - Issue is verified to be resolved to customer's satisfaction

7. Trouble ticket is closed, after complete problem resolution details have been updated in PSA solution

If issue cannot be resolved through tier 1 support:

6. Issue is escalated to tier 2 support

7. Issue is qualified to determine if it can be resolved by tier 2 support

If issue can be resolved through tier 2 support:

8. Level 2 resolution - issue is worked to successful resolution

---

---

9. Quality control - issue is verified to be resolved to customer's satisfaction

10. Trouble ticket is closed, after complete problem resolution details have been updated in PSA soluton

If issue cannot be resolved through tier 2 support:

9. Issue is escalated to tier 3 support

10. Issue is qualified to determine if it can be resolved through tier 3 support

If issue can be resolved through tier 3 support:

11. Level 3 resolution - issue is worked to successful resolution

12. Quality control - issue is verified to be resolved to customer's satisfaction

13. Trouble ticket is closed, after complete problem resolution details have been updated in PSA solution

If issue cannot be resolved through tier 3 support:

12. Issue is escalated to onsite support

13. Issue is qualified to determine if it can be resolved through onsite support

---

If issue can be resolved through onsite support:

14. Onsite resolution - issue is worked to successful resolution

15. Quality control - Issue is verified to be resolved to customer's satisfaction

16. Trouble ticket is closed, after complete problem resolution details have been updated in PSA solution

If issue cannot be resolved through onsite support:

17. Service manager decision point – request is updated in PSA solution with complete details of all activity performed

Equipment and parts ordering

The provider should have a documented request and fulfillment process for ordering, tracking and paying for equipment and parts required for service delivery. Providers can lose valuable scheduling opportunities if this process is not adhered to, not to mention the negative impact to customer satisfaction. It is also vitally important to have a consistent customer billing process for all new hardware installed – the faster the invoice goes out for services not covered under a managed services agreement, the faster it will be paid.

RMA processing
As with all service delivery models, it is incumbent upon the managed services provider to develop and implement an efficient procedure for dealing with RMA's so that they don't pile up in a back office or closet and miss their RMA replacement window. This is an area that can bleed profits for a provider over time, if not managed properly.

Invoicing
One area that should never impact the managed services provider's cash flow is invoicing. The provider should maintain a scheduled, consistent invoicing and accounts receivable collections process for both managed services agreements that go out in advance of the service month as well as for invoices for services that are not covered under a managed services agreement. Some managed services providers are so proficient at this that invoicing for these additional services occurs daily. Customers won't pay without an invoice, and the faster the invoice gets to them, the faster they can process it.

Staff utilization
The ability for the managed services provider to keep their technical staff fully utilized at well over 100% on a consistent basis is critical for profitability and scalability, and could not be accomplished without a professional services automation (PSA) solution and the requirement for all staff to book each minute of their time in it. In fact, the proper implementation

---

and use of RMM and PSA solutions has the potential of increasing managed services staff utilization upwards of 125%, driving more revenue to the provider's bottom line.

The managed services provider's goal now becomes tuning and modifying service delivery processes and procedures to continue to make incremental gains in efficiency, which over time continue to increase profitability.

Costs

As with any service delivery model, the ability to contain, control and reduce costs directly impacts the bottom line. The managed services provider should review all of their overhead costs on a regular basis to make certain that they are getting the absolute best rates on services such as telco, broadband, cell service and HR costs as well, including medical and other employee benefits.

Other ways to minimize costs are to find and utilize dependable contractors for periodic or temporary surges in business. This strategy may save on labor costs in the long run, and delay the necessity to hire additional full-time employees until absolutely necessary. Some managed services providers have gone so far as to only utilize contract labor for onsite service delivery, maintaining their full time employees in their service desk and NOC.

Pricing

An area that is often overlooked by managed services providers and the fastest way to increase revenues across the board in a single day is the practice of raising their rates on a yearly basis. Customers will not balk at a 5% to 8% yearly managed services agreement rate increase, but they will if the provider tries to raise rates 25% to make up for several years without a rate increase.

Vendors and distributors

Another area the managed services provider can explore is working with their vendors and distributors to obtain better pricing and discounts, or other benefits such as marketing development funds that can be used to market for new prospects and grow the provider's business.

Partnering

Another way to maximize and grow revenues for the managed services provider is to partner with other complementary services providers such as telco vendors, copier vendors and the like to trade warm leads. Similarly, the managed services provider can partner with other I.T. solution providers to deliver additional products and services to their customer base and earn added revenues as commissions, increasing their value to their customers as a trusted advisor by marshalling the resources to meet their business needs.

Back office service desk support

With the advent of affordable, 3rd-party back office service desk organizations, the provider has the opportunity to scale their services to a much broader range of customers, and prolong the necessity to hire, train and manage internal full-time staff. This allows a consistent support experience for customers and in many cases increases the provider's profitability due to the low cost of these services. In addition, these organizations can private-label their services, and represent the provider's organization throughout all communications and problem management and resolution activities.

Hardware as a service (HaaS)

The HaaS movement is gaining traction among managed services providers, as it allows the provider to introduce an additional service to their customers which provide them another stream of annuity-based income.

Rather than purchasing servers, software, data center space or network equipment, clients instead purchase these resources on a subscription basis as a fully outsourced service from the provider, who charges them a monthly recurring fee for the customer's use and the provider's maintenance.

This utility computing service model is attractive for the right customers, who leverage tax advantages by claiming the

---

equipment, software and services as operating expenses, rather than capital expenses. Delivered effectively, HaaS offerings are tremendously profitable over time for the provider.

Procurement services

A new service for providers that is gaining momentum is that of procurement services, where a provider partners with an organization to handle the research, pricing, quoting, order fulfillment, invoicing and accounts receivable activities for any and all infrastructure purchases required by the provider for their customers. The management of complex licensing programs, authorizations and support renewals for the provider's customers is also handled by these organizations.

These services streamline the buying and fulfillment process for providers and increase profitability by lowering the expense of procurement by significantly reducing the labor hours currently expended by the provider, as well as leveraging the buying power of the procurement service vendor to reduce costs.

Section 5 – Hiring and Training Technical Staff

If you're like most of our partners – I.T. service providers for whom the process for finding good technical talent is a challenge – and once you do, and invest time, effort and a compensation package in them, find it's difficult to keep them, this section is for you.

In the following chapters we'll discuss effective means for writing employment ads that attract the right talent, using DISC behavioral profiles before the interview to make certain we're interviewing the right candidates, how to interview and which questions to ask, along with putting together the offer letter and employment agreement and developing a compensation plan and training requirements.

These strategies have served us well for over 11 years, and I hope that you will be able to leverage some of these techniques to bring immediate value to your own hiring, retention and management processes.

Writing Effective Employment Ads for Technical Staff

Writing an employment ad for technical staff may be the first HR act we undertake in the early stages of building our organization. Let's take a moment to understand the motivating factors behind technically-oriented people. Our technical staff's ideal work environment may include challenging technical work, ongoing training opportunities and a team approach to problem solving and solution design and delivery, along with appreciation and respect for their contributions to the team; with high monetary incentives ranking lower on the list of needs when seeking employment, or in their decision to remain with their current employer. Technicians' behavior normally falls into the Coordinator/ Supporter/ Relater areas of a DISC (behavioral) profile. A DISC profile is a psychometric testing technique that uses a simple questionnaire as a basis for revealing insights into a person's normal, adapted and work behaviors, and we will explore utilizing DISC profiles to our advantage during the hiring process in the next chapter.

Understanding these motivators for technical staff, effective employment ads highlight these specific areas in the body of the ad. Our job is to effectively promote our employment opportunity to the best technicians available. We're not

Writing Effective Employment Ads for Technical Staff

---

looking for anybody that can fog a mirror – we want seasoned technicians and engineers, whose past performance is an indicator of their future potential.

The best technical staff we've ever hired dove right in to learning every last detail about all of our products and services, and took it seriously to become subject matter experts on everything they supported. There was a clear pecking order with these folks, and you earned their respect by knowing more than they did about a particular subject. These are the type of folks that jumped right in to their positions soon after they were hired, and sucked up information like a dry sponge.

Technicians and engineers see things as black and white problems to solve without a lot of emotion, and the really good ones can build personal relationships with customers and understand that their job is to build rapport with them to establish the trust necessary to elevate the organization's overall perception as that of a trusted advisor that can solve their technical problems and identify solutions to increase their efficiencies, productivity and mitigate their business pain and risk.

These behavioral traits are what we are looking for in our technical staff. Before we developed the hiring process we are about to discuss, I can remember how difficult it was to find

---

Writing Effective Employment Ads for Technical Staff

---

the right staff with the right mix of technical capability, customer service and desire to do the job right the first time.

But first things first – before we have the ability to start DISC profiling and the interview process, we need candidates. And to get candidates interested in our employment opportunity we need to write compelling employment ads.

So we need to structure our employment ad to cover the basics, plus highlight the nuances that will attract the technical professionals we seek. In the old days (pre-Internet), we used to have to excel at "classified ad shorthand" for print ads in the employment section of newspapers. This was the process where we would try to condense full words enough to save on the cost of the ad, while still conveying the gist of our message. Nowadays, we have the luxury of posting just about any size ad we like through online job sites such as Monster, Careerbuilder, Dice, Hotjobs and others for a reasonable fee, in addition to having it run for months at a time, if we wish. Let's look at the basic components of an employment posting for a service desk position:

Our company name and location

Job status – Full Time, Employee

Relevant Work Experience – 3 years minimum

Job Category – Service Desk

Career Level – Experienced

Job Description – Several short paragraphs documenting our desired candidate's qualities, the position's responsibilities and job duties (emphasis on challenging technical work, ongoing training opportunities and a team approach to problem solving)

Minimum Skills Required – A short bulleted list of required skills and experience

Benefits – A short paragraph detailing salary range, bonuses and other benefits

A method of contacting us

Okay, now let's take a look at a representative employment ad that conforms to many of the points in the above layout:

Company: MSP University
Location: Garden Grove, CA 92841
Status: Full-Time, Employee
Job Category: Service Desk
Relevant Work Experience: 3-5 Years
Career Level: Experienced (Non-Manager)

We are currently seeking a highly skilled service desk representative with the drive and determination to help us support our client base. This position reports to our service

---

manager. We are looking for an individual who is a problem-solver and has a proven track record of working within a team environment to successfully address challenging user computing issues, and is accustomed to leveraging technical training opportunities to improve their skills. If you have the experience and the desire, we'd like to talk to you.

Our service desk representatives are responsible for maintaining user uptime and improving their computing experiences through effective remote monitoring, maintenance and problem identification and resolution activities, as well as growing and developing the organization's perception with existing customers through exceptional customer service. Candidates must be energetic and focused with a strong motivation to learn new technologies and management and maintenance processes. This position requires dedication, persistence, follow-up, effective utilization of provided resources and unbeatable customer service.

This position will include identifying user problems and working within a structured problem management and resolution process to remediate issues within established SLAs, and involves working with other resources and vendors to deliver effective support services. Responsibilities include identifying, documenting and troubleshooting user computing issues to resolution and maintaining customer satisfaction.

Job duties include utilizing our remote monitoring and management (RMM) and professional services automation (PSA) solutions along with other service-specific tools and technologies to deliver remote user support services and update service request information, answer technical support calls, assign ticket severity, prioritize work accordingly, and collaborate and work with other staff and vendor support resources to resolve issues. Overall relationship management and the ability to coordinate required resources to respond to complex IT requirements is desired. Other requirements include participating in ongoing training and attainment of manufacturer certifications, developing and maintaining relationships with user and vendor contacts, and preparing and presenting service and monitoring reports to management regularly.

Minimum skills required:

- Minimum three years service desk experience
- Microsoft Certified Professional status
- Excellent knowledge of Microsoft software and technologies
- Strong interpersonal skills required to effectively communicate with users and vendors
- Passion for teamwork, continuing education, problem solving and exceptional customer service
- Must be well spoken, outgoing, organized, detailed-orientated, dependable and flexible

- Experience with HP, Cisco and Citrix technologies a plus
- Valid driver's license and proof of insurance
- Background check and drug screen required
- Reliable transportation

This position entails:

- Troubleshooting user problems over the phone and with remote control technologies
- Accurate documentation of all activities conducted
- The ability to manage, maintain, troubleshoot and support our users' networks, equipment, software and services
- The ability to learn quickly and adapt to changing requirements

The successful candidate must be:

- Professional and articulate
- Interpersonally adept
- Technically proficient
- A relationship builder
- A problem solver

Benefits include group medical/dental insurance, paid vacation, holidays, personal & sick time and training reimbursement. Our generous compensation plans are structured as salary plus bonuses for meeting utilization, compliance and customer service requirements, with initial compensation commensurate with relevant experience.

Qualified candidates please submit a current resume, along with salary history to: hr@mspu.us.

Resources

Careerbuilder.com
www.careerbuilder.com

Dice.com
www.dice.com

Hotjobs.com
www.hotjobs.com

Monster.com
www.monster.com

Using DISC Behavioral Profiles Before Interviewing Candidates

I remember clearly how hit-and-miss our success at hiring the right staff used to be before we discovered the value of utilizing DISC behavioral profiling in our hiring process. Based upon the groundbreaking work of William Moulton Marston Ph.D. (1893 - 1947) in the (then) emerging field of psychology, DISC measures four dimensions of normal human behavior:

- **Dominance** - relating to control, power and assertiveness (how we respond to problems or challenges)
- **Influence** - relating to social situations and communication (how we influence others to our point of view)
- **Steadiness** (submission in Marston's time) - relating to patience, persistence, and thoughtfulness (how we respond to the pace of our environment)
- **Conscientiousness** (or caution, compliance in Marston's time) - relating to structure and organization (how we respond to rules and procedures set by others)

We have not only been able to significantly improve our success rate at hiring the right staff since implementing DISC

Using DISC Behavioral Profiles Before Interviewing Candidates

---

profiling, but we have used DISC profiles to help in team-building efforts. If you haven't read Jim Collins' excellent book "Good to Great", do yourself a favor and pick up a copy. One of the key concepts in "Good to Great" is that of not only "getting the right people on the bus", but "getting the right people in the right seats on the bus". DISC behavioral profiles help us achieve both of these objectives.

Based upon answering a series of twenty-four questions, each with the directive to choose what a candidate is "most like" and "least like", the DISC profile will generate a voluminous report describing the subject's behavior with incredible accuracy. Here is a representative example of the types of questions a subject is asked to answer in a DISC profile:

Each question has two answers – choose one answer that indicates which you are **Most Like**, and one answer that indicates which you are **Least Like**. Each question requires two choices:

The Best I.T. Service Delivery BOOK EVER!

Using DISC Behavioral Profiles Before Interviewing Candidates

Most Like	Least Like	
		Gentle, kindly
		Persuasive, convincing
	x	Humble, reserved, modest
x		Original, inventive, individualistic

		Attractive, Charming, attracts others
x		Cooperative, agreeable
		Stubborn, unyielding
	x	Sweet, pleasing

	x	Easily led, follower
x		Bold, daring
		Loyal, faithful, devoted
		Charming, delightful

Using DISC Behavioral Profiles Before Interviewing Candidates

---

It seems almost unbelievable that merely completing twenty-four questions like this can create a comprehensive behavioral profile that we have come to rely on in each and every one of our hiring decisions. And I've got to admit that when we have gone ahead and made a hiring decision in spite of some red flags uncovered by a DISC profile, we've always come to regret it.

Here's a sample portion of a fictitious DISC profile:

Elizabeth prefers being a team player, and wants each player to contribute along with her. Many people see her as a self-starter dedicated to achieving results. She can be blunt and critical of people who do not meet her standards. She may have difficulty dealing with others who are slower in thought and action. Elizabeth has the ability to question people's basic assumptions about things. She prides himself on her creativity, incisiveness and cleverness. She can be incisive, analytical and argumentative at times. She is aggressive and confident. She tends to have a "short fuse" and can display anger or displeasure when she feels that people are taking advantage of her. Elizabeth is forward-looking, aggressive and competitive. His vision for results is one of her positive strengths. She is comfortable in an environment that may be characterized by high pressure and is variety-oriented.

The Best I.T. Service Delivery BOOK EVER!

Using DISC Behavioral Profiles Before Interviewing Candidates

---

Elizabeth will work long hours until a tough problem is solved. After it is solved, Elizabeth may become bored with any routine work that follows. She is logical, incisive and critical in her problem-solving activities. She sometimes gets so involved in a project that she tends to take charge. She usually takes time when confronted with a major decision; that is, she takes an unemotional approach to analyzing the data and facts. Others may see this as vacillating; however she is just thinking through all the ramifications of her decision. Elizabeth finds it easy to share her opinions on solving work-related problems. Sometimes she may be so opinionated about a particular problem that she has difficulty letting others participate in the process. She sometimes requires assistance in bringing major projects to completion. She may have so many projects underway that she needs help from others. She likes the freedom to explore and the authority to re-examine and retest her findings.

Elizabeth tends to be intolerant of people who seem ambiguous or think too slowly. She usually communicates in a cool and direct manner. Some may see her as being aloof and blunt. When communicating with others, Elizabeth must carefully avoid being excessively critical or pushy. She tries to get on with the subject, while others may be trying to work through the details. She is skilled at asking informed questions and extracting information, but for some people she may need to phrase her questions more tactfully. Her creative and active

---

---

mind may hinder her ability to communicate to others effectively. She may present the information in a form that cannot be easily understood by some people. Others often misunderstand her great ability as a creative thinker. She is not influenced by people who are overly enthusiastic. They rarely get her attention. She may display a lack of empathy for others who cannot achieve her standards.

Here are some other excerpts from Elizabeth's DISC Profile:

Value to the organization:

This section of the report identifies the specific talents and behavior Elizabeth brings to the job. By looking at these statements, one can identify her role in the organization. The organization can then develop a system to capitalize on her particular value and make her an integral part of the team.

- Thinks big
- Forward-looking and future-oriented
- Presents the facts without emotion
- Places high value on time
- Usually makes decisions with the bottom line in mind
- Innovative
- Always looking for logical solutions
- Initiates activity
- Challenge-oriented

Using DISC Behavioral Profiles Before Interviewing Candidates

---

Ideal environment:

This section identifies the ideal work environment based on Elizabeth's basic style. People with limited flexibility will find themselves uncomfortable working in any job not described in this section. People with flexibility use intelligence to modify their behavior and can be comfortable in many environments. Use this section to identify specific duties and responsibilities that Elizabeth enjoys and also those that create frustration.

- Evaluation based on results, not the process
- Non-routine work with challenge and opportunity
- An innovative and futuristic-oriented environment
- Projects that produce tangible results
- Data to analyze
- Private office or work area
- Environment where she can be a part of the team, but removed from office politics
- Forum to express ideas and viewpoints

Perceptions:

A person's behavior and feelings may be quickly telegraphed to others. This section provides additional information on Elizabeth's self-perception and how, under certain conditions, others may perceive her behavior. Understanding this section will empower Elizabeth to project the image that will allow her to control the situation.

Using DISC Behavioral Profiles Before Interviewing Candidates

---

Self-perception:

Elizabeth usually sees herself as being:

- Pioneering
- Assertive
- Competitive
- Confident
- Positive
- Winner

Other's perception:

Under moderate pressure, tension, stress or fatigue, others may see her as being:

- Demanding
- Nervy
- Egotistical
- Aggressive

And, under extreme pressure, stress or fatigue, others may see her as being:

- Abrasive
- Controlling
- Arbitrary
- Opinionated

The Best I.T. Service Delivery BOOK EVER!

Using DISC Behavioral Profiles Before Interviewing Candidates

---

Descriptors:

Based on Elizabeth's responses, the report has marked those words that describe her personal behavior. They describe how she solves problems and meets challenges, influences people, responds to the pace of the environment and how she responds to rules and procedures set by others.

Dominance	Influencing	Steadiness	Compliance
Demanding	Effusive	Phlegmatic	Evasive
Egocentric	Inspiring	Relaxed	Worrisome
Driving	Magnetic	Resistant to Change	Careful
Ambitious	Political	Nondemonstrative	Dependent
Pioneering	Enthusiastic		Cautious
Strong-Willed	Demonstrative	Passive	Conventional
Forceful	Persuasive		Exacting
Determined	Warm	Patient	Neat
Aggressive	Convincing		
Competitive	Polished	Possessive	Systematic
Decisive	Poised		Diplomatic
Venturesome	Optimistic	Predictable	Accurate
		Consistent	Tactful
Inquisitive	Trusting	Deliberate	
Responsible	Sociable	Steady	Open-Minded
		Stable	Balanced Judgment
Conservative	Reflective	Mobile	Firm
Calculating	Factual	Active	Independent
Cooperative	Calculating	Restless	Self-Willed
Hesitant	Skeptical	Alert	Stubborn
Low-keyed		Variety-Oriented	
Unsure	Logical	Demonstrative	Obstinate
Undemanding	Undemonstrative		
Cautious	Suspicious	Impatient	Opinionated
	Matter-of-Fact	Pressure-Oriented	Unsystematic
Mild	Incisive	Eager	Self-Righteous
Agreeable		Flexible	Uninhibited
Modest	Pessimistic	Impulsive	Arbitrary
Peaceful	Moody	Impetuous	Unbending
Unobtrusive	Critical	Hypertense	Careless with Details

Using DISC Behavioral Profiles Before Interviewing Candidates

---

Adapted style:

Elizabeth sees her present work environment requiring her to exhibit the behavior listed on this page. If the following statements DO NOT sound job related, explore the reasons why she is adapting this behavior.

- Precise, analytical approach to work tasks
- Acting without precedent, and able to respond to change in daily work
- Sensitivity to existing rules and regulations
- Limited contact with people
- Disciplined, meticulous attention to order
- Having the ability to see the "big picture" as well as the small pieces of the puzzle
- Careful, thoughtful approach to decision making
- Quickly responding to crisis and change, with a strong desire for immediate results
- Anticipating and solving problems
- Persistence in job completion
- Dealing with a wide variety of work activities
- Calculation of risks before taking action
- Accurate adherence to high quality standards

Using DISC Behavioral Profiles Before Interviewing Candidates

---

Keys to motivating:

Elizabeth wants:

- Evaluation on not only the results achieved, but the quality of the work and the price she paid for performance
- Sincere appreciation for achievements--may interpret as manipulation if overdone
- To explore new ideas and authority to test her findings
- To be part of a quality-oriented work group
- Support staff to do detail work
- To know the agenda for the meeting
- New challenges and problems to solve
- Freedom from controls that restrict her creativity
- To be seen as a leader
- Prestige, position and titles so she can control the destiny of others
- Meetings that stay on the agenda, or reasons for changing the agenda

Keys to managing:

Elizabeth needs:

- To know results expected and to be evaluated on the results
- To adjust her intensity to match the situation
- To be more cooperative with other team members

Using DISC Behavioral Profiles Before Interviewing Candidates

---

- A program for pacing work and relaxing
- To analyze constructive criticism to see if it's true and how it may be impacting her career
- To display empathy for people who approach life differently than she does
- To understand that her tendency to tell it like it is may reduce performance rather than raise it with some people
- To understand her role on the team--either a team player or the leader
- To negotiate commitment face-to-face
- Appreciation of the feelings of others
- To be objective and listen when others volunteer constructive criticism
- The opportunity to ask questions to clarify or determine why

Areas for improvement:

In this area is a listing of possible limitations without regard to a specific job. Review with Elizabeth and cross out those limitations that do not apply. Highlight 1 to 3 limitations that are hindering her performance and develop an action plan to eliminate or reduce this hindrance.

The Best I.T. Service Delivery BOOK EVER!

Using DISC Behavioral Profiles Before Interviewing Candidates

---

Elizabeth has a tendency to:

- Have no concept of the problems that slower-moving people may have with her style
- Be inconsistent because of many stops, starts and ever-changing direction
- Set standards for herself and others so high that impossibility of the situation is common place
- Have difficulty finding balance between family and work
- Have trouble delegating--can't wait, so does it herself

I hope by now you can see how extremely valuable this tool is, and why we choose to include it as a requirement during our hiring process.

So how exactly do we use the DISC profile? Well, we will review all of the resumes that come in for a particular job posting, and then determine who our top candidates are. After this, we will conduct a quick phone interview with each candidate, and the ones that make it to the next cut will be emailed a link to take our DISC behavioral profile online. We then review the resultant report, and decide who to call in for in-person interviews.

For technical staff candidates, in addition to the standard DISC behavioral profile, we will also have them take a specialized

---

---

version of the DISC profile, called the Personal Talent Skills Inventory (PTSI). The PTSI is an objective analysis of the candidate's understanding of themselves, their strengths and their weaknesses. An individual's talents and personal skills are a fundamental and integral part of who they are. The PTSI describes what an individual "can do" in 23 capacities, or personal skills, related to the business environment.

The PTSI is designed to capture how people see themselves and the world around them. To do this, it measures a person from two perspectives, external and internal, and in six dimensions, three in each perspective.

External:

- Empathetic Outlook ⇒ Judgment of people
- Practical Thinking ⇒ Judgment of tasks
- Systems Judgment ⇒ Judgment of systems

Internal:

- Sense of Self ⇒ Judgment of being
- Role Awareness ⇒ Judgment of doing
- Self Direction ⇒ Judgment of becoming

The PTSI report provides a ranking of personal skills that describe an individual's potential for workplace performance by determining their capability in several areas. After

---

---

analyzing the clarity, bias and intensity of each of the six dimensions, one can begin to understand an individual's self view and world view, gaining true insight into the internal and external perspectives that affect superior performance.

Understanding problem-solving techniques, and the ability to implement them effectively during service delivery, is how we define a successful technical resource. We utilize the PTSI to identify a candidate's problem-solving strengths and weaknesses and their ability to perform these functions in the workplace.

The following is a sample of the results from a fictitious PTSI:

Using DISC Behavioral Profiles Before Interviewing Candidates

---

Name: Elizabeth

World View

This is how Elizabeth sees the world around her. This view measures her clarity and understanding of people, tasks and systems. It could also be looked at in terms of feeling, doing and thinking from an external standpoint. The statements below are based primarily on the 3 dimensions on the left side of the dimensional balance page and are in a random order.

- Elizabeth may benefit from improving her relationships with authority figures
- She needs an environment in which contributions are recognized, properly rewarded, and appreciated.
- She has the ability to become action-oriented in order to complete the task at hand
- She performs best in an atmosphere where there is an open exchange of ideas and where feedback is readily available.
- Elizabeth can be versatile and can adapt to different types of people and changing situations
- She may benefit from understanding the importance of interpersonal relationships
- She needs an atmosphere that has structure and a defined chain of command
- She understands how to deal with ideas, knowledge, and systems

---

Using DISC Behavioral Profiles Before Interviewing Candidates

---

- Elizabeth has the ability to use her people skills in order to relate to others

Self View

This is how Elizabeth sees herself. This view measures her clarity and understanding of herself, her roles in life and her direction for the future. The internal dimensions are a reflection of her from both personal and professional viewpoints. The statements below are based primarily on the 3 dimensions on the right side of the dimensional balance page and are in a random order.

- Elizabeth tends to use her internal awareness to achieve the desired outcome during the process of a role change
- She may apply her life planning skills for personal growth
- She has a grasp of her actual and potential accomplishments, life roles and activities
- She has achieved a moderate level of self-understanding
- Elizabeth believes that her own worth is based equally on her sense of self, her life roles, and growing as a person
- She may focus on gaining information to clearly envision herself in the future
- She could get into a comfort zone which could restrict her from developing or applying more of her potential

---

Using DISC Behavioral Profiles Before Interviewing Candidates

---

- She tends to have a balanced understanding of herself, her roles and her future development
- Elizabeth tends to be adaptable, depending on what is called for in the current situation

As you can tell, this portion of the PTSI provides a good understanding of a candidate's perceptions of not only external environments such as the workplace, but of themselves as well, and can also be utilized as a tool to improve an existing technical candidate's skills or interpersonal relationships with others. The following section illustrates the PTSI's findings of a candidate's critical success skills in a visually appealing manner, and ranks the candidate's responses against the population:

The Best I.T. Service Delivery BOOK EVER!

Using DISC Behavioral Profiles Before Interviewing Candidates

Critical Success Skills

ATTITUDE TOWARD OTHERS: The general capacity one has for relating with other people.

```
0....1....2....3....4....5....6....7....8....9....10
```

7.9 *
7.7

MEETING STANDARDS: The ability to perform work according to precise specifications.

```
0....1....2....3....4....5....6....7....8....9....10
```

6.9 *
6.4

JOB ETHIC: The capacity to fulfill the professional responsibilities with a strong sense of moral duty and obligation they have been given.

```
0....1....2....3....4....5....6....7....8....9....10
```

7.3 *
7.2

PROBLEM SOLVING: The ability to identify key components of the problem, possible solutions and the action plan to obtain the desired result.

```
0....1....2....3....4....5....6....7....8....9....10
```

7.5 *
7.5

RESPECT FOR PROPERTY: A measure of the level of respect and appreciation for the property that belongs to others or the company.

```
0....1....2....3....4....5....6....7....8....9....10
```

8.2 *
6.5

RESULTS ORIENTATION: The capacity to clearly and objectively understand and implement all variables necessary to obtain defined or desired results.

```
0....1....2....3....4....5....6....7....8....9....10
```

7.3 *
6.8

* 68% of the population falls within the shaded area.

Using DISC Behavioral Profiles Before Interviewing Candidates

---

The General Employment Skills Summary

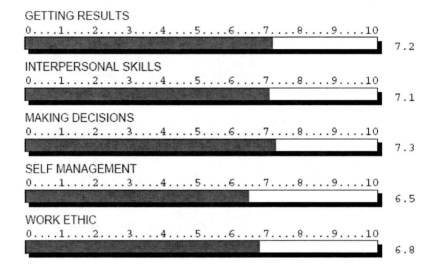

GETTING RESULTS
0....1....2....3....4....5....6....7....8....9....10
7.2

INTERPERSONAL SKILLS
0....1....2....3....4....5....6....7....8....9....10
7.1

MAKING DECISIONS
0....1....2....3....4....5....6....7....8....9....10
7.3

SELF MANAGEMENT
0....1....2....3....4....5....6....7....8....9....10
6.5

WORK ETHIC
0....1....2....3....4....5....6....7....8....9....10
6.8

The Best I.T. Service Delivery BOOK EVER!

Using DISC Behavioral Profiles Before Interviewing Candidates

---

Getting Results

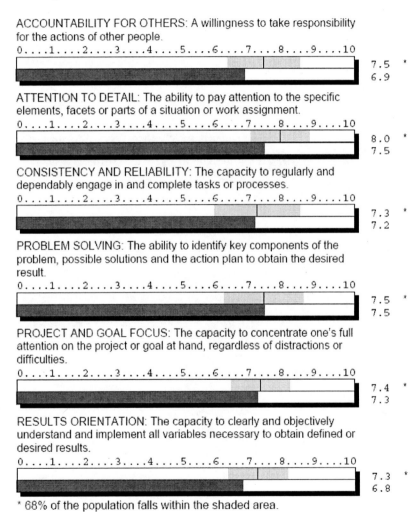

ACCOUNTABILITY FOR OTHERS: A willingness to take responsibility for the actions of other people.

0....1....2....3....4....5....6....7....8....9....10

7.5 *
6.9

ATTENTION TO DETAIL: The ability to pay attention to the specific elements, facets or parts of a situation or work assignment.

0....1....2....3....4....5....6....7....8....9....10

8.0 *
7.5

CONSISTENCY AND RELIABILITY: The capacity to regularly and dependably engage in and complete tasks or processes.

0....1....2....3....4....5....6....7....8....9....10

7.3 *
7.2

PROBLEM SOLVING: The ability to identify key components of the problem, possible solutions and the action plan to obtain the desired result.

0....1....2....3....4....5....6....7....8....9....10

7.5 *
7.5

PROJECT AND GOAL FOCUS: The capacity to concentrate one's full attention on the project or goal at hand, regardless of distractions or difficulties.

0....1....2....3....4....5....6....7....8....9....10

7.4 *
7.3

RESULTS ORIENTATION: The capacity to clearly and objectively understand and implement all variables necessary to obtain defined or desired results.

0....1....2....3....4....5....6....7....8....9....10

7.3 *
6.8

* 68% of the population falls within the shaded area.

Using DISC Behavioral Profiles Before Interviewing Candidates

---

As you can see from these graphical representations, Elizabeth consistently scored highly in almost every area of the PTSI. Based upon the information reflected in this Personal Talent Skills Inventory, along with an evaluation of Elizabeth's DISC behavioral profile, it's immediately apparent that she would make a good candidate for a position on our technical team.

Because we realize the tremendous value the DISC behavioral profile and Personal Talent Skills Inventory offer to any employer, we have created a DISC profile service for our partners which not only allows them to run online DISC profiles for their own staffing requirements, but also affords them the opportunity to re-sell this service to their clients, and earn additional revenue for providing this valuable online service. For more information, and to order a complimentary DISC profile of your own, visit the following link on our website: www.mspu.us/disc.htm.

The Interview Process for Hiring Technical Staff

Now that we've reviewed the DISC behavioral profile and Personal Talent Skills Inventory results of our top candidates, we can decide which of these merit an in-person interview. Note that we have minimized much of the effort we used to expend when hiring staff in the old days. Those were the days when candidates would show up to our offices after sending in a resume that looked promising, and we'd take lots and lots of time out of our busy schedules to interview them. And guess what? Many of the interviews for technical positions went really well – making it difficult for us to choose the right candidate.

Always remember to keep in mind the candidate's current employment situation during the interview and hiring process, and ask pointed questions regarding their prior and current employment history. A great technical candidate should not currently be out of work, unless there is a very compelling reason for it. It's simple logic to assume that successful, aggressive and motivated technical resources worth their salt should currently be employed. And if they are successful, they should look and act the part. A good candidate realizes the value of first impressions and follow-up. If they're not dressed to impress, and speak confidently and articulately during interviews, that's strike one. If they don't initiate good follow-up after interviews, that's strike two. If they are not responsive to your attempts at contact after interviews, that's strike three.

Successful technical candidates will have a firm knowledge of their history at previous employers, and be able to communicate their skill set, certifications and technical experience, in addition to their salaries and bonus plans for the past 3 years. We're also going to ask them specific questions about their daily duties, roles and responsibilities, and how much of their compensation was based upon meeting quotas for utilization, billing, customer satisfaction and adhering to SLAs, and how often they failed to achieve them. If they stutter or stammer, or begin tap-dancing during this line of questioning, that's a red flag. And as with any potential hire, spotty or short tenure at previous employers is always a matter for concern. Read between the lines of the candidate's resume, and don't be afraid to ask the tough questions – be direct and look for the same in return. If you're not good at confrontation, for Pete's sake, please have someone else perform these initial interviews for you. The ultimate effectiveness of your service delivery begins with the decisions you make during the hiring process.

Let's take a look at areas to evaluate when interviewing a technical staff candidate (depending upon their experience and areas of expertise, an experienced technical person will qualify themselves by answering the following questions successfully):

- Ask the candidate to verbalize their basic problem management and resolution strategy
- Is the candidate experienced and trained in PSAs, trouble-ticketing systems and RMM solutions? If so, ask them to describe which ones and their experience with them.
- How does the candidate keep up with new technology?
- What are the candidate's certifications?
- What are the candidate's existing utilization numbers at their current/recent position?
- How many service requests does the candidate close per day/week/month at their current/recent position?
- What is the candidate's current/recent job title and function?
- Does the candidate have experience providing proactive, reactive support, or both?
- What percentage of time does the candidate provide remote support at their current/recent position?
- What percentage of time does the candidate provide onsite support at their current/recent position?
- Does the candidate have experience with producing service reports?

The Interview Process for Hiring Technical Staff

- Ask the candidate to describe successful methods they've used to calm an irate user or customer with specific examples
- Ask the candidate to provide a history of the hardware they have worked with and to rank their expertise in same
- Ask the candidate to provide a history of the software they have worked with and to rank their expertise in same
- Ask the candidate to provide a history of the solutions they have worked with and to rank their expertise in same
- Ask the candidate to provide a history of the vendors they have worked with and to describe their relationship
- What metrics is the candidate's measured by in their current/recent position and how often do they exceed them?
- What support tier does the candidate currently participate in at their current/recent position?
- How many other technical resources comprise the candidate's business unit at their current/recent position?
- What percentage of time does the candidate spend mentoring other technical resources at their current/recent position?
- What percentage of time does the candidate spend troubleshooting an issue before deciding to escalate it?

- Has the candidate ever managed a team of resources? If so, ask them to describe these situations, their role and responsibilities and success at achieving their objective.
- Verbalize several support scenarios specific to the position the candidate is interviewing for, and ask them how they would approach and resolve them

For an exhaustive list of technical questions to ask the candidate, browse to the following links at Daniel Petri's excellent IT Knowledgebase:

- **Networking:**
  http://www.petri.co.il/mcse_system_administrator_networking_interview_questions.htm
- **Active Directory:**
  http://www.petri.co.il/mcse_system_administrator_active_directory_interview_questions.htm
- **Microsoft Exchange:**
  http://www.petri.co.il/mcse-system-administrator-exchange-interview-questions.htm
- **PC Support:**
  http://www.petri.co.il/mcse-system-administrator-pc-technician-interview-questions.htm

The interview questions contained at the links above on the Petri Knowledgebase are comprehensive – take a look at these

---

when developing your interview and testing process for new technical hires and don't reinvent the wheel.

Based upon review of the Personal Talent Skills Inventory and candidate's performance during the initial interview, determine whether the candidate can qualify to join your technical staff, once they understand your particular processes and procedures, tools and technology.

These are the technical-specific areas we will cover during the initial live interview with all candidates, as well as the technical-specific activities they will be asked to perform during the interview (such as taking a written technical test or troubleshooting a test pc, server or network "sabotaged" for this purpose). The best technical candidates will rise to the top of the list naturally. But let me throw out a cautionary note here – we don't want to make the mistake of hiring the best candidate of the bunch just because they are the best candidate of the bunch. We've got to hire the best candidate for our organization. This means we must be prepared to interview many candidates before making the commitment to hire and train one.

Some general questions we would also like to have answered include:

- What do you know about our company?
  - What we are gauging here is their preparation for the interview – a good candidate would have researched our website, at the very least
- Tell me a little bit about yourself and your previous employment history
  - What we are looking for is a brief description of their work history & skills, a narrative of their personal and professional experiences
- What are some of your strengths?
  - This question should not be difficult for the candidate to answer
- What are some of your weaknesses?
  - A good candidate should not have any trouble naming 3 weaknesses – give them plenty of time to answer
- What do you see yourself doing in 3 years? …. how about in 5 years?
  - Is the candidate a goal-setter?
- Tell me about a time when you made a mistake with a client and what steps you took to resolve the issue
  - Look for awareness of fallibility, and gauge the candidate's problem-resolution technique
- What do you get excited about? …. What upsets you?
- What situations make you lose your temper?
  - These last two questions are more personal in nature, and will be explored in more detail

---

when discussing the candidate's DISC Profile with them

- What was one of your greatest successes?
- What are 3 things you do extremely well?
  - A solid candidate will have no trouble answering these questions
- What are 3 things that you need to improve on?
  - A good candidate should not have any trouble naming all 3 things – give them plenty of time to answer
- In a group or team what position do you take on – leader, coordinator or support?
  - We're looking for natural leaders here
- Tell us about a team you have worked in
  - What we are looking for is what their role was, again to determine if they are a leader, facilitator, or socializer
- What are three positive things your last boss would say about you?
  - A good candidate should have no problem answering this question
- How much guidance and management do you like?
  - We are trying to determine how independent the candidate is
- How much do you feel you need?
  - A good candidate will be able to verbalize when they need direction
- What type of people do you work best with?

- o This may elicit a canned response, but we may also get a nugget of insight if the person replies, "People who aren't idiots."
- If budgets were of no concern at your current or previous employer, what would be the first thing you would spend money on and why?
  - o The answer to this question gives an insight as to how involved the person was at their previous job. How quickly candidate responds lets us know how much thought they've put into this subject in the past.
- Can you send us an example of something you've written – a quote or proposal?
  - o We need to gauge the candidate's ability to write quotes and proposals, if required
- Is there anything that would interfere with your regular attendance?
  - o A boilerplate question which may reveal any personal conflicts
- What would your perfect job look like?
  - o This is the candidate's opportunity to push the envelope, and test our response – the more descriptive, the better
- Why should we hire you? …. What makes you more qualified than the other applicants?

- o This is the candidate's opportunity to sell us and try to close the position
- What skills do you possess that you think would benefit our company? ....How do you see yourself fitting in?
  - o A follow-up on the previous line of questioning
- Rate yourself on a scale of 1-10 on Word, Excel, PowerPoint, Outlook, Vista...
  - o We're looking for the candidate's proficiency with our basic office applications
- How do you respond to pressure & deadlines?
  - o There isn't a specifically wrong answer here, but we're looking for the candidate's coping mechanism – we might hear: "It stresses me out when...", to which our follow-up would be: "How do you deal with it"?, to which they might answer: "I just get out of the office for a few minutes, and take a walk to clear my head"
- If you could start your career again, what would you do differently?
  - o We're looking for an honest appraisal
- How would you describe your personality?
  - o Easy going, problem solver, director, like talking to people, make friends easily, etc.
- What is your favorite movie of all time? Why?

- o Just a question to loosen up the mood, we might find a common interest and chat for a bit
- Describe a time when you made a customer/client extremely happy?
  - o A positive, reinforcing question
- Do you mind if we call your former employer?
  - o A good reason for a negative answer here must be offered
- Why are you considering a career change at this time, or leaving your current position?
- What do you like and dislike about your current position?
  - o A couple of basic interview questions meant to provide insight into the candidate's current state of mind and desires
- What about this position do you find the most appealing? .... Least appealing?
  - o We're looking for something in addition to the compensation
- In your present position, what internal problems have you identified and taken action to fix?
  - o We're gauging how deeply the candidate cares to involve themselves as a change agent for the benefit of others besides themselves
- What kind of feedback have you received from past customers?

- - Expect positive reviews here
- How have you handled negative feedback from clients, or team members?
  - We're looking for a truthful response here – ask for a specific incident
- Give an example of a time where there was a conflict in a team/group that you were involved in and how it was resolved.
  - What did they do, how did they handle it? What we are looking for is the ability to go straight to the source. Telling the boss right away, without telling the person concerned or ignoring the situation and hoping it will go away are not good signs.
- Do you have any questions for us?
  - A good candidate will always have questions

These are all excellent questions to pose to potential candidates for our technical position. I'm certain you can now see why we don't just interview anyone that can fog a mirror – the interview and hiring process is lengthy, and deservedly so – we need to be absolutely certain to do everything in our power to minimize the possibility of hiring the wrong person. If we're going to spend the considerable time and money to hire and train a new technical person, we want an excellent return on our investment.

The Best I.T. Service Delivery BOOK EVER!

The Interview Process for Hiring Technical Staff

So let's say we've found one or two candidates that we feel have the "right stuff", and would be a positive addition to our team. Our next step is to schedule an interview with *another member* of our organization. At MSPU, all job candidates for key roles are interviewed by either I or my business partner. If they are a technical candidate, I perform the first live interview, and if they are a sales and marketing candidate, Gary performs the first live interview. Then we swap roles, so Gary gets to perform the second live interview with all technical candidates, and I do the same for the sales and marketing candidates. This second interview will either validate or solidify the decision to hire a candidate, or not. Like it or not, unless we're a seasoned HR or hiring professional, sometimes it's difficult to be completely objective during the interview and hiring process. This is where having another trusted individual available to compare notes with can be invaluable – especially in situations when there needs to be a "tie-breaker" – two equally qualified candidates that we may find challenging to choose between.

In addition, when I'm the second interviewer, I know that the candidate has already passed muster in order to get to me, so I begin exploring other areas that the first interviewer may not have covered – to answer questions about compatibility (will the candidate be able to fit into our culture), and I try to gauge from a gut feeling (I know, the DISC profile doesn't lie!) and comfort level my impression of how easy it will be to work with and integrate the candidate into our organization. I'll ask questions specifically intended to reveal the more personal side of the candidate, like what their taste in movies or T.V. shows is, what they do for recreation, and ask them about their immediate family, as well as their parents and their backgrounds; to get an idea of their stability and support system, and attempt to uncover any stressors that may affect performance on the job. This is all carried out in a friendly, conversational, "get to know me" manner, where I will share personal information with the candidate myself, a la Hannibal Lecter in Silence of the Lambs "...*quid pro quo, Clarisse....*"

If the candidate stands a good chance of joining the team, it's important to begin building a relationship early on. If we really want to win over a candidate, we need to show them the human side of our organization, as well as the career opportunity. Assuming the second interview goes well, we now have a green light to formalize an offer to the successful candidate. During the first interview, items such as compensation and duties and responsibilities would naturally have been discussed, as well as a projected start date of employment, should the candidate be awarded the position.

It's now time to formalize our offer to the successful candidate by means of an offer letter.

The Offer Letter

The offer letter will detail our intent to hire the candidate, what their roles and responsibilities will be, as well as their compensation, bonus and benefits plan. As with any and all forms used in your business practice, please consult with your legal advisor before relying on them.

Let's take a look at a standard offer letter:

Offer of Employment and Employment Contract

Monday, September 1st, 2008

(Employee's Name)

(Employee's Address)

Dear (Employee Name);

We are pleased to offer you a position with MSP University ("Company"). Your start date, manager, compensation, benefits, and other terms of employment will be as set forth below and on EXHIBIT A.

TERMS OF EMPLOYMENT

The Best I.T. Service Delivery BOOK EVER!

The Offer Letter

---

1. **Position and Duties.** Company shall employ you, and you agree to competently and professionally perform such duties as are customarily the responsibility of the position as set forth in the job description attached as EXHIBIT A and as reasonably assigned to you from time to time by your Manager as set forth in EXHIBIT A.

2. **Outside Business Activities.** During your employment with Company, you shall devote competent energies, interests, and abilities to the performance of your duties under this Agreement. During the term of this Agreement, you shall not, without Company's prior written consent, render any services to others for compensation or engage or participate, actively or passively, in any other business activities that would interfere with the performance of your duties hereunder or compete with Company's business.

3. **Employment Classification.** You shall be a Full-Time Employee and shall not be entitled to benefits except as specifically outlined herein.

4. **Compensation/Benefits.**

> 4.1 **Wage.** Company shall pay you the wage as set forth in the job description attached as EXHIBIT A.

> 4.2 **Reimbursement of Expenses**. You shall be reimbursed for all reasonable and necessary expenses

paid or incurred by you in the performance of your duties. You shall provide Company with original receipts for such expenses.

4.3 **Withholdings.** All compensation paid to you under this Agreement, including payment of salary and taxable benefits shall be subject to such withholdings as may be required by law or Company's general practices.

4.4 **Benefits.** You will also receive Company's standard employee benefits package (including health insurance), and will be subject to Company's vacation policy as such package and policy are in effect from time to time.

5. **At-Will Employment.** Either party may terminate this Agreement by written notice at any time for any reason or for no reason. This Agreement is intended to be and shall be deemed to be an at-will employment Agreement and does not constitute a guarantee of continuing employment for any term.

6. **Nondisclosure Agreement.** You agree to sign Company's standard Employee Nondisclosure Agreement, Non-Compete and Proprietary Rights Assignment as a condition of your employment. We wish to impress upon you that we do not wish you to bring with you any confidential or proprietary

---

material of any former employer or to violate any other obligation to your former employers.

7. Authorization to Work. Because of federal regulations adopted in the Immigration Reform and Control Act of 1986, you will need to present documentation demonstrating that you have authorization to work in the United States.

8. Further Assurances. Each party shall perform any and all further acts and execute and deliver any documents that are reasonably necessary to carry out the intent of this Agreement.

9. Notices. All notices or other communications required or permitted by this Agreement or by law shall be in writing and shall be deemed duly served and given when delivered personally or by facsimile, air courier, certified mail (return receipt requested), postage and fees prepaid, to the party at the address indicated in the signature block or at such other address as a party may request in writing.

10. Governing Law. This Agreement shall be governed and interpreted in accordance with the laws of the State of California, as such laws are applied to agreements between residents of California to be performed entirely within the State of California.

---

11. Entire Agreement. This Agreement sets forth the entire Agreement between the parties pertaining to the subject matter hereof and supersedes all prior written agreements and all prior or contemporaneous oral Agreements and understandings, expressed or implied.

12. Written Modification and Waiver. No modification to this Agreement, nor any waiver of any rights, shall be effective unless assented to in writing by the party to be charged, and the waiver of any breach or default shall not constitute a waiver of any other right or any subsequent breach or default.

13. Assignment. This Agreement is personal in nature, and neither of the parties shall, without the consent of the other, assign or transfer this Agreement or any rights or obligations under this Agreement, except that Company may assign or transfer this Agreement to a successor of Company's business, in the event of the transfer or sale of all or substantially all of the assets of Company's business, or to a subsidiary, provided that in the case of any assignment or transfer under the terms of this Section, this Agreement shall be binding on and inure to the benefit of the successor of Company's business, and the successor of Company's business shall discharge and perform all of the obligations of Company under this Agreement.

14. Severability. If any of the provisions of this Agreement are determined to be invalid, illegal, or unenforceable, such

---

provisions shall be modified to the minimum extent necessary to make such provisions enforceable, and the remaining provisions shall continue in full force and effect to the extent the economic benefits conferred upon the parties by this Agreement remain substantially unimpaired.

15. **Arbitration of Disputes.** Any controversy or claim arising out of or relating to this contract, or the breach thereof, shall be settled by arbitration administered by the American Arbitration Association under its National Rules for the Resolution of Employment Disputes, and judgment upon the award rendered by the arbitrator(s) may be entered by any court having jurisdiction thereof.

We look forward to your arrival and what we hope will be the start of a mutually satisfying work relationship.

Sincerely,

MSP University

By: _____
   MSPU Authorized Representative

Acknowledged, Accepted, and Agreed

The Offer Letter

Date: _____

By: _____
    Employee

Once the employee signs the Offer Letter, they will have formally agreed to the terms and conditions of our employment as described. An EXHIBIT A would follow this agreement, stipulating the employee's job description, duties and compensation. Let's review an example EXHIBIT A:

Exhibit "A"

Job Description – Service Desk Analyst

Start Date Is Monday, September 15, 2008

This position will require, but not be limited to the following Essential Responsibilities:

- Provide remote and onsite desktop, laptop, server and network problem management and resolution services to customers and end-users via Company's communications and remote and onsite support solutions, processes and procedures
- Identify, document, prioritize, troubleshoot and escalate service requests per Company's problem management and resolution processes and SLAs
- Perform proactive maintenance of customer and end-user hardware, software and services per Company's established processes and best practices
- Maintain and pursue I.T. training competencies and certifications per Company's established training schedule and requirements
- Maintain Company standards for customer satisfaction, utilization and compliance policies
- Utilize Company's PSA and RMM solutions per Company's established processes to deliver maintenance and problem management and resolution services to customers and end-users
- Interface with customers, end-users and vendor support resources as needed to deliver services within established SLAs
- Maintain communication with all affected parties during problem management and resolution per Company's established processes and procedures

---

The Offer Letter

Base Salary for this position will be ($) per year.

Eligibility to participate in quarterly bonuses will be determined by meeting established Company utilization, process and policy compliance, attainment of training and competencies/certifications, adherence to SLAs and customer service performance metrics:

Utilization requirement score: (%)

Process and policy compliance score: (%)

Attainment of competencies: (%)

Adherence to SLAs score: (%)

Customer service score: (%)

Of course, your particular business model, products, services job requirements and compensation schedules will dictate how you structure EXHIBIT A.

The Employment Agreement

As part of the HR and hiring process, we are going to require our new technical person to sign an employment agreement. The employment agreement will detail the technical person's job title and duties and responsibilities, and will contain non-disclosure and non-compete language in order to protect ourselves from the potential for one of our competitors to hire our technical person away at some later date, and leverage our business plans, processes or other intellectual property against us. Depending upon your local or state laws, NDA and non-compete language and/or agreements will need to be tailored specifically to protect your rights in a court of law. As with any and all forms used in your business practice, please consult with your legal advisor before relying on them.

Let's take a look at a standard Employment Agreement:

EMPLOYMENT AGREEMENT

This Employment Agreement (this "Agreement") is made effective by and between MSP University ("MSPU"), of 7077 Orangewood Avenue, Suite 104, Garden Grove, California, 92841 and (employee's name) ("Employee"), of (employee's address).

The Employment Agreement

A. MSPU is engaged in the business of Providing Information Technology Services. Employee will primarily perform the job duties at the following location: 7077 Orangewood Avenue, Suite 104, Garden Grove, California.

B. MSPU desires to have the services of Employee.

C. Employee is willing to be employed by MSPU.

Therefore, the parties agree as follows:

1. EMPLOYMENT. MSPU shall employ Employee as a (job title). Employee shall provide to MSPU the following services: duties as needed. Employee accepts and agrees to such employment, and agrees to be subject to the general supervision, advice and direction of MSPU and MSPU's supervisory personnel. Employee shall also perform (i) such other duties as are customarily performed by an employee in a similar position, and (ii) such other and unrelated services and duties as may be assigned to Employee from time to time by MSPU.

2. BEST EFFORTS OF EMPLOYEE. Employee agrees to perform faithfully, industriously, and to the best of Employee's ability, experience, and talents, all of the duties that may be required by the express and implicit terms of this Agreement, to the reasonable satisfaction of MSPU. Such duties shall be

---

provided at such place(s) as the needs, business, or opportunities of MSPU may require from time to time.

3. EXPENSE REIMBURSEMENT. MSPU will reimburse Employee for "out-of-pocket" expenses incurred by Employee in accordance with MSPU policies in effect from time to time.

4. RECOMMENDATIONS FOR IMPROVING OPERATIONS. Employee shall provide MSPU with all information, suggestions, and recommendations regarding MSPU's business, of which Employee has knowledge, which will be of benefit to MSPU.

5. CONFIDENTIALITY. Employee recognizes that MSPU has and will have information regarding the following:

- inventions

- products

- product design

- processes

- technical matters

- trade secrets

- copyrights

- customer lists

- prices

- costs

- discounts

- business affairs

- future plans

- marketing plans and methods

- communications

- meetings

- conversations

- training

- emails

- faxes

- documents

- wage and compensation information

- disciplinary actions

- policies

---

and other vital information items (collectively, "Information") which are valuable, special and unique assets of MSPU. Employee agrees that Employee will not at any time or in any manner, either directly or indirectly, divulge, disclose, or communicate any Information to any third party without the prior written consent of MSPU. Employee will protect the Information and treat it as strictly confidential. A violation by Employee of this paragraph shall be a material violation of this Agreement and will justify legal and/or equitable relief.

6. UNAUTHORIZED DISCLOSURE OF INFORMATION. If it appears that Employee has disclosed (or has threatened to disclose) Information in violation of this Agreement, MSPU shall be entitled to an injunction to restrain Employee from disclosing, in whole or in part, such Information, or from providing any services to any party to whom such Information has been disclosed or may be disclosed. MSPU shall not be prohibited by this provision from pursuing other remedies, including a claim for losses and damages.

7. CONFIDENTIALITY AFTER TERMINATION OF EMPLOYMENT. The confidentiality provisions of this Agreement shall remain in full force and effect for a 1 year period after the termination of Employee's employment.

8. NON-COMPETE AGREEMENT. Employee recognizes that the various items of Information are special and unique assets

---

of the Company and need to be protected from improper disclosure. In consideration of the disclosure of the Information to Employee, Employee agrees and covenants that for a period of 1 year following the termination of this Agreement, whether such termination is voluntary or involuntary, Employee will not compete directly or indirectly with MSPU. The term "not compete" shall mean that the Employee shall not, on Employee's behalf or on behalf of any other party, solicit or seek the business of any customer or account of the Company existing during the term of employment and wherein said solicitation involves a product and/or service substantially similar to or competitive with any present or future product and/or service of the Company. This covenant shall apply to the geographical area that includes all of the State of California and any other state in which the Company has customers. Directly or indirectly engaging in any competitive business includes, but is not limited to: (i) engaging in a business as owner, partner, or agent, (ii) becoming an employee of any third party that is engaged in such business, (iii) becoming interested directly or indirectly in any such business, or (iv) soliciting any customer of MSPU for the benefit of a third party that is engaged in such business. Employee agrees that this non-compete provision will not adversely affect Employee's livelihood.

9. EMPLOYEE'S INABILITY TO CONTRACT FOR EMPLOYER. Employee shall not have the right to make any contracts or

commitments for or on behalf of MSPU without first obtaining the express written consent of MSPU.

10. BENEFITS. Employee shall be entitled to employment benefits, including holidays, sick leave, and vacation as provided by MSPU's policies in effect from time to time.

11. TERM/TERMINATION. Employee's employment under this Agreement shall be for an unspecified term on an "at will" basis. This Agreement may be terminated by MSPU at will and by Employee upon 2 Week's written notice. If Employee is in violation of any part of this Agreement, MSPU may terminate employment without notice and with compensation to Employee only to the date of such termination. The compensation paid under this Agreement shall be Employee's exclusive remedy.

12. COMPLIANCE WITH EMPLOYER'S RULES. Employee agrees to comply with all of the rules and regulations of MSPU.

13. RETURN OF PROPERTY. Upon termination of this Agreement, Employee shall deliver to MSPU all property which is MSPU's property or related to MSPU's business (including keys, records, notes, data, memoranda, models, and equipment) that is in Employee's possession or under Employee's control. Such obligation shall be governed by any separate confidentiality or proprietary rights agreement signed by Employee.

The Employment Agreement

---

14. NOTICES. All notices required or permitted under this Agreement shall be in writing and shall be deemed delivered when delivered in person or on the third day after being deposited in the United States mail, postage paid, addressed as follows:

Employer:

MSPU

(MSPU Representative)

(MSPU Representative's title)

7077 Orangewood Avenue, Suite 104

Garden Grove, California 92841

Employee:

(Employee Name)

(Employee Street Address)

(Employee City, State ZIP)

The Employment Agreement

Such addresses may be changed from time to time by either party by providing written notice in the manner set forth above.

15. ENTIRE AGREEMENT. This Agreement contains the entire agreement of the parties and there are no other promises or conditions in any other agreement whether oral or written. This Agreement supersedes any prior written or oral agreements between the parties.

16. AMENDMENT. This Agreement may be modified or amended, if the amendment is made in writing and is signed by both parties.

17. SEVERABILITY. If any provisions of this Agreement shall be held to be invalid or unenforceable for any reason, the remaining provisions shall continue to be valid and enforceable. If a court finds that any provision of this Agreement is invalid or unenforceable, but that by limiting such provision it would become valid or enforceable, then such provision shall be deemed to be written, construed, and enforced as so limited.

18. WAIVER OF CONTRACTUAL RIGHT. The failure of either party to enforce any provision of this Agreement shall not be construed as a waiver or limitation of that party's right to subsequently enforce and compel strict compliance with every provision of this Agreement.

---

19. APPLICABLE LAW. This Agreement shall be governed by the laws of the State of California.

EMPLOYER:

MSP University

By: _____Date: _____

(Authorized MSPU representative name/title)

AGREED TO AND ACCEPTED.

EMPLOYEE:

By: _____Date: _____

The Equipment Loan Agreement

From time to time, and based upon the technical staff's needs, it may become necessary to provide them with company-owned equipment in order to provide them the ability to fulfill their duties and responsibilities. Examples of equipment that can be furnished to employees may include:

- Vehicles
- PCs
- Laptops
- Wireless PC cards
- Cell phones/Smart phones/PDAs
- Pagers
- Security tokens
- Key cards/credentials
- Test equipment
- Inventory

This equipment obviously has value to the company, so it's a good idea to have a solid equipment loan agreement in place documenting it and its value, and holding the employee responsible for keeping it in good condition. The equipment loan agreement also makes it easier to reclaim equipment when an employee leaves the organization, as they agree to forfeit the cost to replace the equipment from their pay should they fail to return it according to the terms of their employment agreement. Let's take a look at a standard equipment loan agreement:

Equipment Loan

Statement of Understanding

I am taking possession of the following equipment belonging to MSP University (Company):

_____

Description

_____

Model Number, Serial Number

which has a replacement cost of $

_____

I will take reasonable and necessary steps to safeguard this equipment from damage and theft.

The Equipment Loan Agreement

If this equipment is damaged or stolen, I will report the relevant facts as soon as possible to my supervisor. I further understand that I have an obligation to pursue recovery for Company from such a loss through my relevant insurance coverage, whether automobile, homeowner's or tenant's.

I understand that I must return this equipment as instructed to Company premises within twenty-four hours of being asked to do so by my supervisor or Company administration.

I understand that I must immediately return this equipment as instructed to Company premises in the event that my employment ends, whether by voluntary quit or involuntary termination.

I agree and hereby give permission to Company to deduct from my pay any amount I owe to Company (up to the replacement cost noted above) due to my failure to return this equipment in working condition to Company as documented in my Employment Agreement.

_____

Employee Signature, printed name and date

_____

Date EQUIPMENT RETURNED:

_____

Received By

Compensation Plans

Throughout the years we've had the opportunity to work with our partners, one of the topics that seem to be the most challenging for them is creating an equitable compensation plan for technical staff. Now, as I.T. service providers, our perception of an equitable compensation plan and our technical staff's perception of an equitable compensation plan may not always match. A generally accepted industry statistic regarding compensation is that a technician should generate two and a half times their W-2 compensation in billable labor time. This means that a technical person earning $60,000 a year on their W-2 should be generating $150,000 in billable labor time per year.

Billable time based on W-2 earnings

W-2 Earnings	Billable Labor
$30,000	$75,000
$40,000	$100,000
$50,000	$125,000
$60,000	$150,000
$70,000	$175,000
$80,000	$200,000
$90,000	$225,000
$100,000	$250,000

Compensation Plans

Salary.com reports the following U.S. national averages for total compensation (base salaries, bonuses and benefits) for the following technical positions as of September, 2008 on their website at http://swz.salary.com/salarywizard/layoutscripts/swzl_newsearch.asp:

Help Desk Support Jr.-Sr. (Service Desk Staff)

Benefit	Median Amount		% Of Total	
Base Salary	$43,683	$50,932	67.7% -	68.4%
Bonuses	$909	$1,131	1.4% -	1.5%
Social Security	$3,411	$3,983	5.3% -	5.4%
401k/403b	$2,765	$3,228	4.3% -	4.3%
Disability	$713	$833	1.1% -	1.1%
Healthcare	$5,328	$5,328	8.3% -	7.2%
Pension	$1,873	$2,187	2.9% -	2.9%
Time Off	$5,831	$6,808	9.0% -	9.1%
Total	$64,514	$74,430	100%	

Source: salary.com

Please note that the median service desk staff's bonuses in the US as reported in September 2008 by salary.com amount to about 1.5% of their total take-home compensation. In our experience, this is extremely low, as we would bonus our service desk staff upwards of 10% of their total salary for achieving goals set for:

Compensation Plans

- Utilization requirements
- Process and policy compliance
- Attainment of competencies
- Adherence to SLAs
- Customer service

We would base customer service scores upon survey responses. In addition, bonuses could be attained individually and by the entire group on a monthly, quarterly and yearly basis. This was designed so that if an individual resource achieved their minimum goals in each area for the month, they would be eligible to receive a bonus. If they achieved the bonus each month for the entire quarter, they would be eligible to receive a quarterly bonus as well. If the entire team achieved their bonuses each month in a quarter, they would be eligible to receive a quarterly team bonus, and if they were able to achieve a quarterly team bonus through 4 consecutive quarters, they would be eligible to receive a yearly bonus. All of these bonuses would be in addition to previously-received bonuses, so the individual service desk staff could potentially be eligible to receive the following bonuses:

- Monthly individual bonus
- Quarterly individual bonus
- Quarterly team bonus
- Yearly team bonus

Compensation Plans

Service Dispatcher Jr.-Sr.

Benefit	Median Amount		% Of Total	
Base Salary	$33,532	$39,745	66.8% -	68.0%
Bonuses	$287	$250	0.6% -	0.4%
Social Security	$2,587	$3,060	5.2% -	5.2%
401k/403b	$2,097	$2,480	4.2% -	4.2%
Disability	$541	$640	1.1% -	1.1%
Healthcare	$5,328	$5,328	10.6% -	9.1%
Pension	$1,420	$1,680	2.8% -	2.9%
Time Off	$4,422	$5,230	8.8% -	9.0%
Total	$50,214	$74,430	100%	

Source: salary.com

Note that the median service dispatcher's bonuses in the US as reported in September 2008 by salary.com amount to about 0.5% of their total take-home compensation. This is low in our experience, as we bonused our dispatcher a small amount based upon meeting SLAs, along with allowing participation in team bonuses, but their bonus did not quite rival the service desk staff's.

Compensation Plans

Hardware Engineer I-V

Benefit	Median Amount		% Of Total	
Base Salary	$52,213 -	$107,891	68.9% -	72.2%
Bonuses	$907 -	$1,081	1.2% -	0.7%
Social Security	$4,064 -	$7,905	5.4% -	5.3%
401k/403b	$3,293 -	$6,762	4.3% -	4.5%
Disability	$850 -	$1,745	1.1% -	1.2%
Healthcare	$5,328 -	$5,328	7.0% -	3.6%
Pension	$2,231 -	$4,581	2.9% -	3.1%
Time Off	$6,947 -	$14,262	9.2% -	9.5%
Total	$75,833 -	$149,645	100%	

Source: salary.com

Note that the median hardware engineer's bonuses in the US as reported in September 2008 by salary.com average about 1.0% of their total take-home compensation. This matches our experience.

Compensation Plans

Field Service Engineer I-V

Benefit	Median Amount		% Of Total	
Base Salary	$44,349 -	$90,859	67.7% -	69.9%
Bonuses	$1,028 -	$3,081	1.6% -	2.4%
Social Security	$3,471 -	$7,186	5.3% -	5.5%
401k/403b	$2,813 -	$5,824	4.3% -	4.5%
Disability	$726 -	$1,503	1.1% -	1.2%
Healthcare	$5,328 -	$5,328	8.1% -	8.1%
Pension	$1,906 -	$3,945	2.9% -	3.0%
Time Off	$5,934 -	$12,284	9.1% -	9.4%
Total	$65,556 -	$130,012	100%	

Source: salary.com

Note that the median field engineer's bonuses in the US as reported in September 2008 by salary.com average about 2.0% of their total take-home compensation. This matches our experience.

Compensation Plans

Engineer I-V

Benefit	Median Amount		% Of Total	
Base Salary	$52,790 -	$105,328	69.0% -	69.5%
Bonuses	$825 -	$5,306	1.1% -	3.5%
Social Security	$4,102 -	$7,928	5.4% -	5.2%
401k/403b	$3,324 -	$6,859	4.3% -	4.5%
Disability	$858 -	$1,770	1.1% -	1.2%
Healthcare	$5,328 -	$5,328	7.0% -	3.5%
Pension	$2,252 -	$4,647	2.9% -	3.1%
Time Off	$7,011 -	$14,468	9.2% -	9.5%
Total	$76,489 -	$151,634	100%	

Source: salary.com

Note that the median engineer's bonuses in the US as reported in September 2008 by salary.com average about 2.5% of their total take-home compensation. This matches our experience.

Compensation Plans

Purchasing Manager

Benefit	Median Amount	% Of Total
Base Salary	$97,951	68.4%
Bonuses	$5,991	4.2%
Social Security	$7,831	5.5%
401k/403b	$6,444	4.5%
Disability	$1,663	1.2%
Healthcare	$5,328	3.7%
Pension	$4,366	3.0%
Time Off	$13,592	9.5%
Total	$143,167	100%

Source: salary.com

Note that the median purchasing manager's bonuses in the US as reported in September 2008 by salary.com averages about 4.0% of their total take-home compensation.

Compensation Plans

Service Desk Manager

Benefit	Median Amount	% Of Total
Base Salary	$83,180	66.2%
Bonuses	$7,480	6.0%
Social Security	$6,936	5.5%
401k/403b	$5,621	4.5%
Disability	$1,451	1.2%
Healthcare	$5,328	4.2%
Pension	$3,808	3.0%
Time Off	$11,856	9.4%
Total	$125,659	100%

Source: salary.com

Note that the median service desk manager's bonuses in the US as reported in September 2008 by salary.com average 6.0% of their total take-home compensation. This matches our experience.

Compensation Plans

NOC Manager

Benefit	Median Amount	% Of Total
Base Salary	$94,595	69.3%
Bonuses	$4,183	3.1%
Social Security	$7,556	5.5%
401k/403b	$6,124	4.5%
Disability	$1,580	1.2%
Healthcare	$5,328	3.9%
Pension	$4,149	3.0%
Time Off	$12,917	9.5%
Total	$136,432	100%

Source: salary.com

Note that the median NOC manager's bonuses in the US as reported in September 2008 by salary.com average about 3.0% of their total take-home compensation. This matches our experience.

Compensation Plans

Project Manager I-III

Benefit	Median Amount		% Of Total	
Base Salary	$65,161 -	$94,720	69.1% -	68.3%
Bonuses	$1,836 -	$5,798	1.9% -	4.2%
Social Security	$5,125 -	$7,690	5.4% -	5.5%
401k/403b	$4,154 -	$6,232	4.4% -	4.5%
Disability	$1,072 -	$1,608	1.1% -	1.2%
Healthcare	$5,328 -	$5,328	5.7% -	3.8%
Pension	$2,814 -	$4,222	3.0% -	3.0%
Time Off	$8,761 -	$13,145	9.3% -	9.5%
Total	$94,252 -	$138,743	100%	

Source: salary.com

Note that the median project manager's bonuses in the US as reported in September 2008 by salary.com average about 3.0% of their total take-home compensation. This matches our experience.

Compensation Plans

Sales Engineer I-V

Benefit	Median Amount		% Of Total	
Base Salary	$51,528 -	$97,157	67.8% -	69.5%
Bonuses	$1,721 -	$7,721	2.3% -	3.5%
Social Security	$4,074 -	$7,845	5.4% -	5.2%
401k/403b	$3,301 -	$6,502	4.3% -	4.5%
Disability	$852 -	$1,678	1.1% -	1.2%
Healthcare	$5,328 -	$5,328	7.0% -	3.5%
Pension	$2,236 -	$4,405	2.9% -	3.1%
Time Off	$6,963 -	$13,715	9.2% -	9.5%
Total	$76,004 -	$144,352	100%	

Source: salary.com

Note that the median sales engineer's bonuses in the US as reported in September 2008 by salary.com average about 3.0% of their total take-home compensation. . This is low in our experience, as we bonused our sales engineers higher commissions for help in closing sales.

Compensation Plans

Inventory Manager

Benefit	Median Amount	% Of Total
Base Salary	$74,533	68.9%
Bonuses	$3,008	2.8%
Social Security	$5,932	5.5%
401k/403b	$4,808	4.4%
Disability	$1,241	1.1%
Healthcare	$5,328	4.9%
Pension	$3,257	3.0%
Time Off	$10,140	9.4%
Total	$108,246	100%

Source: salary.com

Note that the median inventory manager's bonuses in the US as reported in September 2008 by salary.com average almost 3.0% of their total take-home compensation.

A compensation plan for a new technical person will normally be structured as base salary plus bonuses. A base salary is a guaranteed amount of compensation the technical person will receive each month, and if they meet specific goals set by their supervisor during the month, quarter and year, additional bonuses can be realized.

In a base plus bonus compensation plan, we generally see small bonus percentages structured in to support the guaranteed base salary, and engineered in such a manner as to reward the technical staff on activity that helps the

---

organization increase efficiencies, customer satisfaction, and beat project implementation deadlines, among other factors – all of which in one form or another drive additional profits to the bottom line. This is where the bonuses are paid out from – the additional revenues that the technical staff helps to generate.

We feel that technical staff should also be compensated for all services they help sell or influence, as in the sales engineer's role, or field engineers/technicians that can identify needs at customer locations and bring opportunities back for the sales team to follow up on and close.

Now I hope I've done a decent job of presenting different ways of looking at technical compensation and bonus plans for you. Please do not take any of the figures in this chapter as gospel – but rather visit salary.com to drill deep and utilize their filtering capabilities and input your zip code, state or metro area to discover what the median compensation is being reported for the technical roles required for your service delivery model and mode. I've used information gathered from partners, and the rest from our own experience to help you get started.

If you'd like a much more granular compensation report, browse to www.mspu.us/en/tools and pick up the Service Leadership Index™ 2007 Solution Provider Compensation

---

Report™. This 100-page report covers more than 40 positions in solution provider practices and is the only solution-provider-specific salary survey available.

Let me caution you against thinking that by reading this chapter you will be able to save yourself some homework and come away with a ready-made compensation plan that you can simply slap your company's name on, implement and be successful with.

You've got to do your own legwork and investigation into what your true margins and profitability are for each of your services, products and solutions. From there, you've got to dig down deep into your gut and come up with a realistic expectation of how much increased profitability each of your technical resources can achieve, and of this number, what you are comfortable with incenting your staff to qualify for.

Training Technical Staff

The function of training technical staff in an I.T. services organization is obviously much different than training staff in other businesses. In addition to training technical staff in our overall day-to-day operations and functions, we've got to make certain we spend the time necessary, and deliver opportunities for our technical staff to receive the role-specific training required to make them effective, efficient and successful, in order to receive the maximum return on our hiring investment.

Let's identify the common training that we'll deliver to all staff, regardless of their job description, before we get into role-specific technical training topics:

- Company Overview Training
  - o Vision, mission, values, philosophy, goals
- HR Process Training
  - o Overview of compensation, benefits, conduct, sick day and vacation policy, Employee handbook, acceptable use policy
- Administrative Setup and Training
  - o User and email account creation, telco account, extension and voicemail creation,
  - o Use of company equipment (cell phone, PC, laptop, etc.)

  - o Use of company software, Instant Messaging, remote access and remote email
- Formal introduction to management and staff
  - o Tour of facility
  - o Introduction to all management and staff

The above points cover in broad strokes some of the tasks associated with any new employee's basic training and indoctrination to an organization – of course, your policies and procedures may differ from those illustrated.

So what role-specific training do we need to deliver to insure our technical person's success? Let's highlight some of the obvious areas for their managers to address:

- Internal tools and technology training
  - o We'll need to make certain all of our technical staff is trained on our internal tools
    - PSA solution
    - RMM solution
    - Remote control solution
    - Quoting solution
    - Technical drawing solution
    - Project planning/management solution
    - Specialty solutions
    - All others

Training Technical Staff

- Processes and procedures
  - We'll need to make certain all of our technical staff is trained on our processes and procedures
    - Employee handbook
    - Problem management, escalation and resolution
    - Remote monitoring and management
    - Remote control
    - Patching and updating
    - Documentation
    - Parts and equipment ordering
    - Handling RMAs
    - Customer service
    - Reporting
    - Onsite service delivery
    - All others
- Product and Service Training
  - We'll need to make certain all of our technical staff is trained on all of the products and services we sell and install
- Roles and responsibilities
  - We'll need to make certain all of our technical staff is trained on their own, as well as other team members' roles, responsibilities and expectations

---

- Customers
    - We'll need to make certain all of our technical staff is trained on the company's customers and their individual needs, requirements and SLAs
- Fulfillment partners
    - We'll need to make certain all of our technical staff is trained on the company's fulfillment partners, their services and their engagement process
- Vendors
    - We'll need to make certain all of our technical staff is trained on the company's vendors, their services and their engagement process
- Goals and bonuses
    - We'll need to make certain all of our technical staff is trained on their individual and team goals and bonus programs
- Competency and certification achievement
    - We'll need to make certain all of our technical staff is trained on the company's requirements for their attainment of additional competencies and certifications

Role-Specific Training

Service desk staff

In this context, the service desk staff participates in the provider's problem management and resolution process, and can be assigned to deliver remote technical support services to end users. The service desk staff identifies, prioritizes and documents all service requests, and initiates problem management and resolution activity.

Service desk staff will execute the provider's problem management and resolution processes as well as utilize the provider's chosen software and hardware management and remediation tools, processes and procedures during remote technical service delivery.

In addition to the general training requirements for all technical staff previously mentioned, at a minimum, all service desk staff will need specific training in these areas:

- Problem management and resolution
  - o Incident Management
  - o Problem Management
  - o Configuration Management
  - o Change Management
  - o Release Management
  - o Service Level Management
  - o Availability Management
  - o Capacity Management

- IT Service Continuity Management
- Security Management
- Day to day service delivery
  - Receiving all incident notifications and service requests
  - Recording all incidents and service requests
  - Classifying all incidents and service requests
  - Prioritizing all incidents and service requests
  - Troubleshooting all incidents and service requests
  - Escalating all incidents and service requests as necessary to maintain SLA
  - Maintaining consistent communication with all parties affected by the incident or service request
  - Performing all scheduled maintenance activities
  - Reporting on all activities
- Customer service
  - Customer management
  - Setting and adjusting expectations
  - Phone etiquette
  - Utilizing the "hold" button effectively
  - Follow-up and follow-through

NOC staff

In this context, the NOC (network operations center) staff participates in the provider's problem management and resolution process, and can be assigned to deliver proactive remote patching, updating and monitoring services for

---

devices, software applications and operating systems and services in customer environments. Whereas the provider's service desk staff works primarily with end-user issues, the NOC staff's main focus is on managing and delivering scheduled maintenance activities to critical devices and responding to alerts generated by the provider's remote monitoring and management (RMM) solution.

The NOC staff identifies, prioritizes and documents all service activity and will execute the provider's problem management and resolution processes as well as utilize the provider's chosen software and hardware management and remediation tools, processes and procedures during remote service delivery.

In addition to the general training requirements for all technical staff previously mentioned, at a minimum, all NOC staff will need specific training in these areas:

- Problem management and resolution
  - o Incident management
  - o Problem management
  - o Configuration management
  - o Change management
  - o Release management
  - o Service level management
  - o Availability management
  - o Capacity management

- o Service continuity management
- o Security management
- Remote monitoring and management
  - o Installing agents
  - o Configuring thresholds
  - o Configuring alerts
  - o Developing scripts
  - o Incident management
  - o Problem management
  - o Configuration management
  - o Change management
  - o Release management
  - o Service level management
  - o Availability management
  - o Capacity management
  - o Service continuity management
  - o Security management
- Day to day service delivery
  - o Receiving all incident notifications and service requests
  - o Recording all incidents and service requests
  - o Classifying all incidents and service requests
  - o Prioritizing all incidents and service requests
  - o Troubleshooting all incidents and service requests
  - o Escalating all incidents and service requests as necessary to maintain SLA
  - o Maintaining consistent communication with all parties affected by the incident or service request

---

- o Performing all scheduled maintenance activities
- o Reporting on all activities
- Customer service
  - o Customer management
  - o Setting and adjusting expectations
  - o Phone etiquette
  - o Utilizing the "hold" button effectively
  - o Follow-up and follow-through

Field engineers/technicians

In this context, the field engineer/technician participates in the provider's problem management and resolution process, and can be assigned to deliver technical support services at the customer's facilities when necessary.

Field engineers/technicians will utilize the provider's hardware and software problem management and resolution processes as well as the provider's chosen software and hardware management and remediation tools, processes and procedures during service delivery.

In addition to the general training requirements for all technical staff previously mentioned, at a minimum, all field engineers/technicians will need specific training in these areas:

- Problem management and resolution
  - o Incident management

- o Problem management
- o Configuration management
- o Change management
- o Release management
- o Service level management
- o Availability management
- o Capacity management
- o Service continuity management
- o Security management
- Day to day service delivery
  - o Receiving all incident notifications and service requests
  - o Recording all incidents and service requests
  - o Classifying all incidents and service requests
  - o Prioritizing all incidents and service requests
  - o Troubleshooting all incidents and service requests
  - o Escalating all incidents and service requests as necessary to maintain SLA
  - o Maintaining consistent communication with all parties affected by the incident or service request
  - o Performing all scheduled maintenance activities
  - o Reporting on all activities
- Customer service
  - o Onsite etiquette
  - o Customer management
  - o Setting and adjusting expectations
  - o Receiving sign-off
  - o Follow-up and follow-through

- Technology assessments
  - Conducting a granular analysis and evaluation of each component comprising the customer's IT infrastructure, systems, services, processes and vendors and document same

Bench engineers/technicians

In this context, the bench engineer/technician participates in the provider's problem management and resolution process, and can be assigned to deliver technical support services for customer equipment brought in to the provider's facilities when necessary.

Bench engineers/technicians will utilize the provider's hardware and software problem management and resolution processes as well as the provider's chosen software and hardware management and remediation tools, processes and procedures during service delivery.

In addition to the general training requirements for all technical staff previously mentioned, at a minimum, all bench engineers/technicians will need specific training in these areas:

- Problem management and resolution
  - Incident management
  - Problem management
  - Configuration management

- Change management
- Release management
- Service level management
- Availability management
- Capacity management
- Service continuity management
- Security management

Service dispatchers

In this context, the service dispatcher participates in the provider's problem management and resolution process, and assigns resources to and schedules all onsite or bench services. The service dispatcher may also be included in the provider's escalation process and be alerted by their PSA solution should service requests become in danger of falling out of SLA.

Service dispatchers will utilize the provider's chosen software management tools, processes and procedures to manage dispatch functions during technical service delivery.

In addition to the general training requirements for all technical staff previously mentioned, at a minimum, all service dispatchers will need specific training in these areas:

- Problem management and resolution
  - Incident Management

- Problem Management
- Configuration Management
- Change Management
- Release Management
- Service Level Management
- Availability Management
- Capacity Management
- IT Service Continuity Management
- Security Management
- Day to day service delivery
  - Managing all incident notifications and service requests
  - Monitoring all incidents and service requests for proper escalation as necessary to maintain SLA
  - Managing consistent communication with all parties affected by the incident or service request
  - Scheduling all maintenance activities
  - Reporting on all activities
- Customer service
  - Customer management
  - Setting and adjusting expectations
  - Phone etiquette
  - Utilizing the "hold" button effectively
  - Follow-up and follow-through

Service managers

In this context, the service manager is ultimately responsible for maintaining the provider's technical staffing levels, training and certification requirements, problem management and resolution processes and customer satisfaction by strict SLA management, among other responsibilities. Service managers will utilize the provider's chosen software management tools, processes and procedures to manage service delivery.

In addition to the general training requirements for all technical staff previously mentioned, at a minimum, all service managers will need specific training in these areas:

- Problem management and resolution
  - o Incident Management
  - o Problem Management
  - o Configuration Management
  - o Change Management
  - o Release Management
  - o Service Level Management
  - o Availability Management
  - o Capacity Management
  - o IT Service Continuity Management
  - o Security Management
- Day to day service delivery
  - o Responsible for managing all technical staff
  - o Responsible for managing all service delivery
  - o Responsible for managing all customer expectations

- ○ Responsible for reporting on all activities
- Customer service
  - ○ Staff management
  - ○ Customer management
  - ○ Setting and adjusting expectations
  - ○ Follow-up and follow-through

Sales engineers

In this context, the sales engineer is perhaps the most versatile and important role in the provider's practice. The sales engineer participates in both the provider's pre- and post-sales and project planning processes, and can be assigned to assist in the business needs analysis, technology assessment and solution design and specification phases of professional services delivery. All of these functions are critical to insuring smooth project delivery.

In addition to the general training requirements for all technical staff previously mentioned, at a minimum, all sales engineers will need specific training in these areas:

- Review customer needs analyses
- Review customer technology assessments
- Create project scopes
  - ○ Work with customer and internal resources

- - Work with distributors, vendors and fulfillment partners
- Create proposals
  - Create quote
  - Create technical drawings
  - Write proposals
- Act as a sales resource
  - Participate in customer meetings and presentations

Purchasing manager

In this context, the purchasing manager participates in the provider's project quoting and planning process by insuring pricing and availability of hardware, software licensing and services from vendors, distributors and fulfillment partners to meet the provider's requirements.

In addition to the general training requirements for all technical staff previously mentioned, at a minimum, all purchasing managers will need specific training in these areas:

- Purchase order creation and processing
- Manufacturers, vendors and distributors
- Credit and flooring account limits
- Shipping and receiving processes and procedures
- Budget creation, allocation and management

- RMA processes and procedures
- Accounts payable processes and procedures

Project managers

In this context, the project manager participates in the provider's project planning and management process by working with the sales engineer to develop a project scope, then specify methods to be utilized during project implementation, identify all tasks to be completed during project implementation, create a timeline and expected duration for each task's completion and estimate and allocate resources for each task's completion.

In addition, the project manager is normally responsible for creating the risk management plan, change control process and communication and status reporting process utilized during project implementation.

In addition to the general training requirements for all technical staff previously mentioned, at a minimum, all project managers will need specific training in these areas:

- Creating project plans
  - o Project scope review
  - o Project task identification
  - o Project implementation method identification

- o Project timeline and phase creation
- o Project resource allocation
- o Project role, responsibility and task assignment
- o Risk management plan creation
- o Change control process creation
- o Communication and status reporting process creation
- Managing projects
  - o Verification of hardware, software and service order/receipt
  - o Management of internal, customer and vendor resources, their roles and tasks
  - o Managing risk, change and communication
  - o Measuring success of each phase of project
  - o Managing customer expectations
  - o Attaining final project sign-off from customer

Inventory manager

In this context, the inventory manager participates in the provider's service delivery process by insuring adequate inventory availability of hardware, software licensing and services from vendors, distributors and fulfillment partners to meet the provider's service delivery requirements, and handles all returns, RMAs and credits when necessary.

In addition to the general training requirements for all technical staff previously mentioned, at a minimum, all inventory managers will need specific training in these areas:

- Inventory control and management
- Purchase order creation and processing
- Manufacturers, vendors and distributors
- Credit and flooring account limits
- Shipping and receiving processes and procedures
- Budget allocation
- RMA processes and procedures
- Accounts payable processes and procedures

Section 6: Resources

This section contains resources you may find handy in building, maintaining, maximizing and migrating your service delivery model.

RMM Solutions

Handsfree Networks
www.handsfreenetworks.com

HoundDog
www.hounddogiseasy.com

HyBlue
www.hyblue.com

Kaseya
www.kaseya.com

LabTech Software
www.labtechsoft.com

Level Platforms
www.levelplatforms.com

Section 6: Resources

N-able
www.n-able.com

Nagios
www.nagios.org

Secure My Company
www.securemycompany.com

Silverback Technologies (Dell)
www.silverbacktech.com

VirtualAdministrator
www.virtualadministrator.com

PSA Solutions

Autotask
www.autotask.com

ConnectWise
www.connectwise.com

Frontrange Solutions
www.frontrange.com

Kemma Software
www.kemma.com

GWI Software
www.gwi.com

Helpstar
www.helpstar.com.

NetHelpDesk
www.nethelpdesk.com

Novo Solutions
www.novosolutions.com

Results Software
www.results-software.com

Shockey Monkey
www.shockeymonkey.com

Remote Desktop Control Solutions

Bomgar
www.bomgar.com

GoToMyPC
www.gotomypc.com

LogMeIn
www.logmein.com

Remote Helpdesk
www.gidsoftware.com/remotehelpdesk.htm

UltraVNC
www.uvnc.com

I.T. and Managed Services Tools

MSP University
www.mspu.us/en/tools

Back Office Service Desk Providers

Ingram Micro Seismic
www.ingrammicro.com/seismic

MSPSN Virtual Service Desk
www.mspsn.com

NetEnrich
www.netenrich.com

Service Desk USA
www.servicedeskusa.com

Zenith Infotech
www.zenithinfotech.com

Technical Drawing Solutions

Microsoft Visio
http://office.microsoft.com/visio

SmartDraw
www.smartdraw.com

Quoting Solutions

Quotewerks
www.quotewerks.com

Procurement Services

Axis Business Solutions
www.axisbusiness.com

HaaS Solutions

AARC Technology
www.arrc.com

MSPOnDemand
www.mspondemand.com

DISC Profiling Services

MSP University
www.mspu.us/en/services

Blogs

Anne Stanton – CRM Lady
http://www.crmlady.com/

Arlin Sorensen – Heartland Technology Solutions/HTG
http://peerpower.blogspot.com/

Dave Sobel – Evolve Technologies
http://www.evolvetech.com/blog

Eric Ligman – Microsoft
http://blogs.msdn.com/mssmallbiz

Erick Simpson – MSP University
http://www.mspu.us/blog

Joe Panettieri – MSP Mentor
http://www.mspmentor.net/

Josh Hilliker – Intel vPro™ Expert Center
http://communities.intel.com/community/vproexpert

Karl Palachuk – KP Enterprises
http://smallbizthoughts.blogspot.com/

Mark Crall – Charlotte Tech Care Team
http://techcareteam.com

Susan Bradley – The SBS Diva
http://www.sbsdiva.com/

Stuart Crawford – IT Matters
http://www.stuartcrawford.com/

Vlad Mazek – Own Web Now
http://www.vladville.com/

Peer Groups

Heartland Technology Groups
www.htgmembers.com

MSP University
www.mspu.us

Service Leadership, Inc.
www.service-leadership.com

I.T. and Managed Services Publications

MSP University
www.mspu.us/en/publications

Section 7: Forms, Tools and Collateral

We've included on the download available at www.mspu.us/svcbookregistration.htm each and every form, tool and piece of collateral discussed in this book – and then some! These include:

- Hardware Warranty Services Agreement Example
- Managed Services Agreement Example
- I.T. Solutions and Manged Services Proposal Example
- Problem Management and Resolution Process Example
- Employment ad for a service desk engineer
- Employment ad for a NOC engineer
- Employment ad for a service dispatcher
- Employment ad for a field engineer
- Employment ad for a service manager
- Employment ad for a project manager
- Employment ad for a sales engineer
- Employment ad for a purchasing manager
- Employment ad for an inventory manager
- HR Hiring Checklist for a New Technical Person
- HR Interview Questions for a new Technical Person
- Managed Services, Your Business Plan and You PowerPoint Presentation
- Managed Services Business Plan Template

Hardware Warranty Services Agreement Example

- Managed Services Business Plan White Paper
- Bonus Webcast - Developing an Effective Helpdesk SLA and Escalation Process
- Bonus Webcast - How to Prepare an IT Solutions and Managed Services Proposal
- Bonus Webcast - How to Create your Managed Services Agreement
- Bonus Webcast - Pricing and Positioning I.T. and Managed Services
- Bonus Webcast - Managed Services, Your Business Plan and You
- Bonus Webcast - HaaS With Karl Palachuk

To watch these webcasts, you will need the codec found here:

www.gotomeeting.com/codec

Hardware Warranty Services Agreement Example

The following section describes each of these forms, tools and marketing materials in detail, and how to use them.

Hardware warranty services agreement example

A sample hardware warranty services agreement included for instructional and informational purposes only, and is not recommended, or warranted for use. Always have your attorney or legal team review any and all agreements or documents that you use in your IT practice. Local laws and liabilities can never be fully covered by any type of generic document, including this sample hardware warranty services agreement.

Managed Services Agreement Example

A sample managed services agreement included for instructional and informational purposes only, and is not recommended, or warranted for use. Always have your attorney or legal team review any and all agreements or documents that you use in your IT practice. Local laws and liabilities can never be fully covered by any type of generic document, including this sample managed services agreement.

Hardware Warranty Services Agreement Example

I.T. Solutions and Managed Services Proposal Template

A customized, fill-in-the-blanks proposal template for I.T. solutions and managed services.

Problem Management and Resolution Process Example

A basic service desk problem management and resolutions process documenting best practices for incident handling.

Employment Ad for a Service Desk Engineer

An employment ad designed for a service desk engineer.

Employment Ad for a NOC Engineer

An employment ad designed for a NOC engineer.

Employment Ad for a Service Dispatcher

An employment ad designed for a service dispatcher.

Employment Ad for a Field Engineer

An employment ad designed for a field engineer.

Employment Ad for a Service Manager

An employment ad designed for a service manager.

Employment Ad for a Project Manager

An employment ad designed for a project manager.

Employment Ad for a Sales Engineer

An employment ad designed for a sales engineer.

Employment Ad for a Purchasing Manager

An employment ad designed for a purchasing manager.

Employment Ad for an Inventory Manager

An employment ad designed for an inventory manager.

HR Interview Checklist for a New Technical Person

A checklist to utilize when interviewing a new sales candidate in person.

HR Interview Questions for a New Technical Person

A set of questions to use when interviewing a new technical person.

Managed Services Business Plan Webcast

Our webcast with Microsoft's TS2 team focusing on business planning for managed services.

Managed Services, Your Business Plan and You PowerPoint Presentation

The PowerPoint slide deck used in our managed services business plan webcast.

Managed Services Business Plan Template

A customized, fill-in-the-blanks business plan template for managed services.

Managed Services Business Plan White Paper

A supporting document to the business plan template.

Bonus Webcast - Developing an Effective Helpdesk SLA and Escalation Process

Bonus Webcast - How to Prepare an IT Solutions and Managed Services Proposal

Bonus Webcast - How to Create your Managed Services Agreement

Bonus Webcast - Pricing and Positioning I.T. and Managed Services

Bonus Webcast - Managed Services, Your Business Plan and You

Bonus Webcast - HaaS With Karl Palachuk

Hardware Warranty Services Agreement Example

This sample hardware warranty services agreement is included for instructional and informational purposes only, and is not recommended, nor warranted for use.

Always have legal counsel review any and all agreements or documents that you utilize in your IT practice, or distribute to your clients prior to doing so.

Local laws and liabilities can never be fully covered by any type of generic document, including this sample hardware warranty services agreement.

Hardware Warranty Services Agreement Example

Hardware Warranty Services Agreement

1.   Understanding

This Agreement between

_____, herein referred to as
Client, and _____, hereinafter
referred to as Service Provider, covers all obligations and
liabilities on the part of Service Provider, the Client, and other
users of the equipment. The Client (or any user) accepts the
terms of this Agreement. Any changes to this Agreement must
be recorded in writing and have Service Provider's and the
Client's consent.

2.   Responsibilities

The Client agrees to use the equipment in the manner it is
intended, and agrees to take responsibility for their actions
and the results of their actions. If problems arise with the
equipment, Service Provider will make all reasonable efforts
to rectify them. This service may incur a charge, depending on
the nature of the problem, and is subject to the other
conditions in this Agreement.

3.   Intended Use

Equipment supplied by Service Provider is intended for use in
computing environments that are temperature-controlled,
free from excessive moisture, dust, humidity and maintain a

consistent, clean source of power. Unless as otherwise specified, equipment is not warranted for use in extreme environments.

4.   General Limitations

Service Provider equipment is produced to high standards, and is warranted to perform as described in the supplied documentation. No warranty, expressed or implied, other than that contained in this Agreement, is made in respect to Service Provider equipment. Service Provider shall be held blameless for any problems with the computer system not directly related to Service Provider equipment. Service Provider shall not be held responsible for special, consequential or punitive damages of any kind arising out of sale, installation service or use of its equipment.

5.   Hardware Warranty

Service Provider warrants that

---

shall be free of defects in material and workmanship for one (1) year from the date of purchase. Service Provider will repair or replace the equipment as appropriate, and the duration of the warranty shall be extended by the length of time needed for repair or replacement.

Hardware Warranty Services Agreement Example

To obtain service under this warranty, the Client must notify the Service Provider of the defect before the warranty expires. The Service Provider will advise the Client of the address to which the Client must ship the defective equipment at his or her own expense. The equipment should be packed safely, preferably in its original packaging. Service Provider will pay return shipping costs.

6. Hardware Warranty Limitations

This warranty applies only to the hardware specified in this document and used under normal operating conditions and within specification. Third party equipment is covered by the manufacturer's warranty. It does not cover hardware modified in any way, subjected to unusual physical, electrical or environmental stress, used with incorrectly wired or substandard connectors or cables, or with the original identification marks altered. Tampering with or breaking the warranty seal will also void the warranty. Service Provider does not warrant that equipment as suitable for any specific purpose, other than that explicitly stated by Service Provider.

7. Product Types & Warranty Term

Service Provider manufactured equipment covered by one (1) year warranty

Hardware Warranty Services Agreement Example

Service Provider manufactured equipment covered by one (1) year warranty

_____

_____

_____

Third Party Products

Products not manufactured by Service Provider are covered by the manufacturer's warranty.

Accessories and Consumables

Accessories and Consumables are not covered by any type of warranty.

8. Controlling Law and Severability

This Agreement shall be governed by the laws of the State of _____. It constitutes the entire Agreement between Client and Service Provider for equipment. Its terms and conditions shall prevail should there be any variance with the terms and conditions of any order submitted by Client.

Service Provider is not responsible for failure to render services due to circumstances beyond its control including, but not limited to, acts of God.

The Best I.T. Service Delivery BOOK EVER!

Hardware Warranty Services Agreement Example

Accepted by:

Authorized Signature   Service Provider   Date

Authorized Signature   Client   Date

Managed Services Agreement Example

This sample managed service agreement is included for instructional and informational purposes only, and is not recommended, nor warranted for use.

Always have legal counsel review any and all agreements or documents that you utilize in your IT practice, or distribute to your clients prior to doing so.

Local laws and liabilities can never be fully covered by any type of generic document, including this sample managed service agreement.

Managed Services Agreement

1.   Term of Agreement

This Agreement between
_____, herein referred to
as Client, and _____,
hereinafter referred to as Service Provider, is effective
upon the date signed, and shall remain in force for a
period of three years. The Service Agreement
automatically renews for a subsequent three year term
beginning on the day immediately following the end of
the Initial Term unless either party gives the other
ninety days' prior written notice of its intent not to
renew this Agreement.

    a) This Agreement may be terminated by either Party
       upon ninety (90) days' written notice if the other
       Party:

          a. Fails to fulfill in any material respect its
             obligations under this Agreement and
             does not cure such failure within thirty
             (30) days' of receipt of such written
             notice.

          b. Breaches any material term or condition

---

of this Agreement and fails to remedy such breach within thirty (30) days' of receipt of such written notice.

    c. Terminates or suspends its business operations, unless it is succeeded by a permitted assignee under this Agreement.

  b) If either party terminates this Agreement, Service Provider will assist Client in the orderly termination of services, including timely transfer of the services to another designated provider. Client agrees to pay Service Provider the actual costs of rendering such assistance.

2.   Fees and Payment Schedule

Fees will be $_____ per month, invoiced to Client on a Monthly basis, and will become due and payable on the first day of each month. Services will be suspended if payment is not received within 5 days following date due. Refer to Appendix B for services covered by the monthly fee under the terms of this Agreement.

It is understood that any and all Services requested by Client that fall outside of the terms of this Agreement will be considered Projects, and will be quoted and billed as separate, individual Services.

3.   Taxes

It is understood that any Federal, State or Local Taxes applicable shall be added to each invoice for services or materials rendered under this Agreement. Client shall pay any such taxes unless a valid exemption certificate is furnished to Service Provider for the state of use.

4.   Coverage

Remote Helpdesk and Vendor Management of Client's IT networks will be provided to the Client by Service Provider through remote means between the hours of 8:00 am – 5:00 pm Monday through Friday, excluding public holidays. Network Monitoring Services will be provided 24/7/365. All services qualifying under these conditions, as well as Services that fall outside this scope will fall under the provisions of Appendix B. Hardware costs of any kind are not covered under the terms of this Agreement.

Support and Escalation

Service Provider will respond to Client's Trouble Tickets under the provisions of Appendix A, and with best effort after hours or on holidays. Trouble Tickets must be opened by Client's designated I.T. Contact Person, by email to our Help Desk, or by phone if email is unavailable. Each call will be assigned a Trouble Ticket number for tracking. Our escalation process is detailed in Appendix A.

Service outside Normal Working Hours

Emergency services performed outside of the hours of 8:00 am – 5:00 pm Monday through Friday, excluding public holidays, shall be subject to provisions of Appendix B.

Service Calls Where No Trouble is found

If Client requests onsite service and no problem is found or reproduced, Client shall be billed at the current applicable rates as indicated in Appendix B.

Limitation of Liability

In no event shall Service Provider be held liable for indirect, special, incidental or consequential damages arising out of service provided hereunder, including but not limited to loss of profits or revenue, loss of use of equipment, lost data, costs of substitute equipment, or other costs.

5. Additional Maintenance Services

Hardware/System Support

Service Provider shall provide support of all hardware and systems specified in Appendix B, provided that all Hardware is covered under a currently active Vendor Support Contract; or replaceable parts be readily available, and all Software be Genuine, Currently Licensed and Vendor-Supported. Should any hardware or systems fail to meet these provisions, they will be excluded from this Service Agreement. Should 3rd Party Vendor Support Charges be required in order to resolve any issues, these will be passed on to the Client after first receiving the Client's authorization to incur them.

Virus Recovery for Current, Licensed Antivirus protected systems

Damages caused by, and recovery from, virus infection not detected and quarantined by the latest Antivirus definitions are covered under the terms of this Agreement. This Service is limited to those systems protected with a Currently Licensed, Vendor-Supported Antivirus Solution.

Monitoring Services

Service Provider will provide ongoing monitoring and security services of all critical devices as indicated in Appendix B. Service Provider will provide monthly reports as well as document critical alerts, scans and event resolutions to Client. Should a problem be discovered during monitoring, Service Provider shall make every attempt to rectify the condition in a timely manner through remote means.

---

6. Suitability of Existing Environment
Minimum Standards Required for Services

In order for Client's existing environment to qualify for Service Provider's Managed Services, the following requirements must be met:

1. All Servers with Microsoft Windows Operating Systems must be running Windows 2000 Server or later, and have all of the latest Microsoft Service Packs and Critical Updates installed.
2. All Desktop PC's and Notebooks/Laptops with Microsoft Windows Operating Systems must be running Windows XP Pro or later, and have all of the latest Microsoft Service Packs and Critical Updates installed.
3. All Server and Desktop Software must be Genuine, Licensed and Vendor-Supported.
4. The environment must have a currently licensed, up-to-date and Vendor-Supported Server-based Antivirus Solution protecting all Servers, Desktops, Notebooks/Laptops, and Email.
5. The environment must have a currently licensed, Vendor-Supported Server-based Backup Solution.

---

6. The environment must have a currently licensed, Vendor-Supported Hardware Firewall between the Internal Network and the Internet.
7. Any Wireless data traffic in the environment must be secured with a minimum of 128bit data encryption.

Costs required to bring Client's environment up to these Minimum Standards are not included in this Agreement.

7. Excluded Services

Service rendered under this Agreement does not include:

1) Parts, equipment or software not covered by vendor/manufacturer warranty or support.
2) The cost of any parts, equipment, or shipping charges of any kind.
3) The cost of any Software, Licensing, or Software Renewal or Upgrade Fees of any kind.

---

4) The cost of any 3rd Party Vendor or Manufacturer Support or Incident Fees of any kind.

5) The cost to bring Client's environment up to minimum standards required for Services.

6) Failure due to acts of God, building modifications, power failures or other adverse environmental conditions or factors.

7) Service and repair made necessary by the alteration or modification of equipment other than that authorized by Service Provider, including alterations, software installations or modifications of equipment made by Client's employees or anyone other than Service Provider.

8) Maintenance of Applications software packages, whether acquired from Service Provider or any other source unless as specified in Appendix B.

9) Programming (modification of software code) and program (software) maintenance unless as specified in Appendix B.

10) Training Services of any kind.

---

8. **Miscellaneous**

   This Agreement shall be governed by the laws of the State of _____. It constitutes the entire Agreement between Client and Service Provider for monitoring/maintenance/service of all equipment listed in "Appendix B." Its terms and conditions shall prevail should there be any variance with the terms and conditions of any order submitted by Client.

   Service Provider is not responsible for failure to render services due to circumstances beyond its control including, but not limited to, acts of God.

9. **Acceptance of Service Agreement**

   This Service Agreement covers only those services and equipment listed in "Appendix B." Service Provider must deem any equipment/services Client may want to add to this Agreement after the effective date acceptable. The addition of equipment/services not listed in "Appendix B" at the signing of this Agreement, if acceptable to Service Provider, shall result in an adjustment to the Client's monthly charges.

Managed Services Agreement Example

IN WITNESS WHEREOF, the parties hereto have caused this Service Agreement to be signed by their duly authorized representatives as of the date set forth below.

Accepted by:

Authorized Signature   Service Provider   Date

Authorized Signature   Client   Date

The Best I.T. Service Delivery BOOK EVER!

Managed Services Agreement Example

Managed Services Agreement

Appendix A

Response and Resolution Times

The following table shows the targets of response and resolution times for each priority level:

Trouble	Priority	Response time (in hours) *	Resolution time (in hours) *	Escalation threshold (in hours)
Service not available (all users and functions unavailable).	1	Within 1 hour	ASAP – Best Effort	2 hours
Significant degradation of service (large number of users or business critical functions affected)	2	Within 4 hours	ASAP – Best Effort	4 hours
Limited degradation of service (limited number of users or functions affected, business process can continue).	3	Within 24 hours	ASAP – Best Effort	48 hours
Small service degradation (business process can continue, one user affected).	4	within 48 hours	ASAP – Best Effort	96 hours

The Best I.T. Service Delivery BOOK EVER!

Managed Services Agreement Example

Support Tiers

The following details and describes our Support Tier levels:

Support Tier	Description
Tier 1 Support	All support incidents begin in Tier 1, where the initial trouble ticket is created, the issue is identified and clearly documented, and basic hardware/software troubleshooting is initiated.
Tier 2 Support	All support incidents that cannot be resolved with Tier 1 Support are escalated to Tier 2, where more complex support on hardware/software issues can be provided by more experienced Engineers.
Tier 3 Support	Support Incidents that cannot be resolved by Tier 2 Support are escalated to Tier 3, where support is provided by the most qualified and experienced Engineers who have the ability to collaborate with 3rd Party (Vendor) Support Engineers to resolve the most complex issues.

Managed Services Agreement

Appendix A (cont)

Service Request Escalation Procedure

1. Support Request is Received
2. Trouble Ticket is Created
3. Issue is Identified and documented in Help Desk system
4. Issue is qualified to determine if it can be resolved through Tier 1 Support

   If issue can be resolved through Tier 1 Support:

5. Level 1 Resolution - issue is worked to successful resolution
6. Quality Control –Issue is verified to be resolved to Client's satisfaction
7. Trouble Ticket is closed, after complete problem resolution details have been updated in Help Desk system

---

If issue cannot be resolved through Tier 1 Support:

6. Issue is escalated to Tier 2 Support

7. Issue is qualified to determine if it can be resolved by Tier 2 Support

   If issue can be resolved through Tier 2 Support:

8. Level 2 Resolution - issue is worked to successful resolution

9. Quality Control –Issue is verified to be resolved to Client's satisfaction

10. Trouble Ticket is closed, after complete problem resolution details have been updated in Help Desk system

    If issue cannot be resolved through Tier 2 Support:

9. Issue is escalated to Tier 3 Support

10. Issue is qualified to determine if it can be resolved through Tier 3 Support

Managed Services Agreement Example

If issue can be resolved through Tier 3 Support:

11. Level 3 Resolution - issue is worked to successful resolution

12. Quality Control –Issue is verified to be resolved to Client's satisfaction

13. Trouble Ticket is closed, after complete problem resolution details have been updated in Help Desk system

If issue cannot be resolved through Tier 3 Support:

12. Issue is escalated to Onsite Support

13. Issue is qualified to determine if it can be resolved through Onsite Support

If issue can be resolved through Onsite Support:

14. Onsite Resolution - issue is worked to successful resolution

15. Quality Control –Issue is verified to be resolved to Client's satisfaction

---

16. Trouble Ticket is closed, after complete problem resolution details have been updated in Help Desk system

If issue cannot be resolved through Onsite Support:

17. I.T. Manager Decision Point – request is updated with complete details of all activity performed

Managed Services Agreement
Appendix B

Description	Frequency	Included in Maintenance
General		
Document software and hardware changes	As performed	YES
Test backups with restores	Monthly	YES
Monthly reports of work accomplished, work in progress, etc.	Monthly	YES
Systems		
Check print queues	As needed	YES
Ensure that all server services are running	Daily/hourly	YES
Keep Service Packs, Patches and Hotfixes current as per company policy	Monthly	YES
Check event log of every server and identify any potential issues	As things appear	YES
Monitor hard drive free space on server, clients	Daily/hourly	YES
Reboot servers if needed	As needed	YES
Run defrag and chkdsk on all drives	As needed	YES
Scheduled off time server maintenance	As needed	YES
Install software upgrades	As needed	YES
Determine logical directory structure, Implement, MAP, and detail	Revisit Monthly	YES
Set up and maintain groups (accounting, admin, printers, sales, warehouse, etc)	As needed	YES
Check status of backup and restores	Daily	YES
Alert office manager to dangerous conditions -Memory running low -Hard drive showing sign of failure -Hard drive running out of disk space -Controllers losing interrupts -Network Cards report unusual collision activity	As needed	YES
Educate and correct user errors (deleted files, corrupted files, etc.)	As needed	YES
Clean and prune directory structure, keep efficient and active	Monthly	YES
Disaster Recovery		
Disaster Recovery of Server(s)	As Needed	YES

The Best I.T. Service Delivery BOOK EVER!

Managed Services Agreement Example

Managed Services Agreement
Appendix B (cont.)

Networks

Check router logs	Weekly	YES
Performance Monitoring/Capacity Planning	Weekly	YES
Monitor DSU/TSU, switches, hubs and internet connectivity, and make sure everything is operational (available for SNMP manageable devices only)	Weekly	YES
Major SW/HW upgrades to network backbone, including routers, WAN additions, etc.	As needed	YES
Maintain office connectivity to the Internet	Ongoing	YES

Security

Check firewall logs	Monthly	YES
Confirm that antivirus virus definition auto updates have occurred	As Needed	YES
Confirm that virus updates have occurred	As Needed	YES
Confirm that backup has been performed on a daily basis	Daily	YES
Create new directories, shares and security groups, new accounts, disable/delete old accounts, manage account policies	As Needed	YES
Permissions and file system management	As Needed	YES
Set up new users including login restrictions, passwords, security, applications	As needed	YES
Set up and change security for users and applications	As needed	YES
Monitor for unusual activity among users	Ongoing	YES

Apps

Exchange user/mailbox management	As needed	YES
Monitor directory replication	As needed	YES
Monitor WINS replication	As needed	YES
SQL server management	As needed	YES
Overall application disk space management	As needed	YES
Ensure Microsoft Office Applications are functioning as designed	As needed	YES

Managed Services Agreement
Appendix B (cont)

Service Rates

Labor	Rate
Remote PC Management/Help Desk 8am-5pm M-F	INCLUDED
Remote Printer Management 8am-5pm M-F	INCLUDED
Remote Network Management 8am-5pm M-F	INCLUDED
Remote Server Management 8am-5pm M-F	INCLUDED
24x7x365 Network Monitoring	INCLUDED
Lab Labor 8am-5pm M-F	INCLUDED
Onsite Labor 8am-5pm M-F	INCLUDED
Remote PC Management/Help Desk 5:01pm-9pm M-F	$_____/nr
Remote Printer Management 5:01pm-9pm M-F	$_____/nr
Remote Network Management 5:01pm-9pm M-F	$_____/nr
Remote Server Management 5:01pm-9pm M-F	$_____/nr
Lab Labor 5:01pm-9pm M-F	$_____/nr
Onsite Labor 5:01pm-9pm M-F	$_____/nr
Remote Labor All Other Times	$_____/nr
Lab Labor All Other Times	$_____/nr
Onsite Labor All Other Times	$_____/nr

Covered Equipment

Managed Desktops: Desktops/Notebooks
Managed Printers:
Managed Networks:
Managed Servers:

I.T. Solutions and Managed Services Proposal Example

Review

Introduction

YOUR COMPANY NAME has been providing information technology solutions to the SMB market since **YEAR**. Our relationships with partners such as Microsoft, Cisco, Citrix, HP, Dell, Veritas and Trend have allowed us the ability to design, scale and implement effective infrastructure solutions for our diverse client base. Our solution stack includes hosted voice over IP services, application and web development, wireless, local and wide-area networking, as well as managed services. As a Gold Certified Microsoft partner, our core competencies include Information Worker Solutions, Networking Infrastructure Solutions, Advanced Infrastructure Solutions, Microsoft Business Solutions, and we are a Microsoft Small Business Specialist.

The Best I.T. Service Delivery BOOK EVER!

I.T. Solutions and Managed Services Proposal Example

We specialize in educating you in the information technology options available to ease your business' IT concerns in the 21st century. Our professional scope ranges from engineering and implementing local and wide area networking solutions to architecting and designing custom software applications to address your specific business needs. YOUR COMPANY NAME's network and software applications engineers' combined experience allow us the ability to successfully provide custom, affordable solutions to our valued Clients.

Our technical expertise enables us to provide network design and support, as well as application development for office automation, and Internet/Intranet development and support; utilizing technologies such as digital subscriber line, frame relay, point-to-point tunneling protocol and virtual private networking. These technologies provide the ability to securely encrypt data transmission, paving the way for electronic commerce and e-business.

By coordinating and managing all of your technical solutions and vendors, and proactively managing your network, we allow you the ability to completely focus on running your business.

The Best I.T. Service Delivery BOOK EVER!

I.T. Solutions and Managed Services Proposal Example

YOUR COMPANY NAME is uniquely qualified to provide IT project and ongoing service support for YOUR CLIENT NAME. We sincerely appreciate the opportunity to present this proposal.

YOUR COMPANY NAME Bio

Certifications

Microsoft Gold Certified Partner

Microsoft Business Solutions Partner

Microsoft Small Business Specialist

Microsoft Information Worker Competency

Microsoft Networking Infrastructure Competency

Microsoft Advanced Networking Infrastructure Competency

Cisco Partner

Citrix Partner

Partnerships/Affiliations

SMBTN Partner

ASCII Group Member

Vendor Affiliations

Hewlett-Packard Authorized Business Development Partner

Dell Solution Provider Direct

Cisco Reseller

Level Platforms Partner

Zenith Infotech Partner

Symantec/Veritas Partner

ConnectWise Partner

Trend Micro Partner

The Best I.T. Service Delivery BOOK EVER!

I.T. Solutions and Managed Services Proposal Example

General

Physical inspections of **YOUR CLIENT NAME'S** primary location, and meetings with **YOUR CLIENT NAME'S** representative(s) were used to compile the results of this proposal. During our initial site inspection, **YOUR CLIENT NAME'S** local area network, connected client pc's, server(s) and other networked devices were inspected in order to determine their existing configurations and current operating status.

Local Area Network (DESCRIBE YOUR CLIENT'S NETWORK)

YOUR CLIENT NAME'S business operations span between 2 physically displaced buildings, their Main facility and their Irvine Facility. Each of these facilities operates under physically segregated networks, with VPN connectivity to join them. The Main facility's existing local area network is comprised of several 10/100 Network Switches and hubs connected to the new Straitshot DSL router. A Microsoft Windows SBS2003 Server, the client workstations and several network printers and copiers are connected to the inside interface. The IP address on the outside interface of the router is X.X.X.X. DNS Servers being used are X.X.X.X and X.X.X.X. The inside IP address of the router is X.X.X.X. The server is being used as the DHCP server for the network and is Leasing IP addresses in the 192.168.1.x range. The router is

---

---

forwarding traffic from the outside on ports 80, 3389, 110, and 443 to the inside IP address of the SBS Server, X.X.X.X. The router is also forwarding traffic from the outside on ports 80 and 1494 to the inside IP address of the Citrix server, X.X.X.X. In addition the router is forwarding mail traffic from the outside on port 25 to the inside IP address of the Barracuda server, X.X.X.X.

Additionally, there is a D-Link secure wireless access point in the Main facility's server room.

YOUR CLIENT NAME'S Irvine facility's existing local area network is comprised of two Dell 24 port switches connected to a new CyberGuard SG565 firewall router and the facility's ISP's Cox communication DSL router on the outside interface. The new IRVINE server is being used as a domain controller and DHCP server for the network and is leasing IP addresses in the 192.168.2.x range. The router is forwarding traffic from the outside on port 3389 to the inside IP address of the Irvine server, 192.168.2.230.

YOUR CLIENT NAME'S is subletting space in the Main and Irvine facilities, and is sharing the DSL service in these facilities with the tenants.

YOUR CLIENT NAME'S operates two incompatible phone systems at each of their facilities, with the Main facility phone

---

system comprised of an antiquated server-based PBX. While the Irvine facility has temporary off the shelf analog phones.

Existing LAN Diagram (CREATE A DRAWING)

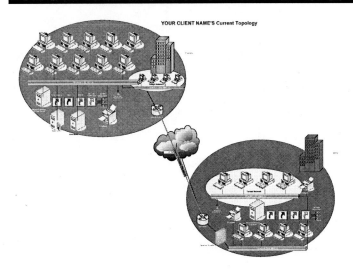

YOUR CLIENT NAME'S Current Topology

I.T. Solutions and Managed Services Proposal Example

Problems at Main and Irvine Facilities (DETAIL AREAS OF CONCERN)

Server

YOUR CLIENT NAME'S new HP Proliant Windows SBS2003 server is configured incorrectly. Upon initial inspection, it was discovered that all of the purpose-built Microsoft Small Business Server tools and wizards have been disabled or ignored. Some of these functions have been manually recreated, contradicting Microsoft's best practices. These purpose-built tools have been specifically designed by Microsoft to properly integrate all the enterprise level features for the operating system. In addition, the domain YOUR CLIENT NAME -Co.com has been improperly named identically to the public YOUR CLIENT NAME'S website domain, www. YOUR CLIENT NAME.com. This can cause name resolution problems and unnecessary network activity, degrading network throughput.

In addition, there are core problems with the server's Internet Information Service (IIS). It was discovered that the server's web component which hosts the company's SharePoint Team Services site, as well as Outlook Web Access and Remote Web Workplace, was not functioning. These features and services are three of the most beneficial attributes of owning Windows Small Business Server 2003. These core components have

---

been removed for no conceivable reason, and will need to be recreated for the restoration of proper functionality to the SBS2003 Server.

YOUR CLIENT NAME'S Citrix application server is not operating properly. This has caused the users much anguish and lost productivity, negatively affecting YOUR CLIENT NAME'S bottom line.

Additionally, YOUR CLIENT NAME'S Blackberry server has no security in place.

Workstations

Most of the laptops in Irvine have expired AntiVirus software and no AntiSpyware software installed.

Licensing

It appears the MS Exchange, email server is licensed only for 20 users. On Wednesday the 19th we saw at least 24 users connected. This will ultimately cause email errors and downtime if the server is not properly licensed.

In addition, it appears that the Microsoft Office software on all the Irvine facility laptops may be pirated.

The Best I.T. Service Delivery BOOK EVER!

I.T. Solutions and Managed Services Proposal Example

Network Backbone

The network backbone has been neglected. There is a 48 port hub stacked on a 24 port switch. Hubs are essentially less intelligent and slower than switches, while the cost difference is negligible. This may be slowing network traffic at the Main facility. Wireless connectivity is also a concern at both facilities due to the wireless access points being off the shelf home user devices, instead of business-class products.

Lastly, **YOUR CLIENT NAME** is subletting space to tenants in both facilities. Since there is no segregation between the tenant networks and the **YOUR CLIENT NAME** networks, the tenants have may be able to access sensitive **YOUR CLIENT NAME** files and corporate data. In addition, the tenants can tax the Internet bandwidth from Citrix during their normal daily operations, as well as unknowingly infect **YOUR CLIENT NAME'S** network and devices with viruses, spyware and worms.

General (DOCUMENT A GENERAL OVERVIEW OF WORK SCOPE)

Phase 1- **YOUR CLIENT NAME'S** representative(s) indicated the need to remediate their new Windows Small Business Server 2003, which hosts several applications, to allow for a stable, secure computing environment, providing both data and hardware fault-tolerance. The quickest way to help the Irvine office is to clean up the Citrix server errors. We will

---

reconfigure the Outlook configuration on the Irvine laptops so they can send and receive mail from any location instead of just the office.

Phase 2- We will upgrade the Citrix server to Windows 2003 Server R2, add 4GB of RAM, and two 200GB hard drives for the DFS synchronization with Irvine.

Additionally, we will correct the wide open security problem on the BlackBerry server. The Irvine laptops will have Symantec AntiVirus and Microsoft AntiSpyware installed on them.

The Blackberry server will be secured.

The tenants network access will be segregated from the YOUR CLIENT NAME network to prevent virus infections or access to YOUR CLIENT NAME data. We will also use the Irvine location's Cyberguard SG565 Firewall to throttle the tenants Internet bandwidth, and in Danville we will move the Tenants to the old SBC Internet circuit. In Danville we will install a new HP Procurve 48 port Switch to replace the aging Hub, and install a CyberGuard SG565 for business class Internet and Wireless access. In Irvine we will use the existing Linksys wireless router for the tenants, and enable the wireless feature on the Cyberguard SG565 router for the YOUR CLIENT NAME Users.

I.T. Solutions and Managed Services Proposal Example

We will purchase and implement 15 new Exchange (SBS) Server licenses and 5 new Microsoft Office Licenses for the laptops.

In addition, the Voice over IP implementation will be completed in Danville in order to provide a solution to the antiquated phone system, and provide the ability to make calls between the Danville and Irvine facilities without incurring Toll charges.

Once these issues have been addressed, we will be able to implement our proactive managed services maintenance plan.

Implementation (DOCUMENT A HIGH-LEVEL PROJECT PLAN)

Approach:

We propose attempting to reconfigure the server by re-running specific portions of the Small Business Server 2003 installation routines. If successful, this will allow the ability to correct the numerous problems detected during our initial inspections. If unsuccessful, we will recommend backing up all of the data on the server, and reinstalling the operating system from scratch. This will be a lengthier and more involved process, and will only be recommended should our initial attempts to repair the server with the first option fail.

I.T. Solutions and Managed Services Proposal Example

We also propose immediately segregating both the Irvine and Danville facilitys' networks from the tenant networks. We recommend purchasing a second Cyberguard SG565 firewall for Danville, to standardize the hardware between both facilities. We also recommend the purchase of an HP Procurve 48 port switch for the Main facility. This switch will improve speed across the network, and allow the best connectivity between facilities.

We will securely encrypt the wireless access points in both facilities, so that only authorized users can utilize these wireless services.

We will redirect both the Irvine and Main users' My Documents folders to their server home folders so that if a workstation dies, the data does not die with it. We will configure the Irvine users' My Documents folders to synchronize between their workstations and the server, in order to eliminate any potential lag time across the VPN. This will allow all users' documents to be backed up by the server. We will configure all users' Outlook applications with Cached Exchange Mode, to further eliminate any lag time across the VPN. Additionally, we will configure RPC over HTTP, allowing the ability for home users to access their email with the full OUTLOOK client, if they so desire.

I.T. Solutions and Managed Services Proposal Example

We also recommend purchasing a spare PC for each **YOUR CLIENT NAME'S** location.

Danville server reconfiguration /troubleshooting   12 Hours

- **A YOUR COMPANY NAME'S** Representatives will spend 12 hours remotely reconfiguring the SBS2003 server and Citrix server, as well as securing the Blackberry server.

- The goal of this phase is to upgrade the Citrix Server to Windows Server 2003 R2 and troubleshoot Citrix functionality, remediate your Windows SBS2003 Server and correct the Active Directory, DNS, IIS and other problems with the server, and insure it is configured and operating per Microsoft's best practices.

Irvine facility network segregation /switch installation /VPN installation & configuration   8 Hours

- One **YOUR COMPANY NAME'S** representative will spend 8 hours at **YOUR CLIENT NAME'S** Irvine facility in the network segregation/switch/VPN installation phase.

- The goal of this phase is to install the new network switches and Cyberguard Firewall VPN routers at each of **YOUR CLIENT NAME'S**

---

buildings and build the VPN tunnel between facilities.

- o The Irvine facility's network will be segregated from the tenant's network by repurposing one of the existing hubs and splitting the DSL circuit behind the two networks.

Secure wireless access point	*2 Hours*

- One **YOUR COMPANY NAME'S** representative will secure the wireless access points and provide **YOUR CLIENT NAME'S** representatives the encryption key, and train them on how to create connections.

Redirect all users' home folders to server /configure cached exchange mode	*12 Hours*

- One **YOUR COMPANY NAME'S** representative will spend 8 hours at **YOUR CLIENT NAME'S** headquarters redirecting all users' My Documents folders to the server's home folders, and configuring Outlook to operate in Cached Exchange Mode.
- One **YOUR COMPANY NAME'S** representative will spend 4 hours at the Irvine facility redirecting all users' My Documents folders to the server's home folders, and configuring Outlook to operate in Cached Exchange Mode.

I.T. Solutions and Managed Services Proposal Example

Proposed Redesign (CREATE AN "AFTER" DRAWING)

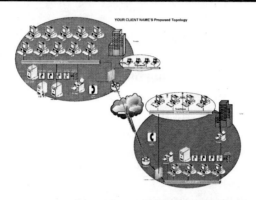

YOUR CLIENT NAME'S Proposed Topology

Proposed Managed Services

After the proposed project scope has been completed, **YOUR COMPANY NAME** will configure **YOUR CLIENT NAME'S** network and all connected Servers, routers, switches, pc's and peripherals to allow us the ability to proactively manage and maintain your network environment.

The core components that comprise our proactive managed services package include:

- *"All You Can Eat" remote helpdesk during business hours*
- *24x7x365 network and critical device monitoring*
- *Vendor management*

I.T. Solutions and Managed Services Proposal Example

Benefits you will receive as a result of our proactive managed services package include:

- *Much faster response time to trouble tickets*
- *Predictive, proactive IT support*
- *Increased operational efficiency*
- *Reduce and control your operating costs*
- *Cost-effectively gain access to enterprise-level support staff*
- *Experience minimized downtime*
- *Regain the ability to focus on running your business, not your vendors*
- *Receive peace of mind knowing that your network is being monitored 24 Hours a Day, seven days a Week*

Summary (SUMMARIZE THE PROPOSAL AND YOUR QUALIFICATIONS)

YOUR COMPANY NAME has installed, configured and manages over xxx Microsoft Small Business Servers, and maintains Microsoft's *Small Business Specialist Certification*, as well as *Microsoft Gold Certified Partner* status, which is achieved by less than 1% of all Microsoft partners worldwide.

YOUR COMPANY NAME will remediate your Microsoft Windows Small Business Server 2003 and reconfigure it according to Microsoft's best practices. When complete,

---

this will allow the users that you designate the ability to remote directly into their workstations to work, check email remotely, and allow you to maintain your own company Intranet, document management and company calendar.

In addition, we will upgrade your Citrix server to Windows 2003 Server R2 to improve your DFS functionality, as well as securing your Blackberry server. We will segregate and bandwidth-throttle your tenant's networks, and re-purpose the existing wireless access points for their use. We will enable and configure the Cyberguard Firewall routers' wireless capability to provide secure wireless access to designated **YOUR CLIENT NAME'S** Users.

We will also implement a secure VPN solution connecting your two facilities, and configure secure wireless access for your locations. Your users' data will be secure, as we will redirect all of their My Documents folders to the server's home folders for nightly backup. We will also configure Outlook Anti-Spam filtering by configuring Cached Exchange Mode on all workstations.

Once these items have been addressed, we will implement a proactive managed services maintenance plan that will allow you the ability to budget your IT service costs as a flat fee each and every month, saving you costs and downtime, and providing predictive, proactive problem resolution through our all you can eat help desk.

Support:

YOUR COMPANY NAME's Technical Support Center answers service calls 24 hours a day, 7 days a week. Our help desk is staffed with experienced technicians from 7am to 5pm. From 5pm to 7am our answering service contacts an on-call engineer who will return your call and diligently work your problem to a successful resolution. Our managed service agreement clients also benefit from remote support, whereby our technicians utilize remote access tools connecting them to your office systems, allowing the ability to diagnose hardware and software failures via dedicated Internet connections. All of our service agreement clients receive priority service.

Requirements:

YOUR COMPANY NAME's personnel will maintain all documentation. This will include recommendations, schematics, drawings, and configuration data. All work possible will be performed during regular business hours. We will not disrupt normal production by performing server work during these hours.

I.T. Solutions and Managed Services Proposal Example

Locations:

Onsite labor will be performed at **YOUR CLIENT NAME'S** facilities as required. All remote labor will be performed at **YOUR COMPANY NAME'S** offices.

Exclusions:

This proposal does not include electrical wiring or panels, network cabling, jacks and related equipment or labor. Other requirements that may be needed, but are not listed in this proposal are deemed outside the scope of this proposal and are therefore not included. Cabling and equipment cannot be quoted until **YOUR COMPANY NAME** is provided with a scope of work.

Installation Dates:

To be determined.

Problem Management and Resolution Process Example

1. Support Request is Received

2. Trouble Ticket is Created

3. Issue is Identified and documented in Help Desk system

4. Issue is qualified to determine if it can be resolved through Tier 1 Support

   If issue can be resolved through Tier 1 Support:

5. Level 1 Resolution - issue is worked to successful resolution

6. Quality Control –Issue is verified to be resolved to Client's satisfaction

7. Trouble Ticket is closed, after complete problem resolution details have been updated in Help Desk system

Problem Management and Resolution Process Example

If issue cannot be resolved through Tier 1 Support:

6. Issue is escalated to Tier 2 Support

7. Issue is qualified to determine if it can be resolved by Tier 2 Support

    If issue can be resolved through Tier 2 Support:

8. Level 2 Resolution - issue is worked to successful resolution

9. Quality Control –Issue is verified to be resolved to Client's satisfaction

10. Trouble Ticket is closed, after complete problem resolution details have been updated in Help Desk system

    ### *If issue cannot be resolved through Tier 2 Support:*

9. Issue is escalated to Tier 3 Support

10. Issue is qualified to determine if it can be resolved through Tier 3 Support

Problem Management and Resolution Process Example

If issue can be resolved through Tier 3 Support:

11. Level 3 Resolution - issue is worked to successful resolution

12. Quality Control –Issue is verified to be resolved to Client's satisfaction

13. Trouble Ticket is closed, after complete problem resolution details have been updated in Help Desk system

If issue cannot be resolved through Tier 3 Support:

12. Issue is escalated to Onsite Support

13. Issue is qualified to determine if it can be resolved through Onsite Support

If issue can be resolved through Onsite Support:

14. Onsite Resolution - issue is worked to successful resolution

15. Quality Control –Issue is verified to be resolved to Client's satisfaction

---

---

16. Trouble Ticket is closed, after complete problem resolution details have been updated in Help Desk system

    If issue cannot be resolved through Onsite Support:

17. I.T. Manager Decision Point – request is updated with complete details of all activity performed

---

Employment Ad for a Service Desk Engineer

Service Desk Engineer

Company: MSP University
Location: Garden Grove, CA 92841
Status: Full-Time, Employee
Job Category: Service Desk
Relevant Work Experience: 3-5 Years
Career Level: Experienced (Non-Manager)

We are currently seeking a highly skilled service desk engineer with the drive and determination to help us support our client base. This position reports to our Service Manager. We are looking for an individual who is a problem-solver and has a proven track record of working within a team environment to successfully address challenging user computing issues, and is accustomed to leveraging technical training opportunities to improve their skills. If you have the experience and the desire, we'd like to talk to you.

Our service desk engineers are responsible for maintaining user uptime and improving their computing experiences through effective remote monitoring, maintenance and problem identification and resolution activities, as well as growing and developing the organization's perception with existing customers through exceptional customer service. Candidates must be energetic and focused with a strong motivation to learn new technologies and management and maintenance processes. This position requires dedication, persistence, follow-up, effective utilization of provided resources and unbeatable customer service.

This position will include identifying user problems and working within a structured problem management and resolution process to remediate them within established SLAs, and involves working with other resources and vendors to deliver effective support services. Responsibilities include identifying, documenting and troubleshooting user computing issues to resolution and maintaining customer satisfaction.

Job duties include utilizing our remote monitoring and management (RMM) and professional services automation (PSA) solutions along with other service-specific tools and technologies to deliver remote user support services and update service request information, answer technical support calls, assign ticket severity, prioritize work accordingly, and collaborate and work with other staff and vendor support resources to resolve issues. Overall relationship management and the ability to coordinate required resources to respond to complex IT requirements are desired. Other requirements include participating in ongoing training and attainment of manufacturer certifications, developing and maintaining relationships with user and vendor contacts, and preparing and presenting service and monitoring reports to management regularly.

Minimum Skills Required:

- Minimum three years service desk experience
- Microsoft Certified Professional status
- Excellent knowledge of our supported software and technologies
- Strong interpersonal skills required to effectively communicate with users and vendors
- Passion for teamwork, continuing education, problem solving and exceptional customer service
- Must be well spoken, outgoing, organized, detailed-orientated, dependable and flexible
- Experience with HP, Cisco and Citrix technologies a plus
- Valid driver's license and proof of insurance
- Background check and drug screen required
- Reliable transportation

This Position Entails:

- Troubleshooting user problems over the phone and with remote control technologies
- Accurate documentation of all activities conducted

Employment Ad for a Service Desk Engineer

- The ability to manage, maintain, troubleshoot and support our users' networks, equipment, software and services
- The ability to learn quickly and adapt to changing requirements

The Successful Candidate must be:

- Professional and articulate
- Interpersonally adept
- Technically proficient
- A relationship builder
- A problem solver

Benefits include group medical/dental insurance, paid vacation, holidays, personal & sick time and training reimbursement. Our generous compensation plans are structured as salary plus bonuses for meeting utilization, compliance and customer service requirements, with initial compensation commensurate with relevant experience.

Qualified candidates please submit a current resume, along with salary history to: hr@mspu.us.

___

Employment Ad for a NOC Engineer

Network Operations Center (NOC) Engineer

Company: MSP University
Location: Garden Grove, CA 92841
Status: Full-Time, Employee
Job Category: Network Operations
Relevant Work Experience: 3-5 Years
Career Level: Experienced (Non-Manager)

We are currently seeking a highly skilled NOC engineer with the drive and determination to help us support our client base. This position reports to our Service Manager. We are looking for an individual who is a problem-solver and has a proven track record of working within a team environment to successfully address challenging network computing issues, and is accustomed to leveraging technical training opportunities to improve their skills. If you have the experience and the desire, we'd like to talk to you.

Our NOC engineers are responsible for maintaining user uptime and improving their computing experiences through proactive remote monitoring, maintenance and problem identification and resolution activities, as well as growing and developing the organization's perception with existing

___

customers through exceptional customer service. Candidates must be energetic and focused with a strong motivation to learn new technologies and management and maintenance processes. This position requires dedication, persistence, follow-up, effective utilization of provided resources and unbeatable customer service.

This position will include identifying hardware, network and service problems and working within a structured problem management and resolution process to remediate them within established SLAs, and involves working with other resources and vendors to deliver effective support services. Responsibilities include identifying, documenting and troubleshooting customer network and computing issues to resolution and maintaining customer satisfaction.

Job duties include utilizing our remote monitoring and management (RMM) and professional services automation (PSA) solutions along with other service-specific tools and technologies to deliver remote network environment support services and update service request information, answer technical support calls, assign ticket severity, prioritize work accordingly, and collaborate and work with other staff and vendor support resources to resolve issues. Overall relationship management and the ability to coordinate required resources to respond to complex IT requirements are desired. Other requirements include participating in ongoing

Employment Ad for a NOC Engineer

---

training and attainment of manufacturer certifications, developing and maintaining relationships with user and vendor contacts, and preparing and presenting service and monitoring reports to management regularly.

Minimum Skills Required:

- Minimum three years NOC experience
- Microsoft Certified Professional status
- Excellent knowledge of our supported software and technologies
- Strong interpersonal skills required to effectively communicate with users and vendors
- Passion for teamwork, continuing education, problem solving and exceptional customer service
- Must be well spoken, outgoing, organized, detailed-orientated, dependable and flexible
- Experience with HP, Cisco and Citrix technologies a plus
- Valid driver's license and proof of insurance
- Background check and drug screen required
- Reliable transportation

This Position Entails:

- Troubleshooting network, equipment and service-related problems with remote control technologies
- Analyzing remote monitoring reports to identify capacity and performance issues and remediate them

---

Employment Ad for a NOC Engineer

- Accurate documentation of all activities conducted
- The ability to manage, maintain, troubleshoot and support our users' networks, equipment, software and services
- The ability to learn quickly and adapt to changing requirements

The Successful Candidate must be:

- Professional and articulate
- Interpersonally adept
- Technically proficient
- A relationship builder
- A problem solver

Benefits include group medical/dental insurance, paid vacation, holidays, personal & sick time and training reimbursement. Our generous compensation plans are structured as salary plus bonuses for meeting utilization, compliance and customer service requirements, with initial compensation commensurate with relevant experience.

Qualified candidates please submit a current resume, along with salary history to: hr@mspu.us.

Employment Ad for a Field Engineer

I.T. Field Engineer

Company: MSP University
Location: Garden Grove, CA 92841
Status: Full-Time, Employee
Job Category: Field Services
Relevant Work Experience: 3-5 Years
Career Level: Experienced (Non-Manager)

We are currently seeking a highly skilled field engineer with the drive and determination to help us support our client base. This position reports to our Service Manager. We are looking for an individual who is a problem-solver and has a proven track record of working within a team environment to successfully address challenging user computing issues, and is accustomed to leveraging technical training opportunities to improve their skills. If you have the experience and the desire, we'd like to talk to you.

Our field engineers are responsible for maintaining user uptime and improving their computing experiences through effective onsite maintenance and problem identification and resolution activities, as well as growing and developing the organization's perception with existing customers through exceptional customer service. Candidates must be energetic and focused with a strong motivation to learn new technologies and management and maintenance processes. This position requires dedication, persistence, follow-up, effective utilization of provided resources and unbeatable customer service.

This position will include identifying user problems and working within a structured problem management and resolution process to remediate them within established SLAs, and involves working with other resources and vendors to deliver effective field support services. Responsibilities include identifying, documenting and troubleshooting user computing issues to resolution and maintaining customer satisfaction.

Job duties include utilizing our professional services automation (PSA) solution along with other service-specific tools and technologies to deliver onsite user support services and update service request information and collaborate and work with other staff and vendor support resources to resolve issues. Overall relationship management and the ability to coordinate required resources to respond to complex IT requirements are desired. Other requirements include participating in ongoing training and attainment of manufacturer certifications and developing and maintaining relationships with user and vendor contacts.

The Best I.T. Service Delivery BOOK EVER!

Employment Ad for a Field Engineer

Minimum Skills Required:

- Minimum three years experience
- Microsoft Certified Professional status
- Excellent knowledge of our supported software and technologies
- Strong interpersonal skills required to effectively communicate with users and vendors
- Passion for teamwork, continuing education, problem solving and exceptional customer service
- Must be well spoken, outgoing, organized, detailed-orientated, dependable and flexible
- Experience with HP, Cisco and Citrix technologies a plus
- Valid driver's license and proof of insurance
- Background check and drug screen required
- Reliable transportation

This Position Entails:

- Troubleshooting user problems onsite
- Accurate documentation of all activities conducted
- The ability to manage, maintain, troubleshoot and support our users' networks, equipment, software and services
- The ability to learn quickly and adapt to changing requirements

---

The Best I.T. Service Delivery BOOK EVER!

Employment Ad for a Field Engineer

The Successful Candidate must be:

- Professional and articulate
- Interpersonally adept
- Technically proficient
- A relationship builder
- A problem solver

Benefits include group medical/dental insurance, paid vacation, holidays, personal & sick time and training reimbursement. Our generous compensation plans are structured as salary plus bonuses for meeting utilization, compliance and customer service requirements, with initial compensation commensurate with relevant experience.

Qualified candidates please submit a current resume, along with salary history to: hr@mspu.us.

Employment Ad for a Service Dispatcher

Service Dispatcher

Company: MSP University
Location: Garden Grove, CA 92841
Status: Full-Time, Employee
Job Category: Dispatcher
Relevant Work Experience: 3-5 Years
Career Level: Experienced (Non-Manager)

We are currently seeking a highly skilled service dispatcher with the drive and determination to help us support our client base. This position reports to our Service Manager. We are looking for an individual who is a problem-solver and has a proven track record of working within a team environment to successfully address remote user issues requiring onsite dispatch. If you have the experience and the desire, we'd like to talk to you.

Our service dispatchers participate in our problem management and resolution process, and assign resources to and schedule all remote, onsite or bench services, as well as growing and developing the organization's perception with existing customers through exceptional customer service. Candidates must be energetic and focused with a strong motivation to learn new technologies and management and scheduling processes. This position requires dedication, persistence, follow-up, effective utilization of provided resources and unbeatable customer service.

This position will include coordinating efficient and timely customer installation and repair assignments through effective management of our field engineering staff and working within a structured problem management and resolution process to complete them within established SLAs, and involves working with other resources and vendors to deliver effective support services. Responsibilities include continuously monitoring and adjusting work assignments to insure optimum tech productivity through efficient routing and maintaining customer satisfaction.

Job duties include utilizing our professional services automation (PSA) solution to monitor remote user support services and update service request information, answer technical support calls, assign ticket severity, prioritize and schedule work accordingly, and collaborate and work with other staff and vendor support resources to resolve issues. Overall relationship management skills and the ability to coordinate required resources to respond to complex IT requirements are desired. Other requirements include participating in ongoing training and preparing and presenting service reports to management regularly.

The Best I.T. Service Delivery BOOK EVER!

Employment Ad for a Service Dispatcher

Minimum Skills Required:

- Minimum three years service dispatch experience
- Excellent knowledge of our supported software and technologies
- Strong interpersonal skills required to effectively communicate with users, staff and vendors
- Passion for teamwork, continuing education, problem solving and exceptional customer service
- Must be well spoken, outgoing, organized, detailed-orientated, dependable and flexible
- Valid driver's license and proof of insurance
- Background check and drug screen required
- Reliable transportation

This Position Entails:

- Heavy scheduling and management of human resources
- Efficient and effective routing of each day's scheduled work to the appropriate field engineer
- Accurate documentation of all activities conducted
- Heavy follow-up and follow-through
- The ability to learn quickly and adapt to changing requirements

---

The Best I.T. Service Delivery BOOK EVER!

Employment Ad for a Service Dispatcher

The Successful Candidate must be:

- Professional and articulate
- Interpersonally adept
- Technically proficient
- A relationship builder
- A problem solver

Benefits include group medical/dental insurance, paid vacation, holidays, personal & sick time and training reimbursement. Our generous compensation plans are structured as salary plus bonuses for meeting utilization, compliance and customer service requirements, with initial compensation commensurate with relevant experience.

Qualified candidates please submit a current resume, along with salary history to: hr@mspu.us.

Employment Ad for a Service Manager

Service Manager

Company: MSP University
Location: Garden Grove, CA 92841
Status: Full-Time, Employee
Job Category: Service Management
Relevant Work Experience: 5-7 Years
Career Level: Experienced (Manager)

We are currently seeking a highly skilled service manager with the drive and determination to help us support our client base. This position reports to our Director of Technical Services. We are looking for an individual who is a problem-solver and has a proven track record of managing a technical team to successfully address challenging user computing issues, and is accustomed to maintaining technical staffing levels, training and certification requirements, problem management and resolution processes and customer satisfaction via strict SLA management. If you have the experience and the desire, we'd like to talk to you.

Our service manager is responsible for maintaining customer uptime and improving their computing experiences through managing our technical staff's effective remote monitoring,

---

maintenance and problem identification and resolution activities, as well as growing and developing the organization's perception with existing customers through exceptional customer service. This position will directly supervise our service desk and staff, provide customer service support, analyze trends in customer inquiries/requests for assistance, recommend improvements in overall service levels and monitor staff performance. Candidates must be energetic and focused with a strong motivation to learn new technologies and management and maintenance processes. This position requires dedication, persistence, follow-up, effective utilization of provided resources and unbeatable customer service.

This position will include managing a structured problem management and resolution process to remediate customer problems within established SLAs, and involves working with other resources and vendors to deliver effective support services.

Job duties include utilizing our professional services automation (PSA) solution to manage technical support services and collaborate and work with other management, staff and vendor support resources to insure effective, efficient service delivery to customers. Overall relationship management skills and the ability to coordinate required resources to respond to complex IT requirements are desired.

Other requirements include participating in ongoing management and strategy meetings and preparing and presenting service reports to management regularly.

Minimum Skills Required:

- Minimum three years service dispatch experience
- Excellent knowledge of our supported software and technologies
- Strong interpersonal skills required to effectively communicate with customers, staff and vendors
- Passion for teamwork, problem solving and exceptional customer service
- Must be well spoken, outgoing, organized, detailed-orientated, dependable and flexible
- Valid driver's license and proof of insurance
- Background check and drug screen required
- Reliable transportation

This Position Entails:

- Management of human resources to meet organizational goals for service excellence
- Administrator of established company policies
- Analysis of service delivery business unit data to seek improvements in efficiency and productivity
- Heavy follow-up and follow-through
- The ability to learn quickly and adapt to changing requirements

The Best I.T. Service Delivery BOOK EVER!

Employment Ad for a Service Manager

The Successful Candidate must be:

- Professional and articulate
- Interpersonally adept
- Technically proficient
- A relationship builder
- A problem solver

Benefits include group medical/dental insurance, paid vacation, holidays, personal & sick time and training reimbursement. Our generous compensation plans are structured as salary plus bonuses for meeting utilization, compliance and customer service requirements, with initial compensation commensurate with relevant experience.

Qualified candidates please submit a current resume, along with salary history to: hr@mspu.us.

Employment Ad for a Sales Engineer

Sales Engineer

Company: MSP University
Location: Garden Grove, CA 92841
Status: Full-Time, Employee
Job Category: Sales Engineering
Relevant Work Experience: 5-7 Years
Career Level: Experienced (Non-Manager)

We are currently seeking a highly skilled sales engineer with the drive and determination to help us support our sales efforts. This position reports to our Director of Sales. We are looking for an individual with a strong I.T. background and the skills to provide pre- and post-sales support for our account managers to help them identify customer needs and develop solutions to address them. If you have the experience and the desire, we'd like to talk to you.

Our sales engineers are responsible for supporting inside and outside sales teams in making technical recommendations to customers and providing information and making technical presentations to help close technical sales. In addition, our sales engineers provide technical training to customers and their staff on hardware and software and will communicate on

The Best I.T. Service Delivery BOOK EVER!

Employment Ad for a Sales Engineer

---

a peer level with IT professionals within customer accounts to quickly and accurately recommend and communicate solution strategies.

Candidates must be energetic and focused with a strong motivation to learn new technologies and management processes. This position requires dedication, persistence, follow-up, effective utilization of provided resources and unbeatable customer service.

This position will include working with our account managers, purchasing manager and project managers to develop project scopes for technical services and solutions implementations.

Job duties include utilizing our quoting, project planning, scheduling and management solutions to collaborate and work with other staff, customer and vendor support resources to insure effective, and efficient service delivery to customers. Overall relationship management skills and the ability to coordinate required resources to respond to complex IT requirements are desired. Other requirements include participating in ongoing sales strategy meetings and preparing and presenting sales reports to management regularly.

The Best I.T. Service Delivery BOOK EVER!

Employment Ad for a Sales Engineer

Minimum Skills Required:

- Minimum five years sales engineering experience
- Excellent knowledge of our supported software and technologies
- Superior writing capabilities
- Strong interpersonal skills required to effectively communicate with customers, staff and vendors
- Passion for teamwork, problem solving and exceptional customer service
- Must be well spoken, outgoing, organized, detailed-orientated, dependable and flexible
- Valid driver's license and proof of insurance
- Background check and drug screen required
- Reliable transportation

This Position Entails:

- Support of organization's sales efforts from a technical perspective
- Heavy quoting, technical drawing and proposal creation
- Effective follow-up and follow-through
- The ability to learn quickly and adapt to changing requirements

The Best I.T. Service Delivery BOOK EVER!

Employment Ad for a Sales Engineer

The Successful Candidate must be:

- Professional and articulate
- Interpersonally adept
- Technically proficient
- A relationship builder
- A problem solver

Benefits include group medical/dental insurance, paid vacation, holidays, personal & sick time and training reimbursement. Our generous compensation plans are structured as salary plus bonuses for meeting utilization, compliance and customer service requirements, with initial compensation commensurate with relevant experience.

Qualified candidates please submit a current resume, along with salary history to: hr@mspu.us.

Employment Ad for a Purchasing Manager

Purchasing Manager

Company: MSP University
Location: Garden Grove, CA 92841
Status: Full-Time, Employee
Job Category: Purchasing
Relevant Work Experience: 3-5 Years
Career Level: Experienced (Manager)

We are currently seeking a highly skilled purchasing manager with the drive and determination to help us support our service delivery efforts. This position reports to our Director of Technical Services. We are looking for an individual with a strong purchasing background and the skills to source I.T. equipment, licensing and services required for efficient, timely service delivery. If you have the experience and the desire, we'd like to talk to you.

Our purchasing manager is responsible for supporting our service delivery and project implementation teams through identification and timely ordering of equipment and products necessary to deliver services within SLA, scope and budget.

Candidates must be energetic and focused with a strong motivation to learn new technologies and inventory management processes. This position requires dedication, persistence, follow-up, effective utilization of provided resources and unbeatable customer service.

This position will include working with our sales engineers, inventory manager, vendors and distributors to coordinate and manage the supply of solution-specific parts, supplies and services.

Job duties include utilizing our quoting, ordering, project planning, scheduling and management solutions to collaborate and work with other staff, customer and vendor support resources to insure effective, and efficient equipment, licensing and service delivery to customers. Overall relationship management skills and the ability to coordinate required resources to respond to complex ordering requirements are desired. Other requirements include managing vendor relationships and participating in project strategy meetings and preparing and presenting reports to management regularly.

Minimum Skills Required:

- Minimum five years sales engineering experience
- Excellent knowledge of our supported software and technologies
- Superior negotiating capabilities

The Best I.T. Service Delivery BOOK EVER!

Employment Ad for a Purchasing Manager

- Strong interpersonal skills required to effectively communicate with customers, staff and vendors
- Passion for teamwork, problem solving and exceptional customer service
- Must be well spoken, outgoing, organized, detailed-orientated, dependable and flexible
- Valid driver's license and proof of insurance
- Background check and drug screen required
- Reliable transportation

This Position Entails:

- Support of organization's service delivery efforts from a logistical and fulfillment perspective
- Heavy ordering, order tracking and management focus
- Effective follow-up and follow-through
- The ability to learn quickly and adapt to changing requirements

The Successful Candidate must be:

- Professional and articulate
- Interpersonally adept
- Technically proficient
- A relationship builder
- A problem solver

Employment Ad for a Purchasing Manager

Benefits include group medical/dental insurance, paid vacation, holidays, personal & sick time and training reimbursement. Our generous compensation plans are structured as salary plus bonuses for meeting utilization, compliance and customer service requirements, with initial compensation commensurate with relevant experience.

Qualified candidates please submit a current resume, along with salary history to: hr@mspu.us.

Employment Ad for an Inventory Manager

Inventory Manager

Company: MSP University
Location: Garden Grove, CA 92841
Status: Full-Time, Employee
Job Category: Warehouse, Inventory
Relevant Work Experience: 3-5 Years
Career Level: Experienced (Non-Manager)

We are currently seeking a highly skilled inventory manager with the drive and determination to help us support our service delivery efforts. This position reports to our Director of Technical Services. We are looking for an individual with a strong inventory control background and the skills to source and stock I.T. equipment and insure adequate levels of inventory at all times for effective, timely service delivery. If you have the experience and the desire, we'd like to talk to you.

Our inventory manager is responsible for supporting our service delivery and project implementation teams through identification and timely ordering of equipment and products necessary to deliver services within SLA, scope and budget.

The Best I.T. Service Delivery BOOK EVER!

Employment Ad for an Inventory Manager

Candidates must be energetic and focused with a strong motivation to learn new technologies and inventory management processes. This position requires dedication, persistence, follow-up, effective utilization of provided resources and unbeatable customer service.

This position will include working with our sales engineers, purchasing manager, vendors and distributors to coordinate and manage the supply of solution-specific parts, supplies and services. The inventory manager is also responsible for the timely and accurate processing of all RMA requests.

Job duties include utilizing our ordering, project planning, scheduling and management solutions to collaborate and work with other staff, customer and vendor support resources to insure required inventory levels of equipment and licensing is available in time for scheduled implementations for customers. Overall relationship management skills and the ability to coordinate required resources to respond to complex ordering requirements are desired. Other requirements include managing vendor relationships and participating in project strategy meetings and preparing and presenting reports to management regularly.

The Best I.T. Service Delivery BOOK EVER!

Employment Ad for an Inventory Manager

Minimum Skills Required:

- Minimum three years inventory management experience
- Excellent knowledge of our supported software and technologies
- Superior negotiating capabilities
- Strong interpersonal skills required to effectively communicate with customers, staff and vendors
- Passion for teamwork, problem solving and exceptional customer service
- Must be well spoken, outgoing, organized, detailed-orientated, dependable and flexible
- Valid driver's license and proof of insurance
- Background check and drug screen required
- Reliable transportation

This Position Entails:

- Support of organization's service delivery efforts from a logistical and fulfillment perspective
- Heavy inventory management, ordering, order tracking and management focus
- Effective follow-up and follow-through
- The ability to learn quickly and adapt to changing requirements

---

Employment Ad for an Inventory Manager

The Successful Candidate must be:

- Professional and articulate
- Interpersonally adept
- Technically proficient
- A relationship builder
- A problem solver

Benefits include group medical/dental insurance, paid vacation, holidays, personal & sick time and training reimbursement. Our generous compensation plans are structured as salary plus bonuses for meeting utilization, compliance and customer service requirements, with initial compensation commensurate with relevant experience.

Qualified candidates please submit a current resume, along with salary history to: hr@mspu.us.

Employment Ad for a Project Manager

Project Manager

Company: MSP University
Location: Garden Grove, CA 92841
Status: Full-Time, Employee
Job Category: Project Management
Relevant Work Experience: 5-7 Years
Career Level: Experienced (Manager)

We are currently seeking a highly skilled project manager with the drive and determination to help us support our client base. This position reports to our Director of Technical Services. We are looking for an individual who is a problem-solver and has a proven track record of managing resources, tasks and schedules to successfully deliver complex I.T. solutions to our customers within scope, timeline and budget. If you have the experience and the desire, we'd like to talk to you.

Our project managers are responsible for working with our sales engineers to develop project scopes, specify methods to be utilized and all tasks to be completed during project implementations, creating timelines and expected durations for each task's completion and estimating and allocating

---

resources for each task's completion, as well as creating risk management plans, change control processes and communication and status reporting processes utilized during project implementation.

Candidates must be energetic and focused with a strong motivation to learn new technologies and management processes. This position requires dedication, persistence, follow-up, effective utilization of provided resources and unbeatable customer service.

This position will include managing, coordinating, directing and supervising personnel, vendors and other resources engaged on projects.

Job duties include utilizing our project planning, scheduling and management solutions to manage resources and collaborate and work with other staff, customer and vendor support resources to insure effective, efficient service delivery to customers. Overall relationship management skills and the ability to coordinate required resources to respond to complex IT requirements are desired. Other requirements include participating in ongoing management and strategy meetings and preparing and presenting progress reports to management regularly.

The Best I.T. Service Delivery BOOK EVER!

Employment Ad for a Project Manager

Minimum Skills Required:

- Minimum five years project management experience
- Excellent knowledge of our supported software and technologies
- Strong interpersonal skills required to effectively communicate with customers, staff and vendors
- Passion for teamwork, problem solving and exceptional customer service
- Must be well spoken, outgoing, organized, detailed-orientated, dependable and flexible
- Valid driver's license and proof of insurance
- Background check and drug screen required
- Reliable transportation

This Position Entails:

- Heavy management of schedules and human resources to meet organizational goals for service excellence
- Planning, coordinating, directing and supervising ongoing projects to insure completion within scope, timeline and budget
- Heavy follow-up and follow-through
- The ability to learn quickly and adapt to changing requirements

---

The Best I.T. Service Delivery BOOK EVER!

Employment Ad for a Project Manager

The Successful Candidate must be:

- Professional and articulate
- Interpersonally adept
- Technically proficient
- A relationship builder
- A problem solver

Benefits include group medical/dental insurance, paid vacation, holidays, personal & sick time and training reimbursement. Our generous compensation plans are structured as salary plus bonuses for meeting utilization, compliance and customer service requirements, with initial compensation commensurate with relevant experience.

Qualified candidates please submit a current resume, along with salary history to: hr@mspu.us.

HR Hiring Checklist for a New Technical Person

1.	Run ad for technical person	Completed
2.	Receive and review resume	
3.	Conduct telephone interview	
	• Use standard interview questions	
4.	Email candidate DISC behavioral profile link	
5.	Email candidate PTSI profile link	
	• Email candidate results of profiles before live interview	
6.	Schedule live interview in office	
	• Complete job application and typing test	
	• Review DISC behavioral profile	
	• Review PTSI profile	
	• Give candidate technical test	
	• Review position requirements	
	• Review training process and timeline	
7.	Schedule second interview with upper management	
8.	Establish start date for candidate (at least 1 week out to check references)	
9.	Email offer letter to candidate	
10.	Conduct criminal background check and reference check	
11.	Schedule appointment for drug screen	
12.	New hire orientation	
	• Issue employee handbook	
	• Schedule company training	
	• Company tour and introduction to staff	

HR Interview Questions for a New Technical Person

Primary Questions*

- What do you know about our company?
  What we are looking for is do they know us or have they at least looked at the web site. (we fill them in if they don't know)
- Tell me a little bit about yourself. If needed clarify (tell me about your previous jobs)
- What are some of your strengths ….. Weaknesses?
- What do you see yourself doing in 3 years? …. how about in 5 years?
- Tell me a time when you made a mistake and what steps did you take to resolve the issue?
- What do you get excited about? …. What upsets you?
- What situations make you lose your temper?
- What was one of your greatest successes?
- What are 3 things you do extremely well?
- What are 3 things you need to work on?
- In a group or team what position do you take on?
- Tell us about a team you have worked in.
- What are three positive things your last boss would say about you?
- How much guidance and management do you like?
- How much do you feel you need?
- What type of people do you work best with?

- If budgets were of no concern, what would be the first thing you would spend money on and why?
- What are your compensation requirements?
- Can we have references?
- Can you send us an example of something you've written?
- Do you have any questions for us?

Additional Questions*

- Is there anything that would interfere with your regular attendance?
- What would your perfect job look like?
- Why should we hire you?
- What makes you more qualified than the other applicants?
- What are the skills that you think would benefit our company?
- How do you see yourself fitting in to our organization?
- Rate yourself on a scale of 1-10 on Word, Excel, PowerPoint, Outlook and Vista
- What type of work environment do you like?
- How do you work under pressures & deadlines?
- If you could start your career again, what would you do differently?
- How would you describe your personality? What is your favorite movie of all time? Why?
- Describe a time when you made a customer/client extremely happy?

The Best I.T. Service Delivery BOOK EVER!

HR Interview Questions for a New Technical Person

- Do you mind if we call your former employer?
- Why are you considering a career change at this time or leaving your current position?
- What do you like and dislike about your current position?
- What about this position do you find the most attractive? .... Least attractive?
- In your present position, what problems have you identified that had previously been overlooked?
- What kind of feedback have you received from past clients and customers?
- How have you handled negative feedback from clients, customers, or team members?
- Give us an example of a time where there was a conflict in a team/group that you were involved in and how it was resolved.

Information Systems Questions*

- Describe your documentation skills
- Rate yourself on a scale of 1-10 on Windows Vista, Windows 2003 Server, Backup Exec, Visio, Trend/Norton AV.
- How comfortable are you working with various hardware?
- What important trends do you see in our industry?
- Do you hold any certifications?
- How do you feel about attaining certifications?
- Do you own a car and have a driver's license?

The Best I.T. Service Delivery BOOK EVER!

HR Interview Questions for a New Technical Person

- Do you mind using your personal vehicle for work?
- What are your hours of availability?
- How do you feel about working some nights and weekends?
- What are the seven layers of the OSI model?
- What sort of cabling is suitable for Fast Ethernet protocols?
- What is the difference between a hub, switch, and router?
- What is a default route?
- What is the difference between TCP and UDP?
- How would you optimize Exchange 2003 memory usage on a Windows Server 2003 server with more than 1Gb of memory?
- What are the standard port numbers for SMTP, POP3, IMAP4, RPC, LDAP and Global Catalog?
- What are the IP address ranges for class A-E? 5.
- What items of information would you request from a user to effectively address a technical problem?
- What command do you use to force the client to give up the DHCP lease if you have access to the client PC?
- What's the difference between forward lookup and reverse lookup zones in DNS?
- How do you breakup a broadcast domain?
- If you were setting up a new PC for an existing user with and existing a PC what steps would you go through?
- What are Levels of RAID 0, 1, 5? Which one is better & why?

The Best I.T. Service Delivery BOOK EVER!

HR Interview Questions for a New Technical Person

- Name key files or directories on a Windows system that should always be backed up.
- What are some things to troubleshoot for an I/O error reported in your backup logs?

Scenario Questions*

- A call comes in to the help desk from a user stating that no one in his or her building can get logged on. The PCs in that building are plugged into a switch and then connected to your building with routers over a T-1 line. What do you do?
- Fifty new PCs are to arrive within two weeks, and you're tasked with installing them. You have a staff of five people. Describe how you would take this project from beginning to end.
- A call comes in from a client that is irate because it has been 3 hours and his/her problem hasn't been fixed yet. Describe how you would deal with this situation step by step.
- What is DHCP and how does it work? What is it used for?
- What is DNS and how does it work? What is it used for?
- Describe what a netmask is. How does it work?

Special thanks to Kurt Sippel from Applied Tech Solutions

Managed Services, Your Business Plan and You PowerPoint

Managed Services, Your Business Plan and You PowerPoint Presentation

www.mspu.us

www.mspu.us

Today's Presenter

Erick Simpson
Vice President/CIO
Intelligent Enterprise/MSP University

- Author – "The Guide to a Successful Managed Services Practice – *What every SMB IT Service Provider Should Know*"

E-Mail: esimpson@mspu.us

Websites: www.ienterprise.us

www.mspu.us

*Intelligent*Enterprise

2

Who is Intelligent Enterprise?

- We're an IT Service Provider just like you!
- In Business Since 1997
- Microsoft Gold Certified Partner
  - Microsoft Business Solutions Partner
  - Microsoft Small Business Specialist
- Microsoft Competencies:
  - Information Worker Solutions
  - Networking Infrastructure Solutions
  - Advanced Infrastructure Solutions
- HTG Peer Group Member
- ConnectWise Partner
- Zenith Infotech Partner
- Authors: *"The Guide to a Successful Managed Services Practice"*
- Founders: MSP University
  - Training MSP's Since 2005

Managed Services, Your Business Plan and You PowerPoint

---

www.mspu.us

Today's Agenda

- Managed Services Business Plan
  - Definition
  - Benefits
  - Purpose
  - Components
  - Tips on Creating your Managed Services Business Plan
  - The Importance of Execution
  - Maintenance
  - Resources
    - Managed Services Business Plan Template Download

Intelligent Enterprise

MSPU

4

---

www.mspu.us

Definition of a Business Plan

- A blueprint and communication tool for your business.
- A device to help you, the owner, set out how you intend to operate your business.
- A road map to tell others how you expect to get there.

-The U.S. Small Business Administration
www.sba.gov

Intelligent Enterprise

MSPU

5

Benefits

- Confirms the viability of your business venture
- Helps you set realistic goals and expectations, based on the market research you conduct
- Provides a roadmap to your success
- Minimizes business risk

Intelligent Enterprise

MSPU

6

Common Purposes of a Business Plan

- Defines your business
  - Vision
  - Mission
  - Goals
- Identifies your
  - Marketing strategy
  - Sources of Revenue
  - Competition
- Can be used to attract
  - Investment opportunities
  - Business financing

Enterprise   MSPU

7

Strategic Planning

- A precursor to writing your business plan
- Helps you match the strengths of your business offerings to available opportunities by requiring you to:
  - Collect and analyze information about your business environment
  - Clearly understand your business' strengths and weaknesses
  - Develop clear goals and objectives
- Forces you to objectively re-evaluate your business

Enterprise

MSPU

8

---

www.mspu.us

Traditional Business Plan Components

- Executive Summary
- Vision, Mission & Goals
- Company Overview
- Marketing Plan
- Key Alliances, Partners and Vendors
- Revenue Sources
- Competition
- Financials

Enterprise   MSPU

9

Executive Summary

- Summary of your business
  - Year of inception, location and areas of expertise
- Company History in the Making
  - Several key highlights in the company's history
- Management
  - A description of your key management team and their backgrounds which qualify them for their positions
- Uniqueness
  - A brief outline of your uniqueness in the industry
- Financials
  - A concise narrative of your current financial position

*Intelligent*Enterprise   MSPU

10

Vision, Mission & Goals

- Your company's Vision Statement
  - A short, inspiring statement of what the organization intends to become and achieve at some point in the future
    - *"There will be a personal computer on every desk running Microsoft software"* – Bill Gates
- Your company's Mission Statement
  - A short, concise statement of your organization's priorities
    - *"To make people happy"* – Walt Disney
- Your company's Goals
  - Several specific, realistic goals for the organization based upon your Vision and Mission Statements

*Intelligent*Enterprise   MSPU

11

Managed Services, Your Business Plan and You PowerPoint

www.mspu.us

Company Overview

- History
  - Briefly document your company history
- Legal Business Description
  - Briefly describe your legal entity – LLC, S-Corp, etc.
    - *"A privately-held California-based S-Corporation, founded in 1997"*
- Board of Directors
  - Briefly state your Board of Directors, titles and responsibilities
- Company Officers
  - Briefly state your Officers, titles and responsibilities
- Notable Clientele
  - Briefly include a few cornerstone clients

IntelligentEnterprise MSPU 12

Marketing Plan

- Address the results of your Strategic Planning and Competitive Analysis
  - Your business
  - Your competition
  - Your uniqueness
- Clearly defines your organization's deliverables
  - Managed Services, Project-based work, Application Development
- Identifies your Target Market
- Ilustrates the methods you will utilize in reaching your Market
  - Microsoft Across America-driven events
  - Direct-response marketing

Intelligent Enterprise   MSPU

13

Key Alliances, Partners and Vendors

- Briefly describe the key alliances, partners and vendors that you will leverage in executing your business plan and marketing strategy
  - Microsoft
  - Strategic Fulfillment Partners
  - Other Key Vendors

Enterprise

14

Managed Services, Your Business Plan and You PowerPoint

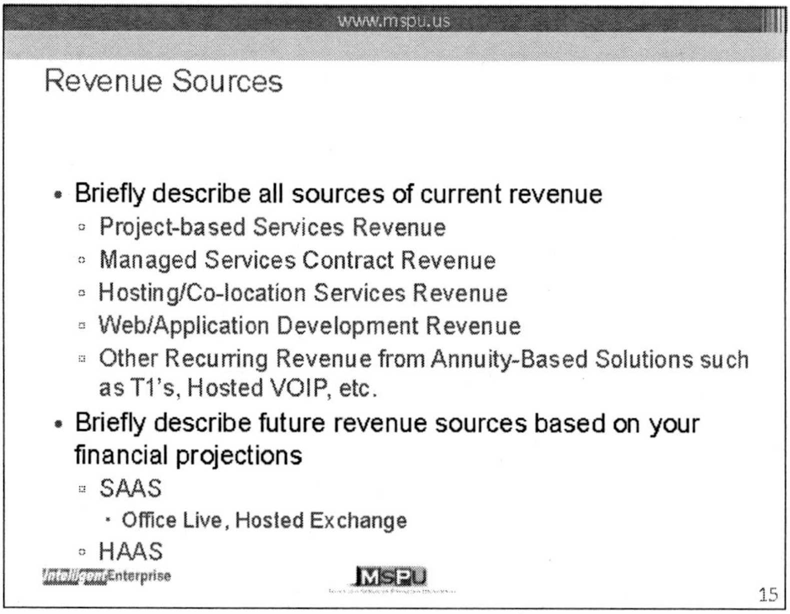

---

www.mspu.us

Competition

- General Competitive Analysis
  - Briefly describe 3 (or more) local sources of competition, and their
    - Marketing Strategy
    - Location
    - Strengths
    - Weaknesses
    - Pricing Structure

Intelligent Enterprise

MSPU

16

Financials

- Financial Projections
  - Briefly describe your financial projections, based upon your financial projections spreadsheet
- Spreadsheet
  - Create and include a spreadsheet supporting your financial projections

*Intelligent*Enterprise

MSPU

17

Tips On Creating Your Business Plan

- Don't skimp on your research
- Be brutally honest with yourself and your assumptions
- Sharpen your pencil
- Keep it brief
- Circulate it for review among trusted business associates or a peer group before execution

Intelligent Enterprise

MSPU

18

---

www.mspu.us

Execution

- *"An organization's ability to learn, and translate that learning into action rapidly, is the ultimate competitive advantage"*

  - Jack Welch

Intelligent Enterprise

MSPU

19

---

www.mspu.us

Maintenance

- Realize that your business plan is a living document – revisit the plan often for review and revision
- Remember that your business plan is your roadmap – understand that maps must adapt to reflect changing road conditions

Intellicom Enterprise

MSPU

20

---

www.mspu.us

Resources

- Visit our website: www.mspu.us
  - Download free Managed Services Webinars
  - Download a sample of *"The Guide to a Successful Managed Services Practice"*
- Attend our next free 1 day Managed Services Workshop
- Email me for:
  - A copy of my white paper on Managed Services Business Planning
  - The complete 11-page Managed Services Business Plan Template we use to train our Partners with

esimpson@mspu.us

Intelligent Enterprise   MSPU

21

Managed Services Business Plan Template

CONFIDENTIAL BUSINESS PLAN

YOUR COMPANY NAME

This business plan has been prepared solely for the benefit of private shareholders of YOUR COMPANY NAME The information contained herein has been supplied in part from trade and statistical services and publications and from other sources that are reliable. YOUR COMPANY NAME makes no representation or warranty as to the accuracy or completeness of such information. This Business Plan may not be used or reproduced for any other purpose.

Anyone accepting delivery of this Business Plan agrees to maintain the confidentiality of the information contained herein, and, upon request, agrees to return this Business plan and all related documents to YOUR NAME, at the address below. Any questions relating to this Business Plan should be directed to:

YOUR NAME

YOUR COMPANY NAME

YOUR STREET

YOUR CITY, STATE ZIP

YOUR PHONE NUMBER

The inclusion of various other corporate icons in this document is intended solely as a graphic supplement to the Business Plan. These companies should not interpret the use of these logos to convey an express or implied endorsement of this business plan. YOUR COMPANY NAME has no relationship with these companies, other than expressly specified in this document.

I.EXECUTIVE SUMMARY

- Summary
- Company History in the Making
- Management
- Uniqueness
- Financials

II.VISION, MISSION & GOALS

- Vision
- Mission
- Goals

III.COMPANY OVERVIEW

- History
- Legal Business Description
- Board of Directors
- Company Officers
- Notable Clientele

IV.MARKETING PLAN

- Creative Strategies

V.KEY ALLIANCES

- Microsoft
- Citrix
- Cisco

VI.REVENUE SOURCES

- Current Revenue Sources
- Future Revenue Sources

VII.COMPETITION

- General Competitive Analysis

VIII.FINANCIALS

- Financial Projections
- Financial Charts

I. Executive Summary

YOUR COMPANY NAME

Summary

WRITE A BRIEF SUMMARY OF YOUR BUSINESS – YEAR OF
INCEPTION, LOCATION AND AREAS OF EXPERTISE.

---

*YOUR COMPANY NAME has been providing Information
Technology Services and Solutions to the Southern
California SMB Market since 1997. Our relationships
with partners such as Microsoft, Cisco, Citrix and HP
have allowed us the ability to design, scale and
implement effective infrastructure solutions for our
diverse client base.*

The Best I.T. Service Delivery BOOK EVER!

Managed Services Business Plan Template

YOUR COMPANY NAME provides Help Desk, 24x7x365 Network Monitoring and Vendor Management Services and Web and Application Development, as well as Network Infrastructure Design, Implementation and Maintenance to a varied Client base, including Small and Medium-Sized Businesses, as well as International Fortune 500 Firms.

- Company History in the Making
  WRITE SEVERAL KEY HIGHLIGHTS IN YOUR COMPANY'S HISTORY (3 SENTENCES).

YOUR COMPANY NAME achieved Microsoft Gold Certified Partner status in 2005, as well as Microsoft's Small Business Specialist Competency in 2006. As a result of our successful methodology and delivery of Managed Services, we have been asked to speak and train at high-level Industry functions and Conferences conducted by Microsoft, Intel and others.

- Management
DETAIL COMPANY MANAGEMENT PERSONNEL AND
THEIR BACKGROUNDS WHICH QUALIFY THEM FOR
THEIR POSITIONS.

*Our Management Team is strong and is composed of
the following experienced individuals:*

YOUR PRESIDENT'S NAME – President and CEO

*YOUR PRESIDENT'S NAME draws upon nearly 20 years
of strong and diverse management experience in
developing strategic operating plans, business
modeling and personnel training and development.
Oversee the company's day-to-day operations.
Maintain clear communication and provide direction to
all key personnel in order to achieve company goals
and objectives Responsible for customer service and
satisfaction. Interface directly with YOUR COMPANY
NAME's clients to maintain clear communication and
develop methods to address individual client needs,
improve relationships and meet expectations.*

*YOUR VICE PRESIDENT'S NAME – Vice President and
CIO*

*YOUR VICE PRESIDENT'S NAME brings over 16 years of
Enterprise-level IT experience to YOUR COMPANY*

NAME, where he oversees all technical aspects of the organization, determining the strategic direction, development and implementation of YOUR COMPANY NAME's Information Technology services and functions as they apply both internally and to its clients. YOUR VICE PRESIDENT'S NAME's previous experience includes overseeing the design, development and implementation of enterprise-level Help Desks and Call Centers for Fortune 1000 organizations, and Industry Certifications include Microsoft MCP, Microsoft Business Solutions and Small Business Specialist Certifications, as well as Microsoft Solutions Framework, Networking Infrastructure, Advanced Networking Infrastructure and Information Worker Competencies.

Etc...

Each dynamic individual on the management team reflects years of experience gleaned from previous environments wherein their specific expertise was developed and refined, thus uniquely qualifying them to supervise their respective departments within the Company.

- Uniqueness

  WRITE A BRIEF SUMMARY OF YOUR UNIQUE SELLING
  PROPOSITION (3 SENTENCES) – THE THINGS THAT
  DIFFERENTIATE YOU FROM YOUR COMPETITORS.

  *YOUR COMPANY NAME's Industry-recognized Managed
  Services Sales, Implementation and Management
  model sets us apart from all other "break-fix" IT Service
  Providers. Based and sold on value received, our
  Managed Services deliverables easily illustrate the
  benefit to our prospects in doing business with our
  organization, easily differentiating us from our
  competition.*

- Financials
  DOCUMENT BRIEFLY YOUR CURRENT FINANCIAL
  POSITION – GROSS SALES, PROFIT, ASSETS AND CASH
  ON HAND.

  *YOUR COMPANY NAME's financial position is strong,
  with gross sales of $_____ for the period ending
  Q107, reflecting gross profit of $_____, with
  available cash on hand of $_____. In addition,
  total company assets are valued at $_____ as of
  the period ending Q107.*

II. Vision, Mission & Goals

- Vision
  WRITE A SHORT, INSPIRING STATEMENT OF WHAT THE ORGANIZATION INTENDS TO BECOME AND ACHIEVE AT SOME POINT IN THE FUTURE.

  To become the leading IT Service Provider to Small and Medium Businesses in Southern California.

- Mission
  WRITE A SHORT, CONCISE STATEMENT OF YOUR ORGANIZATION'S PRIORITIES.

  Our mission is to ease our Clients' Business Pain and increase their productivity and profitability through the use of technology.

- Goals
  WRITE DOWN SEVERAL SPECIFIC, REALISTIC GOALS FOR THE ORGANIZATION BASED UPON YOUR VISION AND MISSION STATEMENTS.

    - *Increase Gross Revenues by 20% quarter per quarter*
    - *Maintain and add new Industry Certifications/Competencies with Microsoft,*

---

*Cisco and Citrix by a minimum of 2 per Vendor
per Year*
- *Hire 3 new Microsoft MCSE's by Q2/07*
- *Develop relationships with 3 new Fulfillment
  Partners in Q207 – Web, VOIP and IP Cameras*
- *Increased Client Satisfaction by 15% as
  measured by Microsoft's next quarterly CSAT
  initiative*

III. Company Overview

- History
  BRIEFLY WRITE A COMPANY HISTORY.

- Legal Business Description
  BRIEFLY DESCRIBE YOUR LEGAL ENTITY.

  *YOUR COMPANY NAME is a privately-held California-
  based S-Corporation, founded in 1997.*

- Board of Directors
  BRIEFLY STATE YOUR BOARD OF DIRECTORS, TITLES
  AND RESPONSIBILITIES.

  YOUR COMPANY NAME'S Board of Directors includes:

- Company Officers
  BRIEFLY STATE YOUR OFFICERS, TITLES AND
  RESPONSIBILITIES.

- Notable Clientele
  BRIEFLY INCLUDE A FEW CORNERSTONE CLIENTS

IV. Marketing Plan

- Creative Strategies

*YOUR COMPANY NAME has declared as its mission
statement to become an industry leader in Information
Technology Services. The following proprietary marketing
campaign will develop and expand YOUR COMPANY
NAME's customer service emphasis; increase the
company's client base; enhance relationships with current*

clients; and grow the company business through measured-response techniques.

The challenges facing YOUR COMPANY NAME are evident: It must attract new business; it must build upon the trust and confidence exhibited by existing clientele; it must brand its customer service ideals among the industry populace, and create an ever-growing "customer pool" from which to develop future business.

YOUR COMPANY NAME has designed a unique marketing plan that will be executed in the following phases:

- *Phase one will be implementation of the small business (1) hour free service review for networking clients. This direct-response marketing campaign will be deployed using DESCRIBE MARKETINGMETHOD HERE. This strategy will yield _____ new client opportunities per month.*
- *Phase two will be the implementation of the Microsoft Across America initiative, which provides a 42-foot truck, fully equipped with the latest innovations from Microsoft, HP, Intel and others; it features complete state of-the-art software and hardware solutions for small and*

---

mid-sized business customers, allowing prospects to experience the technology first-hand and discover the many ways to enhance their businesses. The initiative helps build customer relationships and acts as a tool to answer their questions and address their companies' concerns. This strategy will yield _____ new client opportunities quarterly.

- *Phase three will be the implementation of a Direct marketing campaign of YOUR COMPANY NAME's target market i.e. attorneys, accountants, etc. This will be implemented via marketing cold calls from 500-1000 calls per week. This will be supported by a direct mail campaign and email direct-response campaign. This strategy will yield _____ new client opportunities per month.*

All three phases will be developed concurrently, commencing on _____.

YOUR COMPANY NAME's Services:

- *Monthly Managed Service Contracts*
- *Helpdesk*
- *Network Monitoring*
- *Vendor Management*
- *Microsoft Small Business Services*
- *Back-Up Tape, server upgrades, etc*

- *Microsoft licenses, software support.*

V. Key Alliances

BRIEFLY DESCRIBE YOUR KEY ALLIANCES IN THIS SECTION.

- Microsoft

  YOUR COMPANY NAME is a Microsoft Gold Certified Partner with the following Competencies:

  - *Information Worker Solutions*
  - *Networking Infrastructure Solutions*
  - *Advanced Infrastructure Solutions*
  - *Small Business Specialist (SBSC)*
  - *Microsoft Business Solutions*

- Citrix
  - *Citrix Silver Partner*

- Cisco
  - *Cisco Silver Certified Partner*

VI. Revenue Sources

- **Current Revenue Sources**
  BRIEFLY DESCRIBE ALL SOURCES OF CURRENT
  REVENUE.

  YOUR COMPANY NAME currently enjoys the following revenue streams:

  - *Project-based Services Revenue*
  - *Managed Services Contract Revenue*
  - *Hosting/Co-location Services Revenue*
  - *Web/Application Development Revenue*
  - *Other Recurring Revenue from Annuity-Based Solutions such as T1's, Hosted VOIP, etc.*

- **Future Revenue Sources**
  BRIEFLY DESCRIBE FUTURE REVENUE SOURCES BASED
  UPON FINANCIAL PROJECTIONS SPREADSHEET.

  YOUR COMPANY NAME will earn additional revenue through the development of additional Annuity-Based Products and Services such as Remote Storage and

---

Hosted Exchange, as well as Proxy-based Email filtering, Anti-Virus and Anti-Spam Services.

VII. Competition

- General Competitive Analysis
  BRIEFLY DESCRIBE 3 LOCAL SOURCES OF COMPETITION
  – MARKETING STRATEGY, LOCATION, STRENGTHS,
  WEAKNESSES AND PRICING STRUCTURE.

The Best I.T. Service Delivery BOOK EVER!

Managed Services Business Plan Template

Competitor's Name	Do IT Smarter	Alvaka Networks	Bedrock
Location	San Diego, CA	Orange County, CA	Neenah, WI
Methods of Distribution	Events	Website	Events
Promotional Materials	Brochures Presentations	Brochures Website	Brochures Website
Methods of Advertising	Website Events	Website	Website Events
Pricing Structure	$500/Mo Min.	$500/Mo Min.	$500/Mo Min
Market Share	<1%	<1%	<1%
Strengths	Marketing	20 Years in business	Wrote Managed Services White Paper for Microsoft
Weaknesses	Pricing	Pricing Marketing	Pricing Marketing

At this time, there are only a handful of other organizations providing some flavor of Managed Services nationwide. Among these is Do IT Smarter, based in San Diego California, Alvaka Networks, based in Orange County California and Bedrock, based in Neena Wisconsin.

We do not see these organizations as direct competitors in the key sense, as our services differ dramatically with most of theirs in specific areas, including core services, as well as the manner in which we market to our target market. In addition, we maintain a broad menu of annuity-based products and services that we market, sell and implement. This differentiates us from other organizations that have a small core of highly-priced services that they market to their clients.

Competition market share is growing at this point, and we believe that others will quickly enter this largely untapped market.

In general, the objective reflected by our competitors' services, delivery, training and pricing models skew towards benefiting the competitor more so than the client. While core service offerings such as network monitoring and help desk vary from competitor to

---

competitor, those that do offer it command a much higher price than our offerings

VIII. Financials

- Financial Projections
  BRIEFLY DESCRIBE YOUR FINANCIAL PROJECTIONS, BASED UPON YOUR FINANCIAL PROJECTIONS SPREADSHEET.

  YOUR COMPANY NAME projects Gross Revenue to be $_____ for the period ending Q207, $_____ for the period ending Q307, and $_____ for the period ending Q407, for a total Gross Revenue projection of $_____ for FY07, with Projected Earnings of $_____.

- Financial Charts
  ATTACH YOUR FINANCIAL PROJECTIONS SPREADSHEET HERE.

Managed Services Business Plan White Paper

Many resellers recognize that there's money to be made in managed services, but in their haste to adopt a new business model they forget a step vital to the success of any new business venture: the business plan. Before you take the plunge into managed services, take the time to update your company's business plan. An effective business plan will help you confirm the viability of your venture, set realistic goals based upon the market research that you conduct, and provide a roadmap to your success while minimizing risk.

A managed services business plan requires special attention to areas that may differ from traditional business plans, such as your marketing strategy and financial projections. If you already have an existing business plan in place, it can make a good template that you can modify to address the managed services-specific sections in your plan.

A well-researched and organized business plan need not be lengthy to be effective. As long as your business plan contains the essential components necessary to realize its desired outcome, the more concise and easy to assimilate it is, the better. Your plan may serve many purposes, from defining your company's vision, mission and goals, to identifying your marketing strategy, sources of revenue, competition and

---

more. Some business plans are written specifically to attract investment opportunities, or to seek business financing.

THE MANAGED SERVICES BUSINESS PLAN

Your business plan should begin with an executive summary, which describes the intent of the business plan, as well as contains brief overviews of your company's history, its management team, its uniqueness in the industry and current financial position.

Subsequent sections of your business plan should address your vision, mission and goals, as well as a company overview, including a legal business description of your company, your Board of Directors and company Officers, and any notable clientele that you may have.

Your marketing strategy is a critical component of your business plan, and will need to address the results of the competitive analysis you conduct and include in your business plan. Your marketing strategy and message need to clearly define your organization's proactive deliverables as the answer to your target market's specific pain points; and illustrate your ability to reduce costs, increase productivity and minimize business risk for your clients.

Your competitive analysis will reflect the research you have performed against your top competitors regarding their

---

services, marketing and pricing strategies. Because of the relatively small number of "pure" managed services providers in existence today, it may be a challenge to identify your direct competitors in your target market. In this case you will need to include other, non-managed service providers in your competitive analysis, and demonstrate what makes your services unique in the space, influencing clients to choose you over your competition and justifying your financial projections.

It's a good idea to incorporate a description of strategic vendor relationships and other key alliances that you will leverage in executing your business plan and marketing strategy.

The final required component of your business plan will be your financial projections over the next five years, and should include a breakdown of your current P&L, if available. Your financial projections should reflect the exponential growth you will experience as a result of selling annuity-based service agreements, which will continue to pay predictable dividends month after month, year after year.

Whether you use your business plan as a strategic roadmap to transition your organization to deliver managed services, or as a vehicle to attract financing opportunities for business startup or growth, the benefits you will reap as a result of its

---

creation will far exceed its intended purpose, as it will help you analyze your business opportunity with your bottom line squarely in mind.

Business Plan Components

An effective business plan is comprised of several key sections. Additional components may be included to address specific needs, and to tailor the plan for a specific outcome. The following items comprise a short list of required topics to include in a basic business plan.

EXECUTIVE SUMMARY

- A brief summary of the business
- Key highlights in the company's history
- A description of your key management team
- A brief outline of your uniqueness in the industry
- A concise narrative of your current financial position

VISION, MISSION & GOALS

- Your company's Vision Statement
- Your company's Mission Statement
- Your company's Goals

Managed Services Business Plan White Paper

COMPANY OVERVIEW

- A brief company history
- Your company's legal business description (Corporation, LLC, etc.)
- Your Board of Directors
- Your Company Officers
- A brief summary of your notable clientele

MARKETING PLAN

- Your creative marketing strategies

KEY ALLIANCES AND VENDORS

- An accounting of key relationships that will influence your marketing plan

REVENUE SOURCES

- An illustration of your current revenue streams
- A description of future revenue streams

COMPETITION

- A general competitive analysis

FINANCIALS

- A narrative of your financial projections
- Your financial charts or spreadsheets

MSP University

MSP University specializes in providing managed services training, workshops, and boot camps, as well as sales and marketing services to IT service providers, vendors and channel organizations worldwide through our online Managed Services Provider University at www.mspu.us.

MSP University is a comprehensive, vendor-neutral resource whose sole function is to collect and disseminate as much information as possible and mentor its partners on building, operating and growing a successful I.T. and managed services practice.

Our Mission: To deliver the finest managed services training and support resources available to IT professionals anywhere.

Our Vision: To be recognized as the premier authority on the development and growth of a successful IT managed services practice.

Our Values: Committed to the highest standards of integrity, we fulfill our responsibilities to our partners, our staff and their families in an ethical and professional manner.

The Best I.T. Service Delivery BOOK EVER!

MSP University

What you get: A continuing curriculum dedicated to what every IT service provider needs to know about managed services!

Benefits:

- Access to hundreds of Webinars, teleseminars and forms, tools and collateral – *the most MSP content available anywhere*
- 144 individual MSP Courses and growing!
- Study and participate in these valuable MSP courses at your own speed
- Unlimited email support
- Participation in live "state of the industry" calls every month

Ask about our MSP Boot Camps:

- 3-Day MSP sales & marketing boot camps
- 2-Day MSP annuity-based solution stack boot camps
- 1-Day NOC/help desk boot camps

What is Managed Services University?

MSP University is the answer for all IT service providers either preparing to transition to an annuity-based managed services delivery model, or who are already delivering managed services, and wish to increase their knowledge of managed

---

services vendors, services, solutions and business, technical and sales and marketing best practices.

Why Managed Services University?

The founders of Managed Services University wished to create a single, comprehensive resource to collect and disseminate as much information as possible about building, operating and growing a successful managed services practice.

What are your qualifications to operate Managed Services University?

We are a subsidiary of Intelligent Enterprise, a Gold Certified Microsoft partner and operators of a successful IT Services Practice since 1997, one of the first "pure-play" MSPs in the SMB space who successfully transitioned to a completely managed services delivery model in January of 2005, and developed and "all you can eat" managed services approach focused on 3 core deliverables – remote help desk, proactive network monitoring and we pioneered vendor management.

Through the creation of a managed services sales and marketing approach unique to the industry, Intelligent Enterprise sold well over $2MM worth of managed services agreements before being asked to share their managed services knowledge and expertise with thousands of I.T.

---

service providers and channel organizations worldwide through our MSP University at www.mspu.us.

In addition to real-world experience, our authorship of "The Guide to a Successful Managed Services Practice – *What Every SMB IT Service Provider Should Know...*", "The Best I.T. Sales & Marketing BOOK EVER!", "The Best I.T. Service Delivery BOOK EVER!", and contributions to numerous publications including Microsoft's Expert Column; as well as a series of Microsoft TS2, Cisco and Intel Webcasts and live, in-the-field events with these clients featuring our managed services methodologies, more than qualify us as experts in the field of I.T. solutions and managed services.

What can I expect after joining?

You will gain unlimited access to our hundreds of live and recorded webinars and teleseminars, as well as live regional 1-day workshops, to guide you - no matter where you are on the path to managed services. In addition you will receive unlimited email support from our experienced staff, as well as participation in live group "state of the industry" calls each month to help answer all of your managed services questions.

What types of Courses do you offer?

Unlike other vendor-specific managed services Training offerings, our university curriculum has been consciously

---

designed in a completely agnostic and vendor-neutral manner, allowing us the ability to provide training courses from all MSP vendors who wish to participate, giving you the best opportunity to experience each solution or service to compare head-to-head at your own pace.

In addition to providing access to MSP vendor solutions and services, our courses are a holistic answer to all facets of operating a successful managed services practice, and include:

- Managed Services Concepts
- MSP Vendor Management
- MSP HR Training
- MSP Marketing Process
- MSP Lead Generation
- MSP Sales Process
- MSP Appointment Setting
- MSP Sales Closing Techniques
- MSP Help Desk Best Practices
- MSP Tools
- MSP Service Contracts
- MSP Staffing
- MSP Vendor Solution Partnering
- MSP Additional Annuity-Based Solutions

And more...this is an extremely small sampling of our Courses...

How are University Courses Conducted?

All of our managed services courses, whether they highlight a specific process such as sales and marketing or system monitoring best practices; or spotlight a managed services solution or vendor, are delivered through webinars and teleseminars, which are recorded for offline access.

We also offer regional live workshops and boot camps that deep-dive into specific advanced managed services concepts, as well as one-on-one onsite consulting services.

What other benefits will I receive?

As a MSP University member, in addition to access to all of our live and recorded courses, regional workshops, and email and group call support, you will also receive discounts for all of our boot camp training sessions, and other special offers available only to MSPU members.

How long does MSP University take?

It's completely up to you - our MSP University is a self-paced program delivered through webinars, teleseminars and all-day workshops. It's completely up to you to determine how long it will take to meet your specific needs. Since we are continually adding new content to our university as the managed services industry matures and develops, you may wish to maintain your membership indefinitely.

Do you offer any other Partner Services?

In addition to MSP University, we also provide an economical Managed Marketing Service for our Partners, which handle lead-generation activities for new business in a scheduled, consistent manner.

Our Marketing Department sources Marketing Lists, designs and produces marketing collateral such as your website, letters, postcards and emails, performs the posting and mailing and sets appointments for our partners – allowing them the ability to do what they do best - deliver their services.

We also offer affordable marketing collateral creation services – for those partners who can handle the actual marketing duties themselves, but need help in creating eye-catching collateral, including their website, case studies, white papers, newsletters, line cards, postcards, and developing their marketing message.

How much is Tuition for MSPU?

That's the best part – we've made it amazingly affordable to join Managed Services University! For unlimited access to our entire managed services curriculum of hundreds of courses (and growing every day!), and FREE attendance to any and all

---

The Best I.T. Service Delivery BOOK EVER!

MSP University

---

of our Live regional workshops, and email and group call support, monthly Tuition is only $99!

Sounds great! How do I join MSPU?

Simply visit our website at www.mspu.us and navigate to the "Registration" tab!

If you're not ready to subscribe to our Premium membership, register for a FREE Basic membership to MSP University, which will provide you with access to all of our Non-Premium content including webinars, tools, forms and collateral. Should you wish to access our Premium content at any time, it's easy to upgrade your membership at any time by visiting http://www.mspu.us/upgrade, providing you the following additional benefits:

- Free Audio Book Download of "The Guide to a Successful Managed Services Practice"
- Free Audio Book Download of "The Best I.T. Sales & Marketing BOOK EVER!"
- Unlimited access to MSPU Premium website training content, updated regularly
- Email support
- Deep discounts on all MSPU products and services
  - Other special offers available only to MSPU Premium Members!

...and much, much more!
